The complete journal of

FASHION RETAIL BUYING AND MERCHANDISING

Follow a working store model with comprehensive mini case studies and testing challenges

Charles Nesbitt

The Complete Journal of Fashion Retail Buying and Merchandising

Charles Nesbitt

Published by Charles Nesbitt, 2017.

While every precaution has been taken in the preparation of this book, the publisher assumes no responsibility for errors or omissions, or for damages resulting from the use of the information contained herein.

THE COMPLETE JOURNAL OF FASHION RETAIL BUYING AND MERCHANDISING

First edition. March 17, 2017.

ISBN: 979-8224461622

Written by Charles Nesbitt.

Also by Charles Nesbitt

Fundamentals for Successful and Sustainable Fashion Buying and Merchandising
Fundamentals of Fashion Retail, Technology, Manufacturing and Supplier Management
Fundamentals for Fashion Retail Arithmetic, Merchandise Assortment Planning and Trading
Fundamentals for Fashion Retail Strategy Planning and Implementation
Retail Fashion Procurement Team Roles and Processes
Retail Fashion Arithmetic
Retail Fashion Merchandise Assortment Planning and Trading
Retail Fashion Scenario and Strategy Planning
The Complete Journal of Fashion Retail Buying and Merchandising
Retail Fashion Manufacturing and Technology
Retail Fashion Product Storage and Logistics

Table of Contents

PREFACE

The process of buying and selling in some form or other of goods has been with us since time immemorial. Often when one stands in bewilderment in an elegant shopping mall and wonder how all the stores are able to effectively seduce the many shoppers trawling the wide corridors to readily part with their well-earned money while at the same time enabling them to possibly enjoy a wonderful social experience.

The plan of offering goods to the potential customer is a complicated one and is a science that involves many players whose individual contributions slot seamlessly together and are so perfectly co-ordinated that it provides the perception that it is the result of one individual concerted effort.

It will be illustrated as to how the relationships of the major functions that intertwine from the conceptualisation of a product through to the presentation of a finished garment to the potential customer and in doing this demonstrates how the key areas such as buying, merchandising, technology, production, design, logistics and selling each with their unique specialised operations manage to achieve this.

The book endeavours to try and outline the basic key principles and mechanisms by which this happens and should be helpful to students, people in retailing and those who are maybe considering a career in the industry. For those who already are part of the fashion buying and merchandising community this book will be beneficial in that it provides a complete simplified overview of all the integral activities and roles that go to make up the topic and thereby will provide a broader insight into their own career.

The material of the book, other than that specifically referenced is the result of the author's own exposure to the subject during a career spanning thirty five years at a major retail organisation in

Southern Africa, the support from colleagues, mentors, interaction with suppliers and own research. There has been some cross referencing to other books or technical material but the book focuses largely at a higher level on the key principles, concepts and theories and hence there is none or very little mention of retailers by name or technological packages for some key activities such as planning, allocating, critical path management, logistics and the like.

The fundamental purpose is therefore to provide the basic background that goes into the operational and technical aspects which can be universally applied. While there is merit and great benefits in the use of sophisticated technical packages that live off a common database and also integrate with one another, sadly often the prime emphasis becomes more one of mastering the system and promotes the tendency to live in a silo environment. As a result the importance tends to be focused on that single facet that the system serves rather than the broader picture. The fact that there is a relatively limited amount of material that generally describes the practice commonly known as retailing as an end to end process considering the enormous size of the industry is one of the motivating reasons for the documentation of this book.

INTRODUCTION

Retailing

Retailing is the offer of goods or services for sale by individuals or businesses to an end user. The channels by which these goods reach the final user may vary considerably and arrive via different sources such as wholesalers, trading houses or directly from the manufacturer and there are equally many differing variants in the way the goods are put on sale. Historically it is more likely that shopping would have been done at the village or town market, in a high street shop or at the "mom and pop" store which evolved over time into mass retailing stores that are often housed in shopping malls supported by smaller line shops.

More recently with the advent of the computer utilising various platforms such as the internet or social networks, shopping on line is growing exponentially using electronic payment methods with delivery via the post or with a courier man knocking on the front door of the customer bearing their purchase relatively shortly after the transaction has been processed.

The products that are put on offer will be determined by the demand to satisfy a need in the marketplace. Broadly the merchandise may be categorized into food stuffs, hard or durable goods such as appliances, furniture and electronics and soft goods that have a limited life span typically clothing, apparel and fabrics. Whatever the nature of the product, the key objective will be to acquire and sell the product at a price that will be more than it cost to bring it to the place of offer and thereby make a profit.

Supporting activities such as the storage, movement of the goods, technology, and marketing will endeavour to ensure that the form, function and profit objective is maximised.

In an effort to put in perspective the activities and interaction between the various functional players and their dependency and integration with each other for the end to end process of the product workflow is broadly depicted in the diagram below

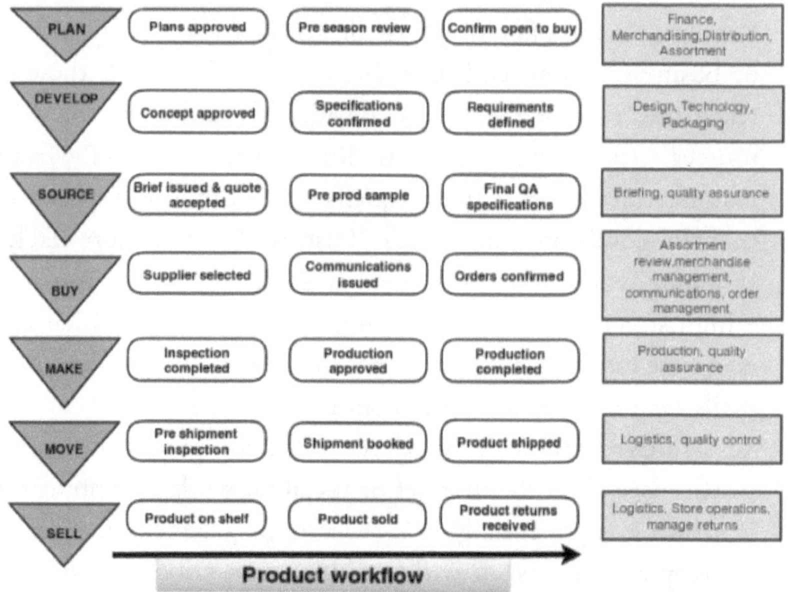

The distinction between supply chain and value chain should be clarified in that it is frequently misunderstood and the interpretation is varied.

Simply put, supply chain is the processes and activities that take place from conceptualisation of styles through to the procurement of raw materials and production process to the logistical operations and the eventual delivery to the end user. The value chain component is the inclusion of those functions that support the supply chain process such as the marketing philosophies. Human resource management, and consultancy resources.

The intimate details of the roles will be exposed in the future chapters as the science of retailing is explored in greater detail.

The retail players

The saying "no man is an island" holds true in many spheres and this is certainly the case in the world of clothing retailing.

Various players, each with very different specialised skills are amalgamated together to deliver a completed outcome which is that of presenting product for sale to potential customers. These players are often very diverse not only in the activities that they perform but also in their personality traits which they possess. The key to a successful team is how maturely the interaction takes place and the mutual respect that every member has for each other's roles.

Below is a brief synopsis of the main player's roles and their dependency and integration with each other. The intimate details of the roles will be exposed in the future chapters as the science of retailing is explored in greater detail.

THE PROCUREMENT TEAM

The foremost players in the clothing and apparel procurement team consist typically of the following members and are described in broad terms.

Designers

Designers have a deep insight into the market they are targeting through the analysis of the changing trends and use these to provide creative direction and develop product designs for the buying teams to consider.

Usually, these participants tend to think out of the box and their creative minds can challenge some of the comfort zones of other team members. What must be kept top of mind is that they need to consistently apply their intellect way ahead of time as to what they think the customer requires as opposed to their personal desires.

Typically, the character traits which they will possess are that they are independent, spontaneous, extroverts, driven by ideas and are confident by nature.

Although the general perception of the word "designer" conjures up a vision of those who work at couture level, the reality is that it also includes those who are involved in creating ranges which may also be exclusive but will be more widely available and therefore can be considered as having been mass produced. Their choices will be influenced by the type of retailer they work for or the product category that they design for. The more traditional retailer which serves predominantly mature customers will be less influenced by radical fashion swings which in contrast will definitely affect the younger market's high fashion boutiques more rigorously.

Work is done at times under enormous pressure to meet critical deadlines, tough meeting schedules and involves frequent international travel. It is not surprising the perception is often one that they live a life of glory and glamour but contrary to this belief the reality is that it is not as extravagant as made out to be.

The fashion and trade shows, whether they be for yarn, fabric or garments are tiring affairs requiring hard work and stamina as is the shopping for appropriate samples, researching fashion magazines, the use of forecasting trend agencies, internet and blogs and out of all of this they need to possess the ability to then distil the emerging trends to create a storybook that will best suit their organisation's customer profiles.

The designer lives with the constant strain of knowing that their level of success will be measured by the eventual amount of money rung up at the till and getting the styling direction wrong or overextending the life of a particular look could have severe financial implications, especially in the cases where volumes are high.

The real challenge is to convince the buying teams and senior management to buy into their vision and have the confidence that what they have in mind will be commercially acceptable to the customer. The designer cannot ignore the technical aspects of the garment production as many problems can be evaded if these are taken cognisance of during the design process.

Retailers in the southern hemisphere do have the advantage that their seasons follow those of countries in the northern hemisphere which allows them to tap into the more successful designs that are trading in volume. However, with globalisation this is not always as clear cut as it was in previous years and the ability to follow as close to the season as possible requires techniques that facilitates the shortening of lead times and attempt to get the product to market as quickly as possible. The advent of communication technologies such as satellite television, internet and social media have brought exposure to different cultures, sports, films, lifestyles and trends such as those generated by specific events, health drives, environmental awareness and technology platforms that can have significant impacts on fashion which sometimes happen at very short notice.

A very important aspect is that the designer must adhere strictly to, is that of copyright. Instances have occurred that other competitor's garments are copied almost identically whether it be by style, print or design. Invariably the driving reason for this is the speed of being able to turn on a replica at a cheaper price. Although it may not be practical to register and copyright every design, any infringement can still be challenged and a consequence could occur of having the offending garments being removed from display and destroyed.

Buyers

The buyer needs to have a clear understanding of the product that is required which is in line with the trend guidelines best suited to their target customer profiles, for both the high fashion segment as well as those that best serve the more traditional customer.

It is a fact is that the role of the designer and the buyer may be a bit blurred in that they research the same fashion forecasting sites and other sources of inspiration in order to put a range of garments together. Both roles must be aware of sizing, quality and costs related to fabrics, trimmings and production. To achieve this successfully they must be flexible enough to develop and buy the most suitable product that is in line with the prescribed strategy and achieves the desired profit margin in keeping with the set down targets. The evaluation of competitive activity and product ranges through regular store visits and comparative shopping provides the knowledge required to keep ahead of the field.

Effective communication and presentation skills are a prerequisite to brief and interact with suppliers as well as presenting product reviews to colleagues within their own group at all levels of seniority. With this comes the need to be able to accept criticism and resolve problems in a mature manner. The sad fact is that frequently when the analysis of the success of the range is evaluated at the end of the season, if the results are disappointing it is not uncommon for the buyer to shoulder the emotional burden of the poor performance. The truth of the matter is that the range was presented on more than one occasion to all team players including senior management all of whom signed the range off but in the final analysis they are more often than not, as is human nature, reluctant to be accept any proper accountability.

Coupled to ability to understand the wants of the customer is the sourcing of the most suitable supplier that will be selected for the specified product types in terms of their particular skills, technical ability, costing efficiency, attitude, transparency, honesty, focus on quality, communications and competitiveness while still meeting the ethical criteria that are acceptable to society.

A large part of the task will be to maintain good relations with suppliers, while at the same time being able to assertively negotiate prices with them and make sure the planned stocks are delivered on time. Communications need to be clear and specific to avoid disputes over issues which may arise through vague and confusing messages. For these reasons they need to be confident, take decisions based on results and be driven by a sense of urgency.

The buyer has to be multi-talented in that as well as being creative they also need to monitor the sales objectively and be flexible enough to react accordingly in terms of turning on or turning off production and transferring fabric and components to more appealing product styles where sales performance and fast emerging trends dictate.

What is key to be a successful buyer is the ability to work as part of the overall team and influence the rest of the team's activities which could be in the form of a managerial and developmental capacity that could also include both their peers and superiors.

The display of emotional maturity and commercial acumen within the controlled parameters as set by the merchandising arm in terms of the budgets, the number of product options and display space constraints is absolutely essential.

The same principle applies to the relationships that need to be maintained with the technical teams in regard to the use of the most appropriate fabrics which meet the product form and function demands in addition to ensuring that the brand standards of the garment are observed.

The fact that potentially the buyer together with the other retail players will be dealing with three to four seasons simultaneously at different stages for each season makes their task even more complicated. To clarify the phenomenon a bit further, the journey of this book attempts to describe the process from beginning to end for one season but while trading in the current season the thoughts and strategies are being developed and documented for two or possibly three seasons ahead followed by the range development leading up to the production taking place for next upcoming season.

The ability to absorb and interpret vast amounts of information from various sources, much of which originates from complex IT systems, can present a challenge to those who are not analytically minded. Systems have altered the scope of the traditional buyer from being a pure "touchy feely art skill" to having to develop basic technical abilities through the continual emergence of innovative systems which have become a great advantage to the role.

Some buyer's, such as those for knitwear, ladies structured underwear, tailoring and footwear will require more expert fabric and garment construction knowledge of their respective industries in comparison to individuals who select the more straightforward cut, make and trim products such as dresses, blouses and casual trousers.

As the trade environment has become more global and through information technology development it is much faster, interactive and has enabled business to be done more effortlessly from a home base interacting with many different countries. A great deal of the job is done amongst many new emerging countries which has led to a need for urgency and nimbleness in order to locate the most effective plants that meet the quality requirements, be able to assess the required technical abilities, understand the economic and cultural demands of the respective countries as well as the logistical peculiarities and government regulations that may exist.

The sourcing of production has to take on different approaches as the pros and cons of dealing internationally needs to be carefully weighed up against those of dealing with the ever-diminishing number of local suppliers. A critical factor is that suppliers must be ethical in terms of labour practices, remuneration, waste management, working conditions and safety. If such conditions are not met it is counter to the interests of the retailer to be associated with such suppliers from both a moral point of view and the exposure of malpractices could lead to negative media reports and the retailer will suffer the consequences that accompany such deeds. The measurement of performance is therefore key to gauging the effectiveness of suppliers.

In larger organisations a buyer will probably be supported by an assistant or trainee buyer who will normally be a person who wishes to pursue a career in the field. They will be largely responsible for the organisation of the ranges, perform some clerical work whilst preparing products for garment reviews, monitoring the product development critical path and production milestones, liaising with suppliers and technology as well as deputising for the buyer when they are out of the office.

A point to note is that the relationship between buyers and suppliers often develops into more than a pure business association since they spend much time travelling together and working closely with one another building ranges. Close familiar relationships frequently make it difficult to maintain a business-like association for the mutual benefit of both parties and can cloud business decision making and judgment. The temptation of bribery and incentives in exchange for placing large orders may be desirous. For newer naïve buyers the rule that the supplier is not your friend should be firmly applied simply because they are more easily seduced by grandiose lunches and gifts as many have unfortunately found out the hard way when they move on and are no longer of great importance to the particular supplier.

A way of balancing the workloads or ranking of buyers and merchandisers is to evaluate the actual number of suppliers, stock keeping units or barcodes being handled by each buyer and then make comparisons regarding workload and productivity of each buyer to established benchmarks.

Merchandisers

There is a novelty t-shirt on the market which has the following statement blazon across the front panel which reads as follows – *"Merchandise Planner – we do precision guesswork based on unreliable data by those of questionable knowledge"*. Although the humour can be appreciated it should be known that this statement is not too far from the truth as the success of merchandising objectives is reliant on many diverse inputs.

The merchandiser or planner applies their focus on maximising profitability from the business end. This is done largely through the analysis of historical sales and the influence of the trend direction to determine the range categories and product breakdown within the overall sales budget.

The role defines what stock levels are required to meet the preset targets such as seasonal stock turnover or forward stock covers based on the sales trends over time. Knowing these requirements, the merchandiser will determine what intake or purchase quantities are needed at any point in time in the season for the total department and each product category.

The level of the budgets will determine the quantity of options in relation to styling, colour palette, size spans, pricing structure and levels of quality per category that will best service the customer for the time that the goods are expected be on offer prior to a new variety of product being introduced in line with the strategic predetermined seasonal themes.

The merchandiser's job has to be to provide guidance to the buyer to procure within the budget parameters. In short it can be described as providing the buyer with a shopping list or range plan that allows them to go out and fill in the blanks on the plan while buying product. This activity requires the careful management of the "open to buy" which can often be a source of tension between the buyer who always tends to want more and the merchandiser who holds the purse strings. A good deal of emotional maturity and teamwork on both sides is therefore critical for a successful partnership.

Sadly, the merchandising role is often branded as a dull, boring number crunching task in accordance with mathematical calculations and while it is this, it can be better described as a creative manipulation of numbers. This task is highly rewarding when positive trade results are achieved or alternatively equally as depressing when these do not materialise. The role can be likened to that of a husband who places his entire salary on a dead cert horse at the races which was by no means appreciated by his wife. However, when the horse won he was similarly unpopular for not putting more money on the horse!

Like the buying role, the merchandiser deals with different activities simultaneously as part of the team across a number of seasons and therefore requires high levels of multi-tasking and re-prioritising in the forward planning, problem resolution, critical milestone management, analysis and timeous action implementation.

As the actual trade takes place the results need to be carefully analysed and immediate action plans initiated in order to maximise the opportunities and minimise the levels of markdowns that erode the profits. For these reasons they need to be logical, reliable, and consistent to take decisions based on fact.

The regular timeous generation of reports detailing sales analysis, stock levels and forward planning needs are distributed to all team members and to senior management. Often numeric information and commercial analysis is demanded on an immediate ad-hoc basis which adds pressure to the job function and can be very disruptive to routines which in such situations requires the merchandiser to adapt quickly and effectively.

The merchandiser plays an integral role during the presentation at product reviews from the numbers perspective which influences the agreed product mix and justification of the levels of sales budgets.

A detailed understanding is necessary of the stores and the customer profile inherent to respective stores that are best met through the attributes of the ranges in terms of styling, colour and size that are put on offer within the store space constraints. The task is best described by the saying "plan each store as if it is your own" which could never be truer.

With sophisticated IT development and the availability of various software packages, some of which may be developed exclusively for the retailer, will provide quick sales analysis, production planning and afford the ability to make sound decisions based on accurate data. This information is especially necessary to give guidance to the allocator or distributor who will be sending the appropriate quantities to satisfy the store's needs as well as give direction as to the level of repeat buys for products that are trading above expectations.

Some organisational structures do differentiate the allocation function between the merchandiser who focuses on the forecasting and production planning and that of the allocator or location planner who will be responsible to distribute the product to the stores in the most appropriate combinations of styles, colour and sizes that meet the store profiles. This function can be housed as an extension within the buying division or may be part of a separate centralised group where an allocator may be responsible for a diverse number of departments. The benefits of such a centralised structure is that there could be a cost saving advantage especially where smaller departments do not warrant a dedicated staff member but added to this is a pool of knowledge which develops a highly skilled team who are able to cross pollinate information, coordinate inter departmental promotions effectively and develop consistent techniques and skills. The identification of common emerging trends will contribute to the optimisation of sales and assist in the control of stock quantities at a very detailed level and thereby maximise profits. Close connections to the departmental merchandisers is maintained to ensure that their actions are aligned to the departmental strategy and plans.

The need for the diversification of the function also makes more sense from the point of view in that where the distribution function is retained within the department it inevitably adds to the increasing workload of the merchandiser. The departmental merchandiser task has more and more been impacted on by the development, the implementation and mastering of complex and sophisticated information systems that analyse sales and stock with added forward planning functionalities.

Many such systems are able to integrate with other supporting IT platforms such as supplier performance, technological measurement, critical path management, ordering, logistical and store systems. The added management of a complex allocation system that is necessary to move the stock to stores is more and more difficult with the result that the incumbent is in danger of being drawn into concentrating on and coping with the intricate detail. As a result, the merchandiser runs the risk of losing sight of the bigger objectives as set out in the strategy and operational plans and the consequent degrading of the inherent merchant intuition becomes very real.

The merchandiser needs to effectively manage and develop the merchandising team which can, not unlike the buying role, consist of an assistant merchandiser or trainee who aspire to be a merchandiser.

The role ensures cohesion of activities that have to be synchronized based on actual sales performance through the formalised interaction with other stakeholders such as the buyers and technologists. This contact is usually in the form of regular, typically weekly, departmental meetings where corrective decisions and plans of action are agreed. Frequent association with the points of sale in stores through written communications and reports as well as formal site visits are critical to keep aligned with the customer's preferences and emerging trends and confirm that the stores are sharing the same vision of the overall strategy.

The need to guide suppliers assertively in terms of prioritisation and the achievement of deadlines is critical to meet the suitable stock requirements at any point in time, particularly in relation to peak seasonal periods or key events. For example, once winter breaks, which it does every year except the exact date is not easy to predict, the objective is to have the right stocks in place such as knitwear, thermal underwear, scarves and the like in sufficient quantities to meet the rush. The usual manner to assist in the anticipation of the weather trend is done through reference to previous years data when the weather changes happened which also help to understand variations in out of ordinary performance at times. The challenge is therefore to have the appropriate quantities in the stores at the vital time while the maintenance of the balance of stocks must be adequate to cater for the demand without overstocking the stores ahead of planned stock targets. Events such as Easter, Christmas, Valentine's Day and Mother's Day are easier to predict and the right levels of stock can be made more accurately available at the right time.

Where suppliers do not meet the required delivery dates, the merchandiser needs to manage the consequences that have to be applied for the underperformance. This can result in some very sensitive and emotional discussions and the negotiation of penalties typically in the form of discounts, sale or return agreements or even total cancellation which will no doubt impact negatively on both parties.

Technology

Technical Teams consist broadly of the fabric and garment technologists. Fabric technologists are highly trained specialists who focus on typically woven or knitted disciplines. Specialised products such as knitwear, tailoring and footwear require added knowledge of components and specific production machinery.

A major portion of the fabric technologist's task is the development and innovation of new fabrics and the enhancement of existing products. New fibres and blends of fibres such as the blending of natural and synthetic fibres, addition of chemicals to finishing process will possibly lead to new inventions and improvements such as better washability, softer handles, easy care properties like easy to iron, crease resistant finishes, rot resistant applications, seamless or seams that are glued that allow for smoother looks particularly for under garments, the evolvement of elastane products such as lycra which revolutionised active and casual wear and the enhancement of thermal properties of winter undergarments. The success of such developments which add to the profitability as well as the form and function necessitates a close working relationship with suppliers, mills and value adders.

Garment technology have the responsibility to ensure that the make-up of the garment meets the set down criteria and the componentry like buttons, interlinings and threads are of the standard that is functional and are not inferior.

Many factories have developed specified technological capabilities that have been built around the production of a particular category of garments relevant to them which vary from factory to factory or even within the same plant. The garment technologist must understand this implicitly and exploit this knowledge to its fullest.

The relationship with the commercial team is sometimes strained as the ideal level of form and function can be challenged by the need to market the product at the most commercially competitive price.

The objective of the garment technologist is to ensure that quality is not compromised. The tasks essential to achieve this can be varied, for example, the assessment of potential manufacturers and fabric mills to ensure that the established standards are achievable, the specification of raw materials, overseeing sampling stages and ensuring that any delays which may result through the process do not compromise the delivery prerequisites.

In safeguarding that all quality standards are met particularly through the inspection of garments, inspectors need to possess specific skills. Quality controllers should be ethical, sincere and honest, open mindedly being willing to consider alternatives, be diplomatic and tactful in their dealings with people and are able to actively observe their surroundings as well as perceive and adapt to varying situations.

The technologist has an intimate knowledge of the supplier base through historical awareness as well as from continually researching new and existing suppliers. As the sourcing specialist they have to guide buying teams in the selection of the most appropriate manufacturer for the various types of product. It is also very essential that they are conscious of the fabric prominence for the forthcoming season as dictated by the strategies and budget levels to ensure that there is sufficient capacities at the relevant mills to meet the overall demands without compromising quality.

The task of assessing potentially new suppliers is a role that may be included in the stable of the technical team or it may be hived off to defined sourcing specialists who are knowledgeable team members that recognise the strengths and weaknesses of suppliers and based on this where best to place orders accordingly.

Suppliers are assessed on various criteria such as their management infrastructure, financial stability, specialised equipment availability, fabric specialty, levels of innovation, fashion or basic production orientation, the other retailers they serve, their flexibility of cost negotiability and social responsibility policies. Other external factors that may well influence the selection of suppliers could be those like prevailing exchange rates, remuneration policies and physical locality.

In summary, the significance must be emphasised that the diverse buying teams all have to have a clear informed understanding of each other's roles and priorities and that they are aligned to ensure all their tasks are integrated to achieve the goal of delivering consistent quality products manufactured by appropriately skilled suppliers on time all the time. This is especially imperative in the case of more complex products such as corsetry, tailored garments and knitwear.

The handling, packaging, storage and movement of the product through the supply channels has to be done in such a way that the quality of the product is not allowed to deteriorate in any way whatsoever. As some product is sourced from more distant locations a newer trend is to contract the technical function out to approved independent technical service providers or to trusted garment and fabric suppliers themselves who understand and are committed to the standards required. These service providers are thereby able to approve samples, perform quality control and be responsible for the eventual release of the finished product.

THE SELLING OPTIONS

There are many ways to expose the product to the customer in the hope that they will take a positive decision during the shopping process. More often than not, the nature of the product will influence the type of channel that is selected but whatever format that the retail store takes, it remains very simply a part of the integrated supply chain whereby goods are purchased in large quantities directly from a manufacturer, wholesaler, trading house or agent to be sold on in smaller quantities to the end user.

Retailing can be done in the more traditional fixed locations like stores or markets but in recent years there has been the evolvement of more innovative ways of selling the product, a typical example being "pop up" shops whereby a temporary location is used in a busy environment which is possibly a sports event, trade show or similar location where large volumes of potential customers are present. It is also an easy way of promoting goods or the carrying out of special launches.

In the modern era of technology the internet is probably the fastest growing medium through which to sell product. Online websites now exist for all types of goods and all the major traders as well as dedicated online retailers are spending large amounts of money to set up their sites in such a way that they are very user friendly, faster and most attractive with secure, easy payment methods.

The main objectives of such sites is to enable the offer of products, create a level of trust and inspire the customer to make a purchase. The establishment of trust can be aided by the use of testimonials whereby the experience of past customers affirm the selling proposition.

Door to door deliveries at an additional fee or which alternatively may be absorbed by the retailer are carried out by sophisticated courier services from various highly efficient distribution centres. International purchases in foreign currencies are also relatively easy to do in this way and customers receive the parcels within a reasonable period of time.

Another option is that the retailer may choose to carry out picking of stock from brick and mortar stores which are in close proximity to the online customer but it should be noted that this choice does bring challenges in sustaining consistent full availabilities and maintaining accurate data integrity. Similarly, some retailers offer the facility of "click and collect" whereby the customer places an order online and at a time convenient to them collects the order from a designated store. There are also outsourced specialised delivery services that can deliver to varied pick up points across a number of facilities which in fact could be another retailer in an area which is not related to the original source of the purchase which allows for greater ease of convenience that suits the lifestyle of the customer.

The problem that customers do have is that they are not able to try on the garments so retailers need to devise some convenient special service options such as the provision of critical body measurements to assist in the determination of an appropriate size.

The fact however remains that there are many online shopping platforms popping up every day but the challenge remains for them remains for all of them is to convert visitors to actual buyers. In order that this is achieved effectively there must be certain fundamentals present. The landing page must be compelling consisting of great visual images and bold statements that highlight the features of the products on offer. The presentation of user reviews inspires confidence in the minds of potential buyers. The personalisation of customer accounts that based on their track record of previous purchases suggest new products that would be suited to their personal profile. What is of paramount importance is the constant striving for excellence through the products that are sold, the experience on the site, as well as the maintenance of great after sales and service.

Marketing teams utilise various types of techniques to effectively expose the product in the most attractive way to the market. Traditional channels in the form of print, radio, television, in house magazines, flyers, and point of sale material as well as the use of innovative medium such as in store digital signage as a tool when they are making purchasing decisions, permeating fragrances and suitable background music or a store branded radio station all attempt to enhance the shopping experience. The use of posters and bill boards, scratch cards and the like are still very prominent in varying formats, however in increasing magnitudes, the creative use of the electronic channels by way of websites, sms, e-mail and social media such as facebook and twitter are now very evident.

The three most popular social media platforms that are utilised to promote the business is Twitter, Facebook and Instagram. Briefly, Twitter allows the targeting the advertising according to interest categories, hashtags, promoted accounts, promoted tweets and promoted trends which allow the business to build followers through greater exposure, building brand awareness, sharing content and offering special deals.

Facebook which has a global membership of 1.5 billion is the largest platform in the world and therefore is like to provide the greatest exposure to the business. Adverts can be specifically directed to specific locations, genders, interests, workplaces, status and relationship statuses. Facebook remains a very cost-effective means of advertising and if the message is accurate it can be extremely successful and effective.

Instagram is the fastest growing platform, and it is estimated that at more than 45% of major brands use this platform to promote their goods. The advertisements can be done in the form of 15 second videos, and photo link advertisements. Typically, Instagram is more suited to brand niche advertising and social media managers need not to tale this forum too seriously but rather sees it as a way to have a bit of fun and actively interact with their community. In this way it can be seen as a tool to build long lasting relationships with the audience and the brand.

It should be noted that today's customers hop from researching products on their smartphones to viewing them physically in a brick-and-mortar store or ordering them online without hesitation. While this has transformed the retail experience compared to a few years ago the merchant's priorities of driving sales, enhancing efficiency and delivering the absolute service have remained the same.

Up until recently the choice of medium was simply based on the sheer traffic volumes that were enjoyed. Fortunately, the approach has changed significantly and the determining factors which influence the decision of what platform to apply is now more customer centralised in that marketing campaigns use those platforms which their target customers frequent the most. In other words, the company realises that the customer data is linked to the people rather than the devices and thereby can create personal experiences across varying channels.

The systematic collection of customers data through the interactive media allows the customer profiles to be analysed and targeted in a more scientific way. Loyalty programmes are very popular and mostly reward the customer either in the form of points which can be cashed in at a later stage for the purchase or provide an immediate discount at the till point. Such programmes are not only extremely effective in significantly improving sales and profits but they also allow the retailer to interpret in detail the buying habits of the customer and consequently thereby are able to better service the consumer needs. Other benefits include providing the retailer's reputation a boost and improve on-line presence and drives additional traffic to the site and thereby gain more customers.

While shopping generally refers to the activity of simply buying a product it has become very much a recreational activity whereby a visit to the shopping mall becomes a wonderful experience which may or may not necessarily result in any purchase being made. Some malls may have added attractions such as theatres, ice skating rinks, stages for entertainment and even larger magnetisms such as aquariums and fun parks while facilities such as gyms are not an uncommon appendage. Restaurant and fast-food eateries are an integral part which are often positioned in centrally located food halls where both the major brands and specialised restaurants are represented.

The dominant tenants are the major retailers who are regarded to be the crowd pullers. The main mix comprise of large food chains together with typical mass clothing retailers while other stores such as general chains provide the bulk of hard and specialist goods like electronics, appliances, stationery, furnishings, jewelry, pharmaceuticals and sports shops.

A complex combination of line shops who derive their name since they flank the interlinking walkways between the major tenants and tend to be more exclusive in their offerings. The rentals are usually at a much higher rate and the closest adjacency to a major tenant comes at a premium. Line shops will typically include outlets such as hairdressers, opticians, beauticians, boutiques, dedicated outdoor gear retailers, accessory specialists, luggage shops, photographic stores, religious retailers selling inspirational product and even tattoo parlours. Other options include the barrow type outlets selling product such as ties and accessories and specialized delicacies.

What is also evolving to a greater degree is the presence of international chains and brands from all over the world as it has become increasingly easy for stores to open due to improved technologies and exposure both from an IT perspective as well as the use of efficient transport methodologies. It has reached a stage where very few major retailers ignore opportunities to trade internationally especially where domestic markets have become saturated and increasingly competitive. The lure of new emerging markets are great but can be challenging in terms of the differing profiles of customers and culture considerations as well as the unforeseen detection of hidden costs.

Malls are strategically positioned close to residential dense areas and the science of the mix of line shops supported by the major tenants are largely influenced by the demographics of the area that they serve. Such malls may be supported by adjacent discount shopping centres which mostly include many clothing, shoe and factory outlet stores. Factory shops enable manufacturers or traders to market over runs, rejects, problem lines at reduced prices in locations that enjoy lower rentals. Liquor outlets, hardware stores and nurseries are also frequently seen adjacent to the main shopping complex.

A factor that should be addressed in the layout of malls is the ease of shopping and the implementation of plans for the free flow of traffic which does not stress the customers particularly during peak times when the mall corridors are jam packed with people. This state of affairs is leading to an ever-increasing trend towards convenience shopping where the establishment of smaller shopping centres on the fringes of suburbs dispenses with the anxiety and lessens the time required to complete the shop.

The mall has largely been the cause of the demise of the "high street" store as is evident by the many major chain stores who have succumbed. The operations have consequently closed or have relocated to the shopping centres outside the city. However, there is still a place in certain instances for these stores to remain as is seen in some cities where there is in fact a reverse trend as there is still a density of office workers as well a growing inclination to live within the city centre which has led to surplus office space being transformed into apartment blocks or new developments being constructed.

Traditional general stores and co-operatives offering a broad range of everything for the community and mom and pop family run shops who purchased from the travelling salesman most found in the rural areas are now very far and few between. Centralised shopping locations consist most commonly of tenants where all the relevant chains being represented with the influx of the discount shops specialising in goods from the East, (some of which may have originated from dubious sources), are now in almost every town. This has sadly relegated these old-fashioned stores to no longer being in existence.

Franchise stores offer the opportunity for individual traders to invest in a mass retail group and enjoy the benefit of the support from the chain's branding, quality products and marketing strategies. The advantage for the franchisee is that the expansion and market penetration can be accelerated with external investment, and they enjoy a commission for goods sold without the risk of stock holding costs, overheads and staffing expenses. The success of a franchise venture will depend mostly on enough working capital, reliable support from the franchisor and the emotional involvement in the business of the franchisee with suitable staff in the right location at affordable rentals.

CASE STUDY

As a hypothetical working example the model of CH Clothing Company chain of stores will be assumed as to have the following characteristics

CH Clothing Company is a mass fashion retailer is a chain of thirty stores spread over the country and also includes an on line facility for the purchase of its products that are on offer.

The breakdown of the thirty types of outlets will consist of the following

Ten mall based stores – based in densely populated towns

Fourteen regional shopping centres based on the borders of suburbs

Five city centre based stores high street units surrounded by offices and city apartments

One on line facility for product purchases

In terms of the retail profile the breakdown of selling units can be illustrated as follows together with a representation as to how the turnover may typically be apportioned per store. Naturally this may well differ in terms of the stores themselves but also across the different product groups as well as the varying customer profiles.

In short the chain of CH Clothing Company can be broadly described as follows:

"CH Clothing Company is a respected mass fashion retailer selling mid-price quality product with a broad representation in malls, regional locations, city centres as well as supporting an on line facility offering core basic product supplemented by on trend mid fashion elements to capture a wide cross section of customer profiles".

Below is a diagrammatic view of the CH Clothing Company which depicts the selling outlet structure and the respective typical sales proportions.

MALL STORES 10 stores 60% sales		REGIONAL STORES 14 stores 20% sales		CITY CENTRE STORES 5 stores 3% sales		ON LINE FACILITY 1 store 17% sales	
Mall 1	12%	Reg 1	6%	City 1	1%	On line 1	17%
Mall 2	10%	Reg 2	4%	City 2	.3%		
Mall 3	9%	Reg 3	1%	City 3	.3%		
Mall 4	8%	Reg 4	1%	City 4	2%		
Mall 5	7%	Reg 5	1%	City 5	.2%		
Mall 6	7%	Reg 6	1%				
Mall 7	2%	Reg 7	1%				
Mall 8	2%	Reg 8	1%				
Mall 9	2%	Reg 9	1%				
Mall 10	1%	Reg 10	1%				
		Reg 11	.5%				
		Reg 12	.5%				
		Reg 13	.5%				
		Reg 14	.5%				

CHALLENGE #1

Based on the different store formats for CH Clothing Company and their relevant contributions to the total company sales consider the following

1. What will the main influences be that will influence the range selection in Mall stores?

2. Regional stores customer profiles may differ from one store to another as a result of different factors that need to be taken into consideration. List four of these factors.

3. City centre stores will not necessarily be evident in all cities. What are at least two drivers that will determine the need to establish a store in a city?

4. The on line facility can have various options of the distribution channels available to deliver the order to the customer. List three possible methodologies of fulfilling the customer orders.

In days gone by the goods were stored in walk-in counters often being displayed behind glass and in drawers with sales assistants serving the customer from within the unit as well as manning a till stationed at each counter. While this way of serving customers was very effective from an interaction point of view it soon became unsustainable due to the demands of mass retailing and convenience for the customer.

The newer formats of stores are well lit, uncluttered and appealing to the customer. They house easy to access product which is in sufficient quantities with well demarcated information through attractive signage. Displays whether on shelves, tables or garment rails are well thought out and coordinated in cameo presentations that are lit in such a way that suggest to the customer how the product pieces can be worn together in terms of lifestyle and colouration. Displays are adjacent to complementary customer needs, for example women's skirts will be located close to the blouse displays which will be adjacent to the ladies trousers. The ladies outerwear will most likely be next to the lingerie department which will lead into ladies sleepwear. There can also be a thread of the chosen similar colour themes throughout which are being promoted at that point in time.

CASE STUDY

CH Clothing Company product offerings consist of the following product types and groupings such as the Menswear, Ladieswear, Girlswear and Boyswear which then are cascaded down into categories or departments. Within each category there is further subdivisions of the parent category which describes the subcategories which then are divided into product groups with similar attributes. Within each product group there must be an optional number of permutations of styling features, fabric types, designs colour ways and size ranges that are selected which consolidates into the entire balanced offer that CH Clothing Company will construct in order to safeguard the broad satisfaction of the customer profile that they seek to satisfy.

The illustration below attempts to describe the construction of CH Clothing Company structure and decision options that are required for their shirt department in their Menswear group. The range construction proportions will be determined by the assortment planning section which will be intensively explored in later sections of the book.

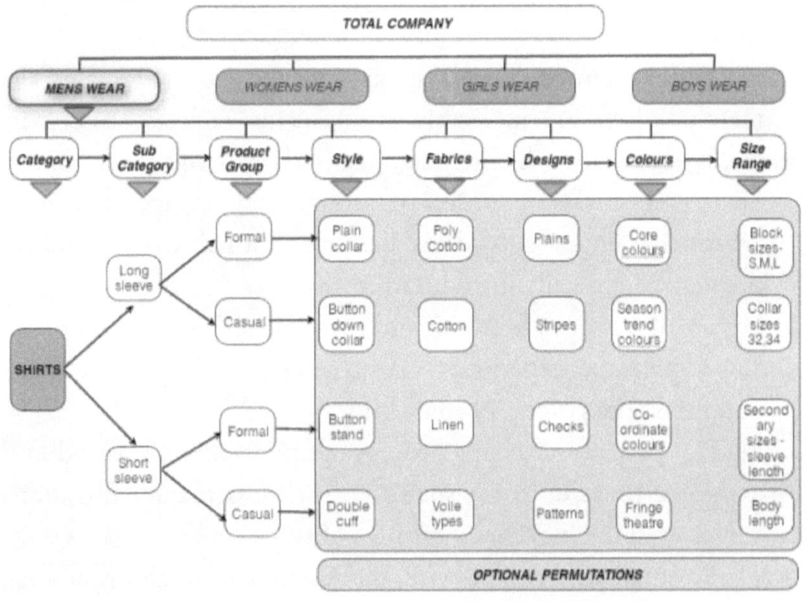

CHALLENGE #2

In the hierarchy of product selection for Menswear shirts illustrated above with the intention to create a balanced selection option for the customer comment on the following:

1. Consider an alternative method of creating the subcategory and product group splits for shirts.

2. In the more conservative older customer profile type of stores versus the high fashion stores serving the younger markets list the comparative percentage proportions of fabric types for each customer personality.

3. In the size category where provision is made for secondary sizes such as in addition to the collar size there may be a choice of different sleeve lengths. Name other types of products which may also offer similar different choices of secondary sizes.

Focus cameo displays as created by specialist visual merchandisers are in highly visible areas such as aisles, window displays or walls which change regularly to convey the message of prevailing stories in order to attract and engage the customer. Seasonal changes, special events, promotional activity and colour themes are typically introduced in this way and thereby sustain the impact of newness, freshness and excitement. The customer not only has a pleasant experience considering the proposition, but the potential opportunity of a sale is maximised.

Pay points and change rooms are conveniently placed and the design of these units are such that they lessen the frustration that comes with the inevitable waiting periods.

Personal interaction with the customer by any staff member whether they are the sales assistants or management can never be substituted. Service remains of paramount importance in ensuring that they can illustrate to the customer the ways in which styles and colours of the different components can tastefully be worn together.

Payment methodologies are also focused on to ensure that the customer has an enjoyable experience and is not frustrated by the task of having to stand in long queues. Technologies are advancing at a rapid pace to minimise long queues and newer examples are in the form of a shopping basket being scanned in total which eliminates the individual handling of each product, the evolvement of the contactless card which does not require the customer having to swipe cards, provide pin numbers or sign any slips. All that is required is the simple tapping of the card against a card reader for payment to be processed. Another innovative process is the establishment of self-service pay points whereby the customer checks out their own goods and thereby saves considerable time. Whatever the sophistication of the payment methodologies there is one basic requirement that retailers need to make provision for and that is having a card facility. Without such a facility they will not survive for the following simple reasons. Cards are now a global form of payment and are particularly important to international travellers. They are convenient for everyone as they minimise the necessity to carry cash and are therefore less of a security risk and should the card get lost or stolen the can be quickly cancelled via a telephone call which makes them safer than carrying cash. Card payment also enables bigger purchases, which may or may not be a good thing, but research shows that customers tend to make about thirty percent bigger purchases as opposed to only using cash. Because a card leaves a trace it allows for accurate tracking of transaction history and enables more responsible management of financial resources.

For the retailer, the advantages of card facilities is that they enable real time transactions which includes reporting and reconciliation. Added to this they empower the acceleration of transactions, tighten control and security and most importantly reduce costs across the board.

The unfortunate downside is that they are a soft target for cyber criminals and therefore need to be carefully protected through disciplined usage and password or pin code control.

The need for refurbishment and revitalisation of stores and displays is an ongoing process, which although being costly, regularly presents the customer with a fresh and exciting environment to enjoy the shopping experience and avoid being faced with stale, run down and drab looking stores that undermine even the most attractive merchandise.

As with the buying teams, the selling teams also consist of a mix of skills that are coordinated in such a way that the customer has a most satisfying shopping experience.

The team is spearheaded by general manager who is the head of the store. This position maybe supported by an assistant officer, and they will ensure that the overall co-ordination of all the roles will deliver the most efficient running of the operation. A classic structure that they will manage consists of commercial or departmental managers each of whom will be responsible for a segment of the store.

Their role will focus on ensuring that the displays are constantly fully stocked and that they are optimally positioned and displayed proportionately appropriate to the customer demand. By way of illustration the most popular product will normally be in the front of the racks and displayed at the eye level of the customer. The size of the display will be proportionate to the relative demand, in other words, in the ideal world a product that represents twenty percent of the sales will enjoy twenty percent of the space of the relevant display area. Exceptions to this principle may occur where the product may be bulky and will have to be pallet stacked on the floor. An example of this would be nappies, duvets and cushions.

CASE STUDY

CH Clothing Company has a basic layout format of the various groups and departments and product which will accommodate the flow of the customer in such a way that the greatest exposure is provided. A typical layout is reflected below.

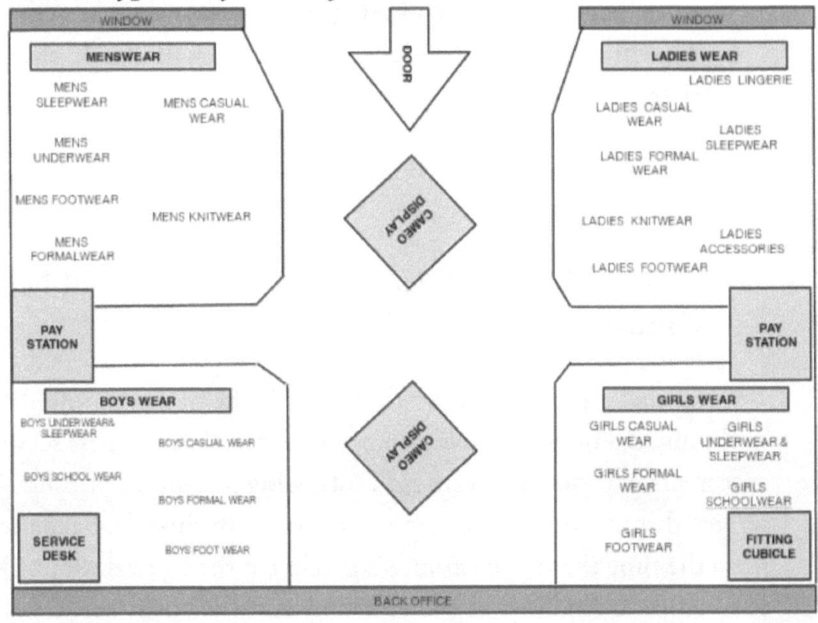

CHALLENGE #3

Based on the basic layout plan for a CH Clothing Company store answer the following questions

1. In each of the product group sections what will determine which product groupings will flank the aisle?

2. What product will be featured in the cameo displays and windows?

3. What factor will determine which group will be situated at the door?

The challenge is to ensure that there is the optimum number of well trained, knowledgeable and positive staff that can best serve the customers without the overhead costs being put under pressure. The service disposition should apply for the entire shopping experience from the time that the customer is greeted at the front door until the transaction is finalised at the till point and the customer leaves the store with the added objective being that the customer will always look forward to returning to the store. Even where a sale may not transpire the offering of advice or patiently helping consider alternatives is part and parcel of ensuring that the customer will return.

Selling teams are supported by other staff functions such as the human resource officer who will be responsible for the personnel functions as well as the shift scheduling of staff. This task is imperative to ensure optimum staffing which is appropriate for the inconstant number of customers over the various times during the day, week month and year of trade. A flexible, part time work force is required which can be more than two thirds of the total store staff and because some of the hours of work are unsocial such as weekend or after normal hours variable rates of remuneration or extra time off will apply.

TRAINING

One of the common requirements of each role that has been outlined is that in order to achieve the highest degree of proficiency there should be a structured methodology of training which will include on the job training where the incumbent is mentored by a qualified and experienced more senior specialist who in turn has had exposure to effective training methods and performance management techniques. Ideally as the trainee progresses they will take on the responsibility for a small section of their department in order to gain the confidence and skills that will stand them in good stead going forward and also serve as a contingency in the event of the loss of senior personnel.

Coupled to on the job training is the formal classroom style lecturing as is necessary and can be performed by either internal or external tutors who will provide the theory that is matched to that which has been learnt on the job. This is of great importance as it is not uncommon that with on the job training exclusively the poor habits of the trainer are frequently transferred downwards.

Equally important is for new appointees to have an understanding and appreciation of the roles of their counterparts in other areas of the business. In order for this to be achieved they should spend adequate time attached to specialists in other fields. An example would be where a buyer in training would need to spend time in stores interacting with customers, at suppliers, with merchandisers, technologists, the marketing team and packaging specialists, in the warehouse and with the logistical experts including forwarding agents. These attachments should be well thought out with specific objectives in mind and followed up in formal reviews in front of a panel of experts from each area who test their understanding. An independent representative from human resources should also be present to ensure that the consistency of standards applied across the business is maintained and the assessment is objective without any personal bias of trainers subjectively influencing the conclusions either positively or negatively.

Overall, in order to guarantee the creation of professional teams is that the training needs to be consistent and that the outcomes deliver broadly the same standard of qualified appointees. An outstanding illustration of this is where the customer enjoys the same high level of service from sales personnel in whatever store they frequent, or suppliers enjoy similar levels of proficiency across different buying teams.

Two common errors that are made which dilute the depth of knowledge is firstly, the situation where managers are appointed over areas where they have had none or very little exposure or experience. This leads to them being unable to assess the information presented with authority and makes the mentoring role required to develop juniors in some cases ineffective.

The second error that is relatively common is the assumption that because the person may be extremely proficient in performing their task it will automatically mean that they will be equally good in being the boss. The truth is that the exact reverse may well apply in that they may not have the inherent management skills and invariably will over focus on the detail and still have the desire to continue doing the work themselves.

Both such scenarios will lead to the situation where the officeholders will lose confidence in themselves and the respect of their subordinates will be weakened.

CASE STUDY

A typical training pack and formats at CH Clothing Company will probably look as follows

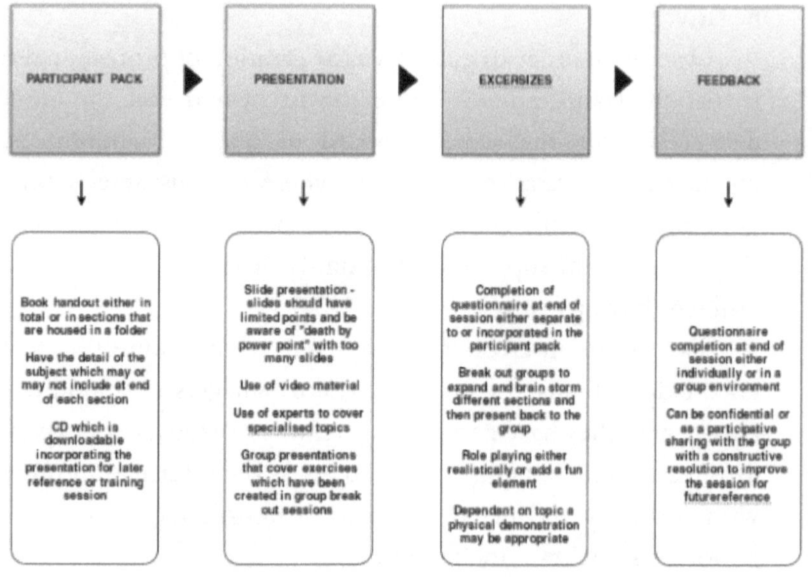

CHALLENGE #4

Comment on the advantages or disadvantages of the use of following the options highlighted in the scenario above

1. The benefit of the CD option for the participant pack

2. The dangers of "death by power point " in presentations

3. The advantage of break out group excersize

4. The advantage of groups in the feedback for the improvement of the session

PROCESS FLOW OF KEY RETAIL ACTIVITIES

While a lot of activities are required from conceptualisation to the eventual offering of a completed product to the customer they do nevertheless follow a relative set sequence of events even though there may be at any point in time where they can possibly overlap each other.

In the sections that follow, the detail required for each key activity will be explored and their relationships and dependencies on each other will be highlighted.

The journey commences broadly with strategy formulation and the strategic planning for each stakeholder area, the creation of a merchandise plan through to the buying of the product within the budgetary parameters. The commercial team have the support of the technology teams to establish the technical requirements as well as the sourcing of appropriate suppliers in order to enable the production of the product.

The packaging is detailed to assist in the marketing of the product and protect the garments in transit and storage. Orders are initiated and the critical production milestones are managed in such a way to ensure delivery deadlines are met timeously.

During production the quality inspection and supplier performance management takes place and once the order is complete the products will be allocated and delivered either directly to stores or to a storage facility. In some instances, there may be value added processes applied to the goods after which they will be transported to stores.

Once the goods are on offer to the customer the sales are analysed and reviewed in order to adjust where necessary. At the end of the season the lessons learnt are noted and applied to the strategy development for the new season.

SCENARIO PLANNING

From a broader perspective it is wise to evaluate the forecasts of your own and respected scenario planners to attempt to understand any possible impacts on the business and trading environment that may or may not evolve in the future. Scenario analysis is used to formulate a picture of the potential trading landscape in the longer term. Previously strategic planning was almost simply the financial extrapolation of past history going forward with hardly any qualitative discussion about the social conditions where the combined effect of various factors can have a significant impact. Some of these that we think we know about are forward trends, demographic shifts and the impact of new technologies. Those which we have no knowledge of are the uncertainties which are almost unpredictable such as currency rates, interest rates, outcomes of elections, impact of dominant political leaders, effect of political sanctions and the road ahead in terms of high risk hotspots such as the circumstances currently being experienced in the middle east, the consequence of an overwhelming influx of refugees into various countries, fads and fashions and technological innovations.

The changing of the way we work

There is a well-worn saying about change and that is certain is that there will be change. In talking about change it is unusual to understand what is unlikely to change and there are elements that will not change soon.

Included in these elements are items such as certainty where we know we need assurance that it is possible to avoid pain and gain pleasure. A basic need is also that we need variety to keep up the levels of stimulation through continuous change as well the desire to feel significant through recognition and develop a feeling of belonging or being loved and respected. The need to continually wishing to grow and expand our capacities and capabilities will never change and the contribution that we make will satisfy the sense of delivering to the best of our ability. Building a feeling of trust amongst all those with whom we interact is a major factor. All these elements will remain static while the environment wherein we operate will without doubt keep on changing on a continuous basis.

The way we work in the longer term is highly likely to dramatically change. There is no dispute that the way tasks are completed is rapidly adapting to suit a totally new environment. The advancement of technology, connectivity and the expectations of both employers and employees are demanding that the economic activities be radically reviewed.

There is an ever-increasing trend to relocate resources from the traditional high density centres such as Hong Kong, Tokyo, London, Paris and the like because of high living costs, fast increasing rentals, and salaries which are being outpaced by costs. As a result the purchasing power of residents is being severely diminished and therefore this tendency is forcing organisations to relocate to areas where it is cheaper to live and conduct business. Technology has aided this process as it is easier to operate from remoter areas and still have access through tools such as Google, Dropbox, Skype and the like which makes it just as easy to service customers as effectively no matter where the base location is. The base link ups could also be temporary in that desks could be rented with all the required technological facilities, boardroom or conference facilities supported by the appropriate equipment and catering requirements thus saving investment in permanent structures.

Apart from being able to conveniently work from different sites the necessity for a substantial portion of the workforce no longer have to negotiate the traffic or use public transport daily and therefore the surplus time saving can be productively utilised. There are instances that those firms who find it difficult to adapt to this newer culture and stubbornly maintain a level of mistrust have experienced a depletion of suitable staff and productivity as the workforce prefer to pursue a flexible option. It is important that the mind shift of acknowledging that the quality delivery of tasks should be the measure of productivity and not the actual time spent in the office.

The trend has evolved that an incumbent is no longer a specialist in one field all their life. With the ongoing development of new processes, technologies and systems to be successful there is a continual need for education and re-education. One big degree for a lifelong job at one corporation is being replaced by a culture of a repeatable cycle of learning then work, then learn again and work to sustain competitiveness in the labour market. It is fact that where in the past job hopping carried a considerable stigma, this is now more than ever becoming the norm.

In days gone by, the evidence of consistent job hopping on an applicant's resume hinted that in all likelihood presented a negative perception that the candidate probably had a people issue and did not get on with others, could not hold down a job, was disloyal and could not commit to a long-term relationship.

The reality is that the opposite is becoming the actuality especially with regard to advancing through a continual learning and relearning process and the new job-hopping millennia's are now perceived to possess a higher learning curve, perform better and deliver above expectations as they pursue the drive to make a favourable impression and assert themselves in a shorter time period with each employer.

Because such employees are continually challenging themselves outside their comfort zones they are typically over achievers who deliver a significant contribution to the bottom line which stands them in good stead before they move on to new opportunities every two to four years. It is believed that the learning curve tends to flatten after three years so in fact regular job hopping has become crucial to ensure a stable career growth.

It nevertheless can remain a concern for companies as there is a continual requirement to invest in new staff, but the upside is that the rapid growth of the organisation and the worry of the loss of intellectual property to competitors is less threatening because the swift change makes the impact of the loss of such intellectual assets soon to be outdated.

The world is also seeing an exponential growth of entrepreneurs who with their specialised knowledge, offer their services on a short-term basis simply by working as freelancers or contractors. With a wide-ranging exposure they enhance their skills and are thereby able to raise their rates or acquire additional freelancers to assist them and consequently grow their personal wealth.

Preparation of a Scenario Plan

Scenario planning can be defined as the blending of the known and unknown into a consistent future point of view. All our knowledge that we have is about the past, most of which can be described as we don't know what we don't know, a smaller percentage is knowing what it is that we don't know, and the smallest percentage is being aware of what it is that we actually do know. The conclusion is therefore the knowledge that is required in order to make good decisions is mostly beyond our comprehension.

Coupled to the knowledge base, the different types of futures can be categorised into "possible" or that which might happen based on future knowledge, that which is "plausible" which is what could happen and therefore depends on current knowledge, that what is "probable" based on current trends and lastly that which is "preferable" which is what we want to happen based on value judgments.

The proportionate levels of knowledge inputted into the different types of future

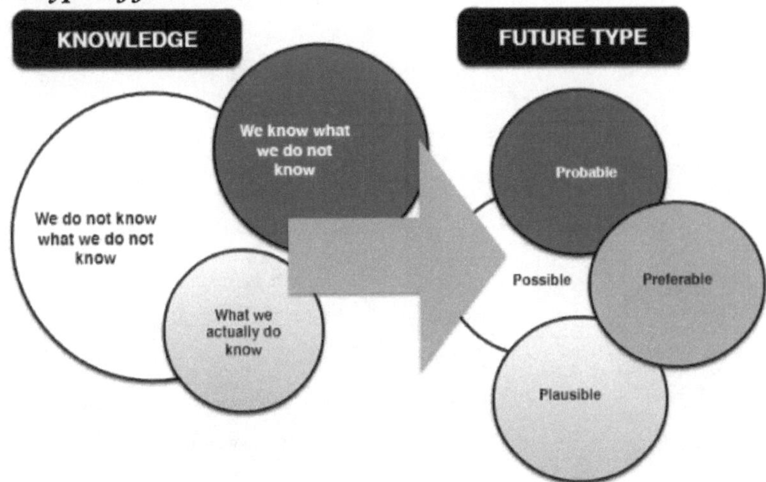

Scenarios can be described as possible views of the world in a narrative or story form which enables better informed forward decisions being able to be made which is likely to assist in the formulation of a successful strategy. It should be noted that scenarios do not predict the future but rather highlight those drivers that are most likely to influence the future and form part of the strategic management toolbox which consists of traditional methods which focus on the past while scenario planning tools focus on the future. By combining both the past and future the strategic thinking process is therefore stronger and enables better responsiveness, improved flexibility as well as generates a competitive advantage

CASE STUDY

The CH Clothing Company scenario plan could possibly reflect the   *following*

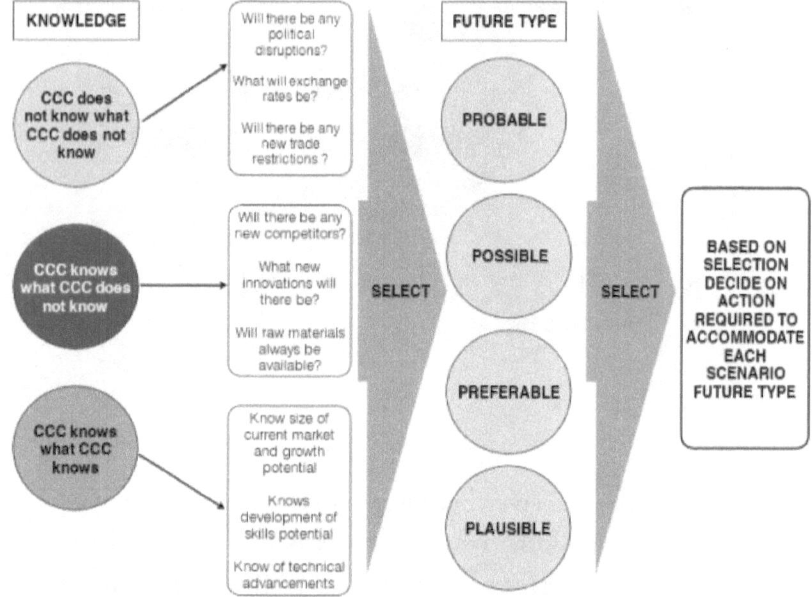

CHALLENGE #5

Based on the CH Clothing Company individual landscape diagramme above complete the following

1. Utilizing the three types of knowledge and the examples of the situations, select for each one those that will be either PROBABLE, POSSIBLE PREFERABLE or PLAUSIBLE

2. Once the selections have been made list what possible actions could possibly be taken for each item "CCC knows what CCC does not know" knowledge grouping.

The creation of such scenarios follow a simple structured sequence of events where conscious long term judgments such as the identification of the major influences and factors within varying situations can bring about significant changes to the way business is done and deliver a diversity of results. Scenarios can be created through the grouping of complimentary influences into a framework of a number of "what if" situations. The number of these may then be reduced to an amount through amalgamation or elimination to end up with a manageable quantity of scenarios which would possibly have the greatest effect should they occur.

Selection of key drivers

After both an internal and external environmental scan is done, the consequence is the identification the key factors or subjects which may well decide the future nature of the environment in which the organisation will be operating. These forces will form the pillars of the areas which need to be examined and the specific definition of those drivers that will form the base of the different scenarios. Once the important topics are acknowledged, they are used to create scenarios which deliver alternative outcomes and should include the important predictable as well as the unknown outcomes. Typical examples of such drivers are those that represent the social, economic, technological, environmental, globalisation and political aspects.

The environmental scan will include an internal analysis of the company in terms of the strengths and weaknesses as well as an external scrutiny of the threats and opportunities which may or may not exist. Part of the scan will include an exploration of the industry that the business operates within. This will include the examination of the barriers that exist to enter the industry, the existing supplier infra-structure, customer base and evidence of substitution products as well as the rivalry intensity that is present amongst the participants.

After assessing the environmental scan, the firm will match those strengths they possess to their benefit and address the weaknesses as well as acknowledge the threats to the possible opportunities that may exist.

The macroeconomic environment factors also need to be taken into consideration, sometimes referred to as the PEST analysis (which is the acronym for political, economic, social and technological) that will impact on the firms operations.

Political factors include government regulations and legal issues under which the company must operate such as tax policy, employment laws and regulations, environment boundaries that may exist, trade restrictions and tariff structures as well as the overall political stability.

Economic facets that will influence the scenario planning process will be the economic growth, interest rates, inflation and exchange rates.

Social factors such as demographic and cultural aspects in the macroeconomic environment which will affect the customer needs and market penetration are typically health consciousness, population growth, the spread of age distribution and attitude to careers.

Technological factors such as automation, research and development will have significant impacts on production efficiencies and the extent that tasks need to be outsourced.

The CH Clothing Company key drivers and factors identified during the environmental scan is illustrated below

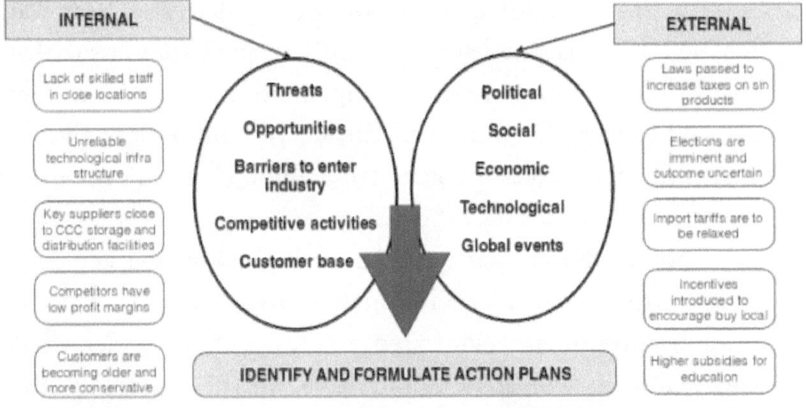

CHALLENGE #6

From the illustration above you are required to perform the following

1. Identify and categorise the factors under the internal and external headings to those depicted in the respective circles.

2. Once the categorisation is completed, formulate action plans that will either maximise the opportunities or minimise the risks that may or may not exist.

Brainstorming

Before we proceed any further it is valuable to describe a simple brainstorming process.

There are many techniques of brainstorming, some of which are more sophisticated than others. A very popular, basic and easy to use methodology, although it may be slower than other processes, is through the use of common sticky notelets.

All that is required is an isolated room with a clear wall and maybe a flip chart to list comments and park some issues for later discussion. The number of participants should not be too few but also not too large. In most cases the ideal quantity should be no more than fifteen which is a controllable amount that normally can be comfortably managed by the facilitator.

Prior to the commencement of the session the key drivers or pillars which were identified in the environmental analysis stage must be prominently indicated as the headings under which the sticky notelets will be randomly stuck on the wall which have the advantage that they can be removed or relocated as discussion progresses.

As is the case with the majority of brainstorming sessions, the generation of ideas invariably stimulate the creation of others which are pasted on the wall and the participants can move the posts around the wall under the designated headings as they wish. The process is relatively user friendly and therefore it is also easy for newcomers to grasp the concept and enjoy participating.

The illustrated example below assumes that the key drivers that will serve as the headings on the clear wall have been defined as political, social, technological, economic and environment.

The participants are then able to actively write their ideas on the notelets and paste them under the relevant heading.

Once all the ideas are exhausted and are evident on the wall under the appropriate headings the next stage will be to identify those that are important versus those that are not in terms of their levels of impact and uncertainty on the future. In order that this is done effectively the application of the eighty twenty rule is critical so that only those factors which are most relevant are focused on. Just allowing a number of topics to be randomly selected in terms of their perceived importance often results in those topics which are purely of interest being selected as opposed to those that are prioritised according to the commercial significance.

The eighty twenty rule

The eighty twenty rule, also known as the Pareto principle, recognises that a principle of eighty percent of the result is delivered by twenty percent of the effort or participants. It should be recognised that this is not a precise formula but is more an illustration of the principle and therefore the bulk of the results will be produced by a much lower number of participants.

CASE STUDY

In the case of CH Clothing Company if we refer to the illustration of the distribution of the percentage sales percentage contribution across the total catalogue of stores. This graphic representation clearly depicts the Pareto principle where in this example eighty percent of the sales occur in the top eight of the total thirty stores.

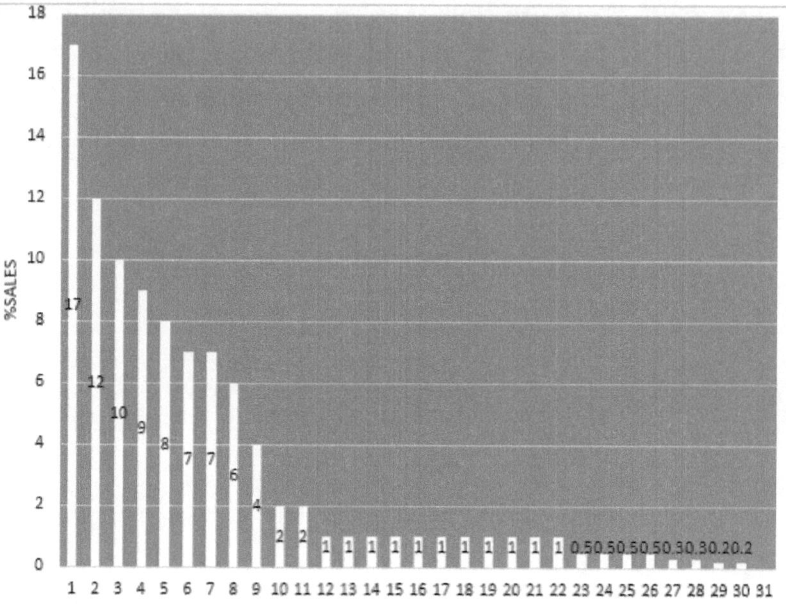

CHALLENGE #7

Taking into account the above example of the distribution of sales turnover across the total number of stores respond to the following

1. Provide two other examples where the eighty twenty principle may apply

2. What commercial decision may be taken should the tail-enders with low results be considered unviable?

Prime examples in retailing is, for example, in the context of stores it is probable that twenty percent of the stores deliver eighty percent of the sales and deserve the proportionate dedication of energy and focus, as does the thick middle sizes such as medium and large and therefore should always be in stock. Core base colours such as white, black, naturals and greys also contribute largely to the sales and should always be evident in volume. It is clear that certain styling features will likewise guarantee the bulk of sales and should be finalised first and certain peak trading periods such as holidays or special events will contribute largely to the total seasonal sales and must be managed very carefully in terms of production planning and delivery scheduling.

Once the important topics are identified, the use of them to create scenarios which deliver alternative outcomes should include the important predictable inferences as well as fictional conclusions.

The next step is to integrate these key influences and thereby create a framework or scenario matrix. The linking of some of the influences can take place where the characteristic of one factor may be relevant to another while, on the other hand this may not always be the case. The brainstorm participants therefore arrange the elements into groups that have relevance and make some sense. The amount of groups that emerge will be dependent on the number of elements available to contemplate. While this process is in progress it is possible that new groupings may be added while others could be removed. As these clusters of elements materialise, the creation of the mini scenarios may be linked together based on their similarities or mutual influence and eventually a process of rationalising and absorption can take place to condense the mini scenarios into two or three core scenarios. All of the above will entail extensive debate before common ground is met in order to agree the fundamental insights into what the really imperative issues are applicable to the organisation. Once this stage is achieved, because of the intimate understanding of the participants that has developed, it will be almost instinctive without any reference to any formal report to know how to cope with potential issues should and when they materialise.

Presentation of scenarios

The final two or three scenarios that are constructed need to be written up in a formal format to serve as a consistent guideline for team leaders to base their strategy on. The report will in essence be more qualitative rather than be peppered with intense detail although reference may be made to tabular work and diagrams but in whatever emphasis this happens, the report needs to remain factual.

An example of the simplistic building of a scenario plan using the process described above is depicted below

Key headings and notelets pasted below on the clear wall with the annotation of importance of each comment in terms of impact relative to uncertainty is depicted as follows

POLITICAL	SOCIAL	TECHNOLOGICAL	ECONOMIC	ENVIRONMENT
Influence of global governments	Increasing population	Increasing reliance on technology	Declining trade of traditional commodities	Increasing acceptance of environment awareness
1 Li/Hu	**2** Mi/Mu	**3** Hi/Lu	**4** Li/Mu	**5** Mi/Mu
Influence of dominant world leaders	Aged more economically active	Improved health environment through better technologies	Globalisation	Continued degradation of natural environment
6 Mi/Mu	**7** Hi/Lu	**8** Mi/Mu	**9** Mi/Lu	**10** Hi/Lu
Global conflict	Cultural transformation through globalization, immigration and technology	Newer and cleaner renewable energy resources now viable	New technologies creating channels for empoyment	Declining water quality
11 Hi/Mu	**12** Li/Mu	**13** Hi/Hu	**14** Li/Hu	**15** Hi/Mu
Terrorism	Increased life expectancy and quality health support	Increasing technological devices making shopping easier	Evolution of single global currency	Declining air quality and increased energy consumption
16 Hi/Hu	**17** Mi/Lu	**18** Li/Hu	**19** Mi/Hu	**20** Mi/Hu
Influence of key election results	Rural areas being developed increased urbanisation	Combination of technologies to make on line trading become economically efficient	Traditional employment approach creating unemployment	Impact of global climate change
21 Li/Lu	**22** Li/Lu	**23** Mi/Lu	**24** Li/Lu	**25** Li/Mu
Influence of non government organisations				
26 Li/Hu				

Uncertainty

Low (Lu) – very that activity will happen in the way that we expect

High (Hu) – no certainty as to what will happen

Med (Mu) – somewhere in between

Impact

Low (Li) – effect of activity will deliver low results

High (Hi) – effect of activity will deliver high results

Med (Mi) – somewhere in between

A Scattergram below illustrates according to the corresponding shapes the relative significance of impact and uncertainty of each comment

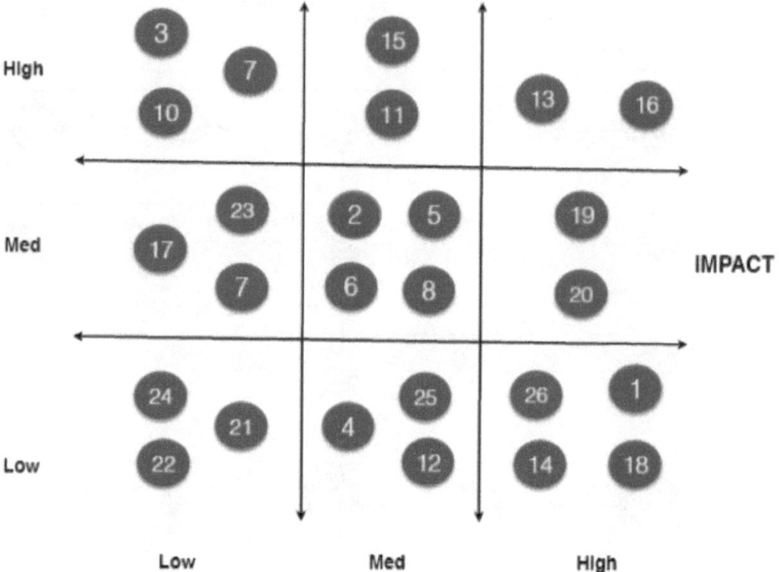

The two highest uncertainty and highest impact critical external factors (right top of the matrix) which will be selected according to our model will be

- Terrorism

- New and cleaner renewable energy resources which are now economically viable

The three most critical internal factors in terms of impact and uncertainty which will be selected are

- Increase in market penetration through innovative and technological methodologies

- Availability of safe retail space

- Supplier management and sustainability

In the scenario workshop the participants will need to consider the world of the future taking into account the external and internal factors and the influence they will have in creating the environment in which trade will take place.

During the process of imagining the world of the future it is essential that participants are not influenced by personal opinions such as not believing it possible, mistrust and relying on intuition but should rather focus on the plausibility perspective. By way of illustration the drafting of the scenario of the future period must be therefore be done taking into account the following types of points

- What will the world be like going forward? To do this take into account the events that brought change to where you are now and project those events that will influence the world going forward.

- In building a picture of a future world consideration should be given to the effect of current indicators are not necessarily a foregone conclusion should they change significantly. As an example, if the borrowing interests increase, the growth of the economy will probably be undermined and consequently the currency in relation to other currencies will be worth less. However even if the interest rates are conversely reduced unless the domestic demand for product is strong enough, the currency could still deteriorate. The possibility of exporting more product, or attracting more tourism will have a positive influence on growth as will attracting foreign investors. Commodity prices will also change the landscape dramatically such as a weak oil price will enable cheaper costs but it may not be weak but is gaining strength so in this case will have the reverse effect.

- Will your organisation exist in this new world going forward? What would you look like? Are you going to be global? Will you be virtual or physical? What will your customer look like? What will your organisational structure look like?

- The drafting and presentation of the scenario does not have to be off the wall but above all should be creative.

The main uses of scenarios is to provide a common language for ongoing forward discussions, assess the risks involved when taking specific decisions, assist in the evaluation of current strategies as well as in the development of new strategies.

Scenarios provide clues as to what the strategic drivers of the future might be, how they may interact and in what way they may affect the organisation. The identification of robust strategies that will be able to survive future scenarios is key and are able to assist in detecting early warning indicators to know what to do in the occurrence of such events, some of which may be catastrophic beyond control, wide in scope and rapidly moving. Examples of such events could be a stock market collapse, a terrorist attack or disrupted water and electricity supply.

One certain conclusion about change is that change will happen. The skill is, through scenario planning is to identify in what way organisations will change. Examples of how they are likely to change could be such as from an autocratic environment to an empowerment one, from a structured life to an unstructured life, from a volume based production base to a need for speed to market base, from high predictability based on historical trends to a world of uncertainty, from slow change to rapid change and ambiguity, from reliance on processes to reliance on people, from structured hierarchical organisations to alliances and coalitions, from avoiding risk to managing risk.

The final message to take note of is that the traditional strategic planning processes are no longer sufficient on their own but need the support of well thought out perceptions of the future.

CASE STUDY

Below is a simplified example of a CH Clothing Company scenario view which under the key driver groupings certain events are listed and tagged in terms of the levels of certainty that are prevalent. Added to this, comment is made as to the form and impact that these events may take.

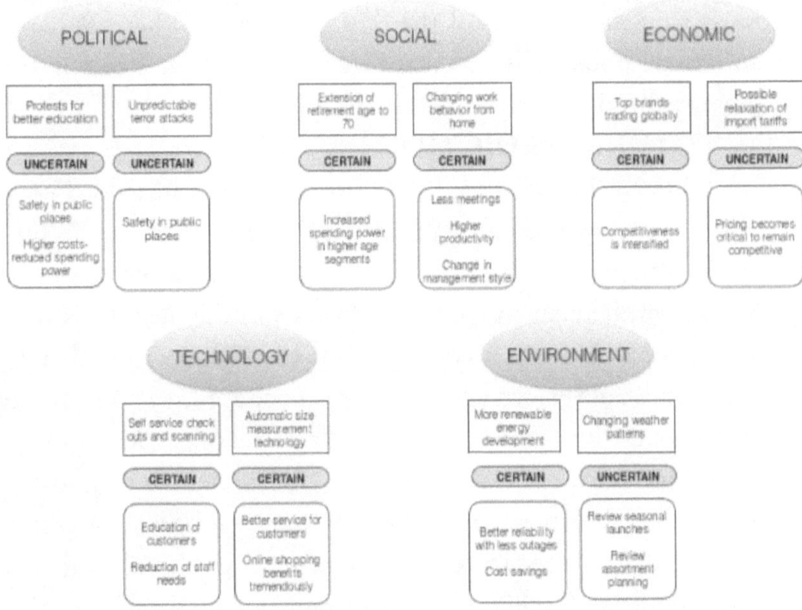

CHALLENGE #8

After assessing the possible impacts that the possible events may have describe what action or preventative could be taken in the following situations

1. Under the political grouping what action can be taken to make shopping more secure?

2. In terms of the changing work behaviour what are examples of the different technical options available to enable these changes?

3. With the changing weather patterns what methodologies can be applied to confirm the validity of these theories?

During some of my research, I came across an article written by Robert M. Goldman MD, PhD, DO, FAASP that had such an impact on me in terms of the illustration as to what has happened and what potentially can happen in our world, I felt it best be presented verbatim to maximise the message.

FUTURE PREDICTIONS

In 1998, Kodak had 170,000 employees and sold 85% of all photo paper worldwide. Within just a few years, their business model disappeared and they went bankrupt. What happened to Kodak will happen in a lot of industries in the next 10 years - and most people don't see it coming. Did you think in 1998 that 3 years later you would never take pictures on paper film again? Yet digital cameras were invented in 1975. The first ones only had 10,000 pixels, but followed Moore's law. So as with all exponential technologies, it was a disappointment for a long time, before it became way superior and got mainstream in only a few short years. It will now happen with Artificial Intelligence, health, autonomous and electric cars, education, 3D printing, agriculture and jobs. Welcome to the 4th Industrial Revolution. Welcome to the Exponential Age.

Software will disrupt most traditional industries in the next 5-10 years.

Uber is just a software tool, they don't own any cars, and are now the biggest taxi company in the world. Airbnb is now the biggest hotel company in the world, although they don't own any properties.

Artificial Intelligence: Computers become exponentially better in understanding the world. This year, a computer beat the best Go player in the world, 10 years earlier than expected. In the US, young lawyers already don't get jobs. Because of IBM Watson, you can get legal advice (so far for more or less basic stuff) within seconds, with 90% accuracy compared with 70% accuracy when done by humans. So if you study law, stop immediately. There will be 90% fewer lawyers in the future, only specialists will remain. Watson already helps nurses diagnosing cancer, 4 time more accurate than human nurses. Facebook now has a pattern recognition software that can recognize faces better than humans. By 2030, computers will become more intelligent than humans.

Autonomous Cars: In 2018 the first self-driving cars will appear for the public. Around 2020, the complete industry will start to be disrupted. You don't want to own a car anymore. You will call a car with your phone, it will show up at your location and drive you to your destination. You will not need to park it, you only pay for the driven distance and can be productive while driving. Our kids will never get a driver's license and will never own a car. It will change the cities, because we will need 90-95% fewer cars for that. We can transform former parking space into parks. 1.2 million people die each year in car accidents worldwide. We now have one accident every 100,000 km, with autonomous driving that will drop to one accident in 10 million km. That will save a million lives each year.

Most car companies may become bankrupt. Traditional car companies try the evolutionary approach and just build a better car, while tech companies (Tesla, Apple, Google) will do the revolutionary approach and build a computer on wheels. I spoke to a lot of engineers from Volkswagen and Audi; they are completely terrified of Tesla.

Insurance Companies will have massive trouble because without accidents, the insurance will become 100x cheaper. Their car insurance business model will disappear.

Real estate will change. Because if you can work while you commute, people will move further away to live in a more beautiful neighbourhood.

Electric cars won't become mainstream until 2020. Cities will be less noisy because all cars will run on electric. Electricity will become incredibly cheap and clean: Solar production has been on an exponential curve for 30 years, but you can only now see the impact. Last year, more solar energy was installed worldwide than fossil. The price for solar will drop so much that all coal companies will be out of business by 2025.

With cheap electricity comes cheap and abundant water. Desalination now only needs 2kWh per cubic meter. We don't have scarce water in most places, we only have scarce drinking water. Imagine what will be possible if anyone can have as much clean water as he wants, for nearly no cost.

Health: There will be companies that will build a medical device (called the "Tricorder" from Star Trek) that works with your phone, which takes your retina scan, your blood sample and you breathe into it. It then analyses 54 biomarkers that will identify nearly any disease. It will be cheap, so in a few years everyone on this planet will have access to world class medicine, nearly for free.

3D printing: The price of the cheapest 3D printer came down from $18,000 to $400 within 10 years. In the same time, it became

100 times faster. All major shoe companies started 3D printing shoes. Spare airplane parts are already 3D printed in remote airports. The space station now has a printer that eliminates the need for the large number of spare parts they used to have in the past.

At the end of this year, new smart phones will have 3D scanning possibilities. You can then 3D scan your feet and print your perfect shoe at home. In China, they already 3D printed a complete 6-storey office building. By 2027, 10% of everything that's being produced will be 3D printed.

Business Opportunities: If you think of a niche you want to go in, ask yourself: "in the future, do you think we will have that?" and if the answer is yes, how can you make that happen sooner? If it doesn't work with your phone, forget the idea. And any idea designed for success in the 20th century is doomed in to failure in the 21st century.

Work: 70-80% of jobs will disappear in the next 20 years. There will be a lot of new jobs, but it is not clear if there will be enough new jobs in such a small time.

Agriculture: There will be a $100 agricultural robot in the future. Farmers in 3rd world countries can then become managers of their field instead of working all days on their fields. Agroponics will need much less water. The first Petri dish produced veal is now available and will be cheaper than cow-produced veal in 2018. Right now, 30% of all agricultural surfaces is used for cows. Imagine if we don't need that space anymore. There are several startups that will bring insect protein to the market shortly. It contains more protein than meat. It will be labelled as "alternative protein source" (because most people still reject the idea of eating insects).

There is an app called "moodies" which can already tell in which mood you are. Until 2020 there will be apps that can tell by your facial expressions if you are lying. Imagine a political debate where it's being displayed when they are telling the truth and when not.

Bitcoin will become mainstream this year and might even become the default reserve currency.

Longevity: Right now, the average life span increases by 3 months per year. Four years ago, the life span used to be 79 years, now it's 80 years. The increase itself is increasing and by 2036, there will be more than one year increase per year. So we all might live for a long long time, probably way more than 100.

Education: The cheapest smart phones are already at $10 in Africa and Asia. Until 2020, 70% of all humans will own a smart phone. That means, everyone has the same access to world class education.

Robert M. Goldman MD, PhD, DO, FAASP

www.DrBobGoldman.com

World Chairman-International Medical Commission

Co-Founder & Chairman of the Board-A4M

Founder & Chairman-International Sports Hall of Fame

Co-Founder & Chairman-World Academy of Anti-Aging Medicine

President Emeritus-National Academy of Sports Medicine (NASM)

Chairman-U.S. Sports Academy's Board of Visitors

STRATEGIC PLANNING

The commencement of the process to draft and implement a strategic plan follows a set sequence of events that form the foundation of a blueprint that needs to be followed to develop a sustainable plan of action going forward.

The type of points that need to be addressed in the drafting of a plan is to know what the vision together with the corresponding mission is. The relevant customer and their desires specific to the retailer have to be intimately clear.

The strategy ought to be aimed specifically at them in order that the purpose and values of the business is linked by the strategy to the right customer and the other stakeholders. It is therefore important that the strategy is sustainable over the longer term through clear communication, that it directs the focus and effort and thereby energises and inspires people to consistently perform at optimal levels.

Competitors should be clearly identified as well as the factors that will influence both the customer and the competitors of the future. Added to this the competitors are becoming increasingly hostile in a global market which adds complexity bringing with it more challenges requiring additional thought to transform ideas into action in a much shorter space of time often with limited resources. It is therefore absolutely imperative that the retailer should know as much about their competitors as possible and should in fact construct a dossier on each of their foremost challengers. Knowing who the direct and indirect contenders are and how they are performing in the market place, what can be learnt from their operations, what their strengths and weaknesses are, how different they are, the frequency and what media is used to advertise as well as what pricing strategy is employed will assist in the intimate understanding of competitors.

There are two basic types of competitive advantage which are the cost factor whereby the product is the same or similar in form and function to competitors but is made available at a lower price. The second advantage is the difference in the form of added value the product possesses compared to other products on offer in the market. The strategic activities may include plans to create the competitive advantage in one way or the other through the processes as outlined below.

In the strategic planning process the weaknesses need to be emphasised in order to minimise risks, the strengths must to be continuously capitilised upon while at the same time the appreciation of any threats to the business which may hamper the progress has to be taken into account. With all these factors in mind the plan of appropriate operational activities must be formulated in such a way that they are aligned to the vision of the company and support the basis of the strategy.

A firm's strengths are its resources and capabilities to gain competitive advantage and typical of these are patents, reputable brands, reputation, cost advantages and access to effective distribution networks.

The absence of certain strengths can be interpreted as weaknesses and could include factors such as absence of patent protection, weak brands and lack of reputation, high cost structures and poor distribution channels.

The external environmental analysis may result in the identification of the emergence of opportunities for growth and profit as well as certain threats. Examples of opportunities could be the evolvement of new customer needs, development of new technologies, the relaxation of regulations and the possible removal of international trade barriers. The opposite of the opportunities could in turn be seen as the threats to the firm such as the shift away from the products by the customers, the emergence of substitute products, new regulations and the imposition of international trade barriers.

This dependable interpretation of the strategy will enable the planning of management activity that is used to set the priorities, focus energy and resources, strengthen the operational events while ensuring all the key stakeholders are aligned in such a way that the overall company strategic goals are achieved. A documented strategic plan is formulated which communicates the goals and the operational activities that are required to achieve them. Management of the plan must ensure that the processes are systematically coordinated and the resources and actions are aligned with the mission, vision and strategy throughout the organisation.

The framework and methodologies of managing the strategic plan broadly follow the same sequence of phases which are that the understanding of the external and internal environments is developed, the formulation of the strategy is documented, a corresponding operational plan of activities required to achieve the strategic goals is drafted and lastly, the evaluation and sustainability of the plan is managed and continually refined through performance measurement, communications and data reporting.

Diagrammatically the process cycle of strategic planning can be depicted as follows

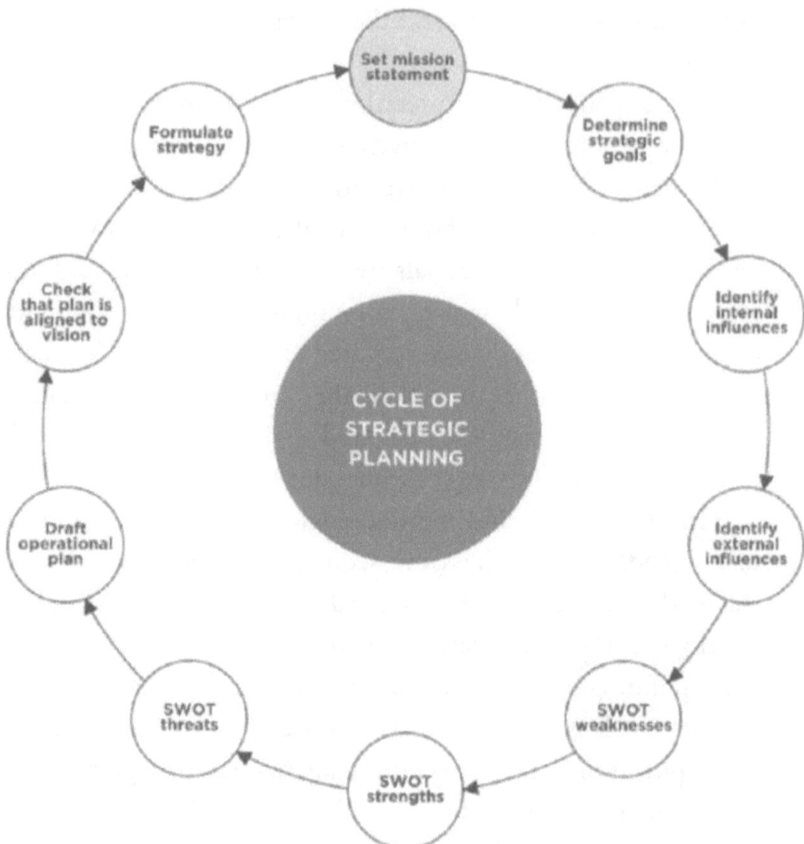

By way of illustration a hypothetical retailer has been formed which follows the creation of the strategy and the subsequent operational plan. In broad terms the business firstly documents its vision which describes the blue sky dream of becoming a preferred retailer which offers clothing that represents exceptional value, is up to date with current trends and is purposeful in both form and function.

The company has a mission to expertly fulfill the customers' needs transparently in such a way that they can be trusted and sustain a high level of integrity.

In order that this can be achieved adequately the set of goals need to be identified that are realistic, are able to be benchmarked and measured. In the simplistic model outlined below there are basically three goals that need to be focused on which are growing market penetration by one percent through the optimum use of media, expand real estate to cater for all regions and develop and implement tools of measurement of supplier performance to ensure the optimum delivery of product to maximise profit opportunities.

In order to remain focused it is imperative to identify where the strong points are such as a loyal customer base and trustworthy and reliable suppliers and constantly focus on protecting these qualities. On the other hand it should be acknowledged that they may well be behind the rest of the field in terms of technologically advanced competitors who are reaping the benefits of digital retail channels and should grasp the potential development of such vehicles as a wonderful opportunity to acquire similar benefits that the competitors do.

CASE STUDY

A simplistic example of the strategic plan of CH Clothing Company can be as outlined below

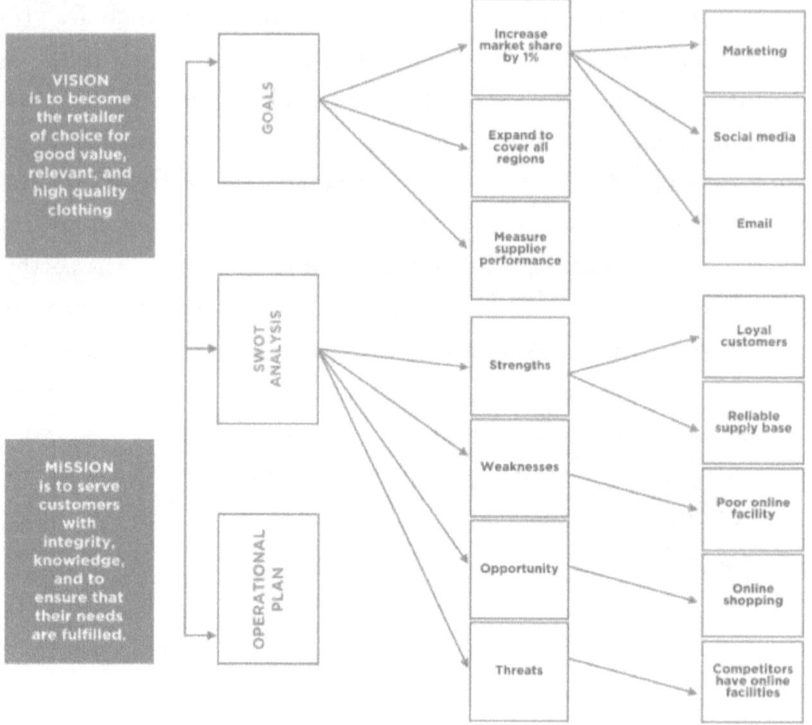

CHALLENGE #9

1. In order to try and achieve the goal of the measurement of supplier performance list three factors that could be monitored to evaluate performance of the supplier

2. A strength that is highlighted is that of a reliable supplier base. What attributes are essential to the making of a dependable supplier

3. One of the weaknesses is noted as a substandard on line facility. Name three factors that are essential to rate the facility to be above standard

As has been stated, the strategic thinking delivers what is desired to be delivered while the operational aspect provides guidance as to how the objectives are going to materialise. The example of the hypothetical retailer who wishes to be a retailer of choice may wish to use the advantage derived from loyalty programmes which could be in the form of discount coupons, the publication of own brand magazines and derive the benefit of sophisticated analysis of the consumer data base to gain better understanding of their customer profile.

The desired sales outlet expansion will have to be achieved through opening of new stores, the remodeling and enlargement of existing stores, expansion of newer formats with the exploitation of those categories which offer the most potential opportunities and the development of an on line sales channel all of which will demand additional location sites, design and IT resources.

The effective measurement of supplier efficiencies will require measurement tools and a reporting infrastructure which will preferably be available on line and provide for a system of penalties for underperformers and incentives for those suppliers who exceed expectation.

CASE STUDY

The corresponding operational plan of CH Clothing Company strategic plan above will therefore possibly look like

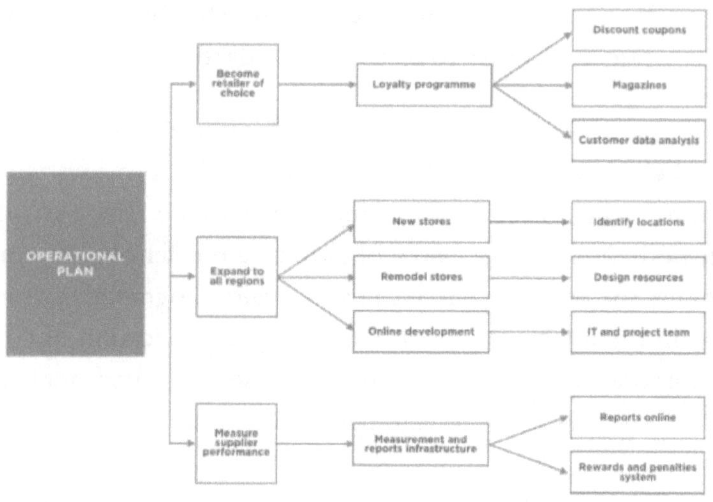

CHALLENGE #10

1. Three examples of different types of loyalty programmes are listed. Note an additional two types of loyalty programmes that could be beneficial.

2. Implementing a store expansion programme, in the identification of new locations, list three components that would make for suitable locations

3. In the measurement of supplier performance provide an example of an incentive reward and three models of penalties systems

The consequences of poorly thought out strategies can be devastating. There are many examples of once extremely successful chains whose buildings that were landmarks are today parking garages. Retailers who have a tendency to doubt outlooks are often displayed through the rear view mirror images which tells us from where we have come has always worked and the subsequent question asked is more often than not "if it is not broken why change?"

The very successful, intelligent captains of such firms often succumb to the destruction of once successful business for a number of reasons. The fear of change is more often than not the cause because the potential is not viewed as an opportunity but rather seen as a risk. When there is a trend being followed by competitors or new entries to the market an air of arrogance takes hold and the dogged belief is upheld that the current trading philosophies which are set in concrete will withstand the onslaught and any other unfamiliar options are doomed to failure.

Taking the importance of new strategic objectives seriously is seen at times as just another routine task on the calendar which needs to be completed but in reality the focus quickly apathetically returns to complete the current responsibilities as before to sustain the operation.

The lack of the leaders who see the big picture and miss out on the benefits in total can be extremely damaging. In their place is only those who resolutely continue the practice of working within their own relevant areas of control and comfort zones and do not consequently contribute to the achievement of an overall vision. Invariably it is the personal objective that dominates which is one of self-preservation as is reflected in the view that as long as their area has performed within the required parameters any failures that may arise cannot be attributed to them.

Similarly some organisations, characteristically those that are family driven or are by nature very staid with autocratic leadership frequently lack imagination to foresee change or are reluctant to "think out of the box" and consequently there is an unwillingness to innovate. When such an approach is challenged it is often met with obstinacy to hold on to what's more certain, defined and secure which is in the present. The effect is that the argument for change is often justified by making the situation sound less critical than it really is and is stereotypically confirmed by erroneous comparisons to other existing case studies.

The success of retailers is frequently measured by the scale of operations and share value rather than by the product quality, shopping experience and resultantly the usage of the phrase "customer service" becomes trite and is nothing but just a throw away statement.

In many circumstances operations were in recent years dominated by the availability of easy credit at stores where the needs of the customer were broadly projected and the product was bought in high volumes across a limited number of categories to lever better prices from vendors. The driving force was to sell them as quickly as possible using mediocre service. Consequently innovation and revitalised selling formats were almost totally stagnant for many years.

The reality is that the consumer has become conscious to this fact and it does not inspire them any longer to remain loyal to a specific brand but rather to source out the retailers who are sincere in their messages, offer service of difference whereby the customers can truly appreciate a better experience. Much of the success of the newer revolutionary retailers is that they have identities that the consumer associate with which may be cultural such as an eastern philosophies, sporting associations with an emphasis on lifestyle and role models where the markets are not dependent on mass and discount but on meaning and have become communities in themselves.

The point needs to be made that it takes some bold mind shifts when the writing is on the wall that failure is imminent and the need to manage the way out of the situation calls for outside interventions, new strategies and tactics and respect in order to emerge on the other side of the storm successfully.

There are some key philosophies that need to be applied to rescue struggling businesses and it is only through embracing these that will possibly provide the essential lifeline. Innovation or evaporate is an ultimatum that cannot be ignored because unless there is some form of reinvention it is without doubt that through doing the same thing over and over again it is guaranteed that oblivion will be the consequence. Knowing your market and their expectations is critical and working within these parameters is paramount and venturing outside these boundaries is likely to lead to confusion and mistrust. Often success can in itself be a stumbling block as it leads to a sense of euphoria and invincibility with an element of complacency. This is a reason why great leaders will continually be questioning as to what is next. Updated systems are key to keeping up with the pack and so often the neglect to adopt newer applications results in calamity and often enforces urgent catch up programmes to remain relevant.in the market place. Lastly but without doubt the most important point is to remember that the customer is king and if an attitude is adopted that they can be dictated to often leads to rejection unless focus is fully maintained on their changing desires, requirements and needs.

Key performance indicators

There have been many portrayals of key performance indicators over time such as "what is measured gets done", "if you do not measure results you are unable to distinguish between success and failure", and "if you are not able to measure it you cannot manage or improve it". In summary it is the true identification of strategic measurements of inputs, project and operational processes which results in the degree of successful or unsuccessful deliverables.

For stakeholders to be able to check whether the performance is on track to achieve the strategic objectives it is measured against a suite of pre-set performance indicators. The most common performance pointers which are assigned targets that will deliver the desired financial requirements, are the following.

Sales
Markdowns
Buying margin
Sales margin
Stock forward cover
Stock annual turn
Return on inventory investment

It is absolutely imperative that these indicators are clearly understood by all members of the retail team both in the head office and stores and what the role is that they individually play in the support of them.The measures are almost always referred to in financial reports as share holders utilise these to determine their level of confidence in the company performance.

CASE STUDY

CH Clothing Company has set their key performance indicators as follows which are typical of their type of trading profile in that they cater for the middle of the road customers with balanced ranges.

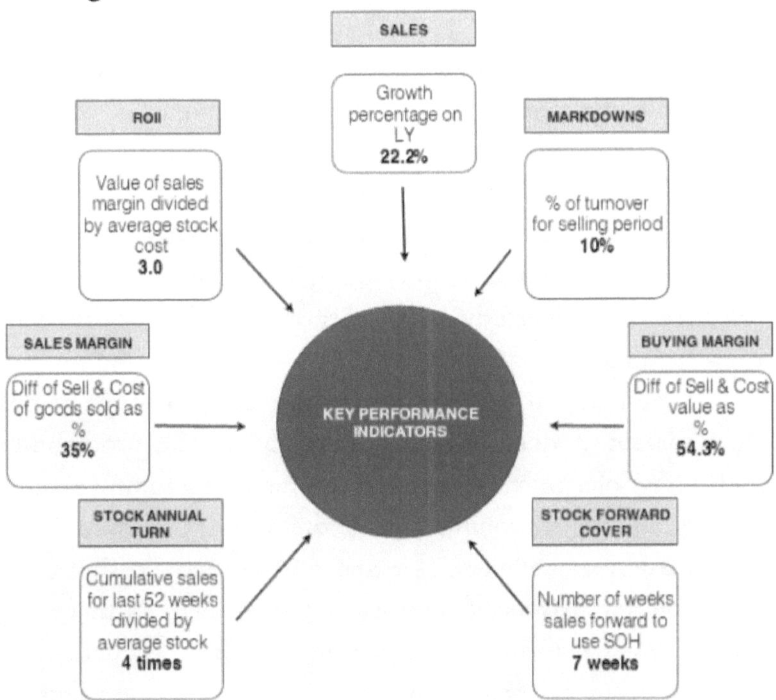

CHALLENGE #11

In the above setting of performance indicators for the middle of the road retailer how will the following be affected how if they were a high fahion retailer?

1. Markdowns?
2. Buying margin?
3. Stock forward cover?
4. Stock annual turn?

The market share measurement is a key performance indicator which is a simple calculation of the company's proportion of the total market. It is essential to consider it in detail as part of the strategy planning process as sales figures independently do not necessarily reflect how well the company is performing relative to its competitors.

The value of the total market is not always readily available and often the involvement of market research companies which have as many retail companies subscribed as they can recruit and through accumulation of each subscribers sales defined in various categories and total are able to determine relatively accurately each subscribers share and communicate the individual retailers results in detail, usually on a quarterly basis, without divulging other member's information.

Although market share reflects the strength of the company in the market it does not necessarily reflect the profitability. The advantage of a high market penetration is that it improves the buying power and higher volumes enable the benefit of economies of scale and thereby the retailer is able to negotiate keener cost prices.

The key drivers of improving market share is that of quality in terms of form and function of the product, the price competitiveness, the effectiveness of marketing campaigns and the network of stores that expose the products to the customer.

In a number of cases it may be preferred to actually decrease market share of product such as where there may be a low margin strategy and therefore the more that is sold the higher is the pressure on the overall profitability and a price war may be provoked.

However it is not only the monetary results that are the key deliverables. There are also the qualitative perceptions of the strategic intent that indicate the the degree of of success of a plan.

Other qualitative performance indicators may exist such as a reduction of the customer waiting time factor where the actual can be measured to a set target which will translate into improved customer retention.

Internal strategic objectives could be the introduction of enhanced systems or processes which will improve efficiency, effectiveness and time savings against set targets.

Organisational capacity improvement might be achieved through intensified training, resources investment and operational processes design which can be expected to deliver efficiency and logistical time saving.

Brand awareness can be improved through technological system enhancements with strategic marketing techniques.

Social awareness and programmes may be established with specific targets being set in terms of goodwill perception and is compared to actuals derived through various means such as data collection from loyalty programmes, questionnaires, membership enrolment and social media analysis.

Good KPI's provide an objective way to see if a strategy is working, offer a comparison to guage the degree of performance change over time, focus employees attention as to what matters that are most probable to succeed, they provide a common language for communication of results that are valid to ensure the measurement of the right things and are certifiable with reference to accurate data integrity.

The balanced scorecard

KPI's are the progress indicators in terms of achieving a successful outcome through the monitoring of the implementation and effectiveness of an organisation's strategy.

The creation of a balanced scorecard may be done through the establishment of target values for each identified KPI and an actual score based on historical values and trends. A certain amount subjectivity is established through applying some weighting to the strategical intent. This activity provides a framework that not only provides performance measurements but also identifies what should be done and be measured which truly enables the execution of a strategy.

Apart from ensuring that the financial funds are in place as a priority to allow for the efficient operation of the company through resourceful and accurate provision of data, the balanced scorecard recommends the analysis of the organisation from other perspectives as well. These include the learning and growth perspective which comprises of employee training and corporate cultural attitude related to both individual and corporate self improvement. In the current rapid technological change it is becoming increasingly necessary for knowledge to be acquired through a continual learning process. It is therefore essential for metrics to be put in place to ensure that sufficient funds are in place in order to accommodate this.

The third business process perspective is to have metrics in place in order to assess whether or not the the business is running well enough to have the products and services that sufficiently conform to the customer requirements. The design of these measurements need to be determined by the right people who intimately understand the mission of the company.

Lastly, the customer perspective has been developed by a retail management philosophy that stresses the importance of customer focus and service. Poor performance from this perspective can only lead to the decline of trading performance even though current sales performance may not immediately indicate this.

CASE STUDY

An example of the CH Clothing Company balanced scorecard can be digrammatically set out in terms of the qualitative assessments as opposed to the pure monetry measures and a form of metric measurement attatched to these in order that they can be rated and actions identified to improve any shortcomings.in order that the achievement of the strategic intent is maximised

CHALLENGE #12

1. Add under the qualitative factors of customer satisfaction and brand awareness an additional key factor for each

2. What additional action can be taken in the case of the shortcoming of organisation capacity?

3. What means of communication would be effective in promoting environmental awareness?

STRATEGIC STAKEHOLDERS

In a clothing retail environment the typical individual stakeholder areas need to focus on their independent strategies for a specific period of time that together must be aligned to meet the overall company strategic objectives. It is therefore imperative that the different areas are scrutinized and activities are adapted to ensure that this objective is achieved.

Illustratively the various pertinent strategic focus areas are depicted as follows

Business unit strategy

The leaders representing each of the key areas will construct the overall company strategy more often than not on an annual basis with interim updates for a specific period as well as for an extended future time thereafter up to as much as three years.

The corporate strategy development and co-ordination is concerned with the definition of the issues that are corporate responsibilities. These may be in the form of the definition of the overall goals as well as the way in which the key stakeholders are integrated and managed.

Fundamental for the company's success is the need to nurture an environment wherein all employees are able to conduct their business in pleasant conditions with fair remuneration enjoying personal recognition and job security. Coupled to this will be the investment of finances across the various components and the development of synergies by the sharing and co-ordination of resources and staff across the different units across the company. The way the units will be governed, either in a centralised or decentralised format will influence the effectiveness of the sharing of resources and staff and therefore this should be considered very carefully in the formulation of the corporate strategy.

Factors which that need to be taken into account in the construction of the overall strategy will be the historical trading performance, current business trends, competitor activity, customer demographics, the growth of new emerging markets, economic trends like increasing fuel prices and interest rates, and evolving trends which can translate into new business opportunities, as is the case of procuring better value goods from off shore suppliers and initiatives like the exponential increase of on line shopping.

Using internal and external research with the evaluation of past performance will determine the budget targets, key performance goals and market penetration potential.

Out of the strategic workshop including the identification and management of the synergies between the key operating areas a corporate operational plan will be developed and disseminated to the relevant business areas to give guidance in the construction of their own individual strategies to ensure that the overall objectives of the company are met. This would include the need for shifts in retail, financial, marketing, information technology, real estate strategies, the sourcing of suppliers, logistical processes and provide individual operational plans that will ensure that the modifications and new initiatives are all catered for. Examples of changes may include action to penetrate new or better serve customer profiles, expand retail channels such as on line, to open new stores in new locations, implement innovative systems and reduce lead times. Fresh initiatives may be in the form of adding new product types, acquisitions, enhancing logistical operations and implement an innovative variation of loyalty programmes.

CASE STUDY

The CH Clothing Company diagrammatic business unit strategy in terms of the development of a corporate operational plan that will give guidance to the critical key areas would probably resemble a format with action plans to ensure new initiatives will be catered for as follows

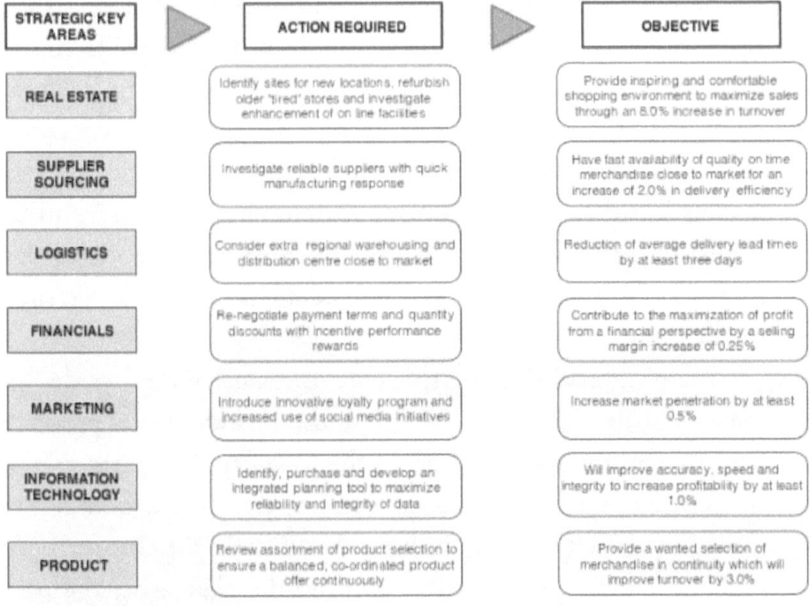

CHALLENGE #13

1. Should a regional store consist of a predominantly more mature age group, name at least three modifications that will be applied to enhance their shopping experience.

2. List three optional loyalty programme methodologies that can be employed to improve the marketing strategy.

3. Apart from assisting the efficiency of a marketing strategy name two other benefits that loyalty programmes bring.

Brand strategy

A considered view of the external and internal retail landscape has to be documented and understood. In order to enable this, team members in the buying groups, marketing, sourcing, technology, packaging, the store's visual team and designers will workshop the information gathered from past sales performance and take on board lessons learnt from the previous season, market share information, loyalty programme data analysis together with trends evident at global trade shows, catwalks, other retailers, suppliers, internet and social media.

From a planning perspective, the analysis of trade at the conclusion of the season which must include space productivity analysis and the modification of the merchandising targets need to be accounted for in terms of the impact on the brand. Typical examples of such aspects would be the effect on the customer profiles and the market penetration opportunities that arise, the open to buy reserve quantities to enable flexibility and impact on stock management and other key performance indicators which may need to be modified.

The task that is undertaken is the formulation of the direction of emerging trends in designs, core fabrics, colours, technical innovation and packaging, marketing communication as well as the highlighting of key global customer and lifestyle trends. These developments can be applied to the future season together with the identification of potential customer penetration opportunities which is vital in the input for the construction of the group buying strategies.

Service is very much a critical component of branding particularly where the retailer is own brand active and that if unsatisfactory service persists it will be unlikely that the operational expectations will be delivered. Experience shows again and again that excellent customer service lowers customer attrition rates, fosters positive messaging via word of mouth and with this comes significant increases in sales.

Some of the key ways that retailers can make their customers feel more valued include the following. It is paramount to always say thank you whether it is verbally or in the form of a token it must be sincere. In order to boost your brand reputation. In instances where disputes may arise it is critical to give the customer the benefit of the doubt and work with the customer to resolve their concerns and offer great service in the process. Satisfying the customer is everyone's priority, including the executive leadership and understand that the company needs the customer more than the customer needs the company.

It is a proven fact that across a number of countries where there is an offer of digital service options such as e-mails, SMS, internet sites or social media vehicles nearly eighty percent of customers prefer the direct contact with humans either directly or via the telephone as the preferred channel of customer service when engaging with brands or service providers. This is in spite of the fact that consumers are becoming increasingly familiar with digital channels.

The positioning of the brand in the market place amongst all other competitors is determined by the attributes that make up the character of the product which helps to evaluate the product positioning in relation to other retailers and assist in ensuring that the right emphasis is achieved in order to maximise opportunities. It is critical that fashion retailers have a clear perception as to where they are positioned otherwise customers will become confused and will drift away to alternative contenders who give a clearer message as to what they stand for through the distinctive branding that identifies them.

The market positioning provides the customer with an awareness of the borders wherein the products fall and decree what they would expect to buy from the retailer. A prime example would be where a high fashion retailer introduces a traditional and conservative range of merchandise which would then send out a message that there is an older profile customer shopping in the store. It is therefore important that when a retailer consciously makes changes whether it be style, price or new ranges to reposition themselves that this intention is clearly communicated through appropriate marketing channels to the customer. Failure to do so effectively could result in them running the risk of significant write downs.

In terms of the advertising of your product, it should be noted that advertising itself does not physically sell the product but rather the idea and basis a scenario that fulfils the customer needs in order to persuade them to buy. This objective makes the realistic, honest descriptive copy and illustrative content of prime importance.

It is also important to have a good logo that will establish the brand identity, enhance the customer loyalty and can influence purchase decisions. In order to achieve this, there are some important guidelines that should be adhered to during the creation of a logo. For a start the colour of the logo ought to convey the right mood or message to your target audience. For example, studies in the psychology of colour deduce that green is associated with nature and life while blue expresses community and trust while black is linked to elegance. It is therefore paramount to choose a colour that reflects the company personality. The logo has to be versatile in that it must be adaptable for all vehicles from billboards to business card and brochures and should look equally good in both multi-colour and black and white formats. The typography also reflects the personality of the brand and needs to be accepted by the right target market, for example, script typefaces project young and fun images while serif typefaces convey a sense of dignity and power. The logo must be unique in that it stands out from the competition while at the same time be able to stand the test of time.

The positioning of the brand in the market is best communicated to the customer by building a marketing mix matrix which will be perceived and understood by the customers and will also facilitate benchmarks as points of reference for the retailer to compare with competitors. Distinctive branding is achieved through precise marketing, commendable public relations, a sound corporate identity and consistent messaging and image building through consistent advertising.

In the illustration below the attributes are positioned on the varying extreme scales of fashionability and value in the market and serves as a check for the retailer to ensure that they are best catering for their target customer profile by ticking off the qualities that suitably represent their products

The brand can be described as the personality of the retailer.

A brand positioning model in the market can be illustrated as follows

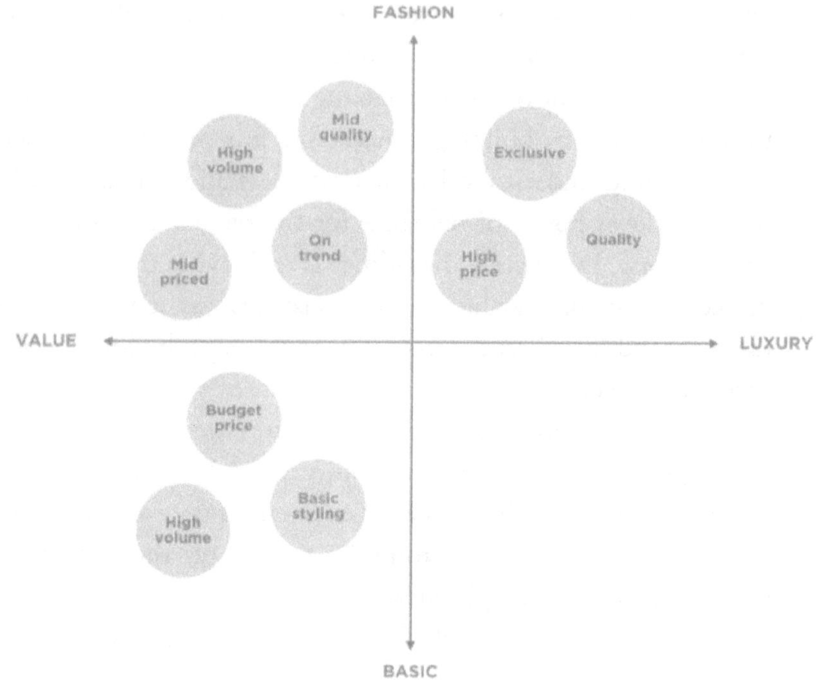

CASE STUDY

If the broad description of CH Clothing Company philosophy is as stated in the first case study which is repeated below it can be used in determining what type of retailer CH Clothing Company is:

"CH Clothing Company is a respected mass fashion retailer selling mid-price quality product with a broad representation in malls, regional locations, city centres as well as supporting an on line facility offering core basic product supplemented by on trend mid fashion elements to capture a wide cross section of customer profiles."

CHALLENGE #14

After considering the definition of the CH Clothing Company profile determine in which quadrant and roughly where in the selected quadrant the following attributes will live

1. Mass retailer
2. Price
3. Quality
4. Location
5. Customer
6. The total chain

Buying group strategy

The buying group is a strategic business unit which as a profit centre can be planned independently and are less about the co-ordination of operating units but are more focused on the development and sustaining a competitive advantage for the goods that are put on offer for sale.

The formulation of the strategy is therefore more focussed on the positioning of the group against the rivals, the anticipation of the changes in demand and innovating competitive advantages such as the creation of new distribution channels or pursuing new technologies, improving product differentiation and streamlining the manufacturing processes.

Utilising the total company strategy as an input into the buying group strategy for the season will ensure that they stay aligned to the higher level objectives. The similar focus points will be considered and interpreted as they pertain to the specific buying group. Customer and trend direction must be adapted accordingly and the financial budgets, product mix of the group will need to be reviewed as a result. For a six month season period which may be split into sub seasonal periods, in other words, the six month winter period may well consist of a transitional three month autumn period and a high season winter time.

The trading performance and lessons learnt from the previous season as well as the customer penetration opportunities together with the competitor activity and economic landscape has to be assessed. Adjustments to the targets of the key performance measurements may have to be made to align the strategy. The customer profile relating to lifestyle and the trend forecast for the specific target market pertaining to the specific business unit will be analysed as will the financial budgets and import versus local procurement.

The strategy has to be tested against the other supporting stakeholders such as logistics, marketing, IT initiatives, human resources, trend sourcing plans and packaging revisions to ensure that these will accommodate the buying group vision.

IT initiatives may have to be reassessed to ensure that they are robust enough to meet the basic requirements that the newer applications demand in terms of response times, storage capacities, design flexibility and ease of integration with other platforms. Many such systems are able to integrate with other supporting IT applications such as supplier performance, technological measurement, critical path management, ordering, logistical and store systems.

Organisational hierarchical design must be guided by human resource expertise to enable the most efficient structures that will deliver the end in mind objectives.

CASE STUDY

A typical buying group organisation chart which is applied in the CH Clothing Company is outlined below where the mainstream buying and merchandising function cascades down from the highest platform to the lower department level details. Service areas as depicted on the right hand side of the diagram support the core functions.

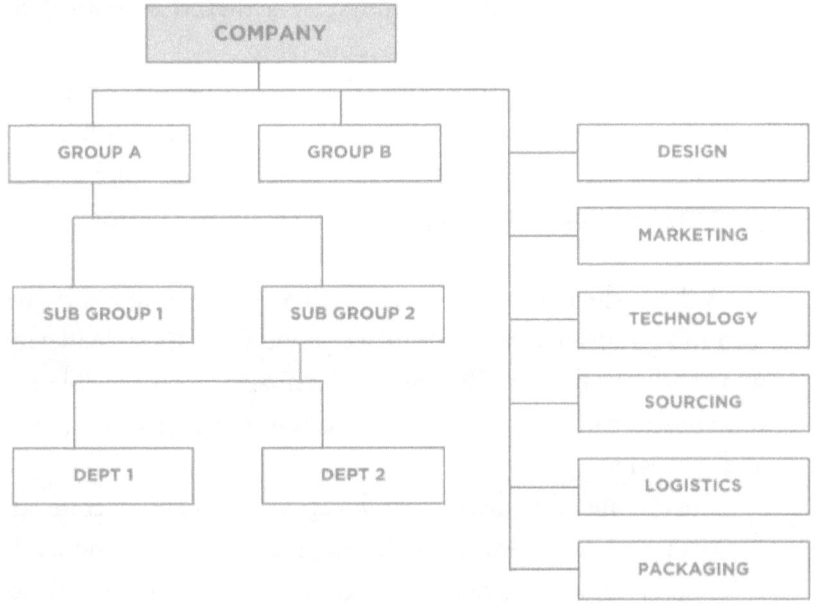

CHALLENGE #15

Using the earlier example of the Menswear group product division provide examples that could be applied to the following blocks as depicted in the illustration.

1. Company
2. Group A
3. Sub Group 2

4. Dept 1

5. Dept 2

The basic hierarchical staffing roles of all the key players in a mainstream buying structure is outlined diagrammatically below.

The chief executive officer is clearly the leader together with the board of directors who ensure that the overall company strategic intent is delivered and the profits are achieved as reward to the shareholders to whom they are accountable.

Group executives look after the broad category types such as menswear, ladieswear and childrenswear. The responsibility is to ensure that the group delivers to the set strategy and is reacting properly to changing trading conditions while still meeting the profit objective.

Within the mainstream groups such as menswear a sub division into sub groups may well take place probably by lifestyle like formal wear and casual wear. The category manager is responsible for the mini business or sub group with set turnover targets, profit objectives and strategies.

Buyers, merchandisers and location planners operate at the departmental level down to the lowest degree of product being colour and size and are responsible that the management of the detail delivers the eventual goals at all the higher levels.

It must be emphasised that there is a very definitive collaborative process between the buying and merchandising team where an appropriate measure of tension may exist. The same environment may apply between the finance departments and the buying team in terms of the financial budget.

CASE STUDY

Key staffing hierarchy posts of the buying organisation in the illustration of the CH Clothing Company are illustrated as follows

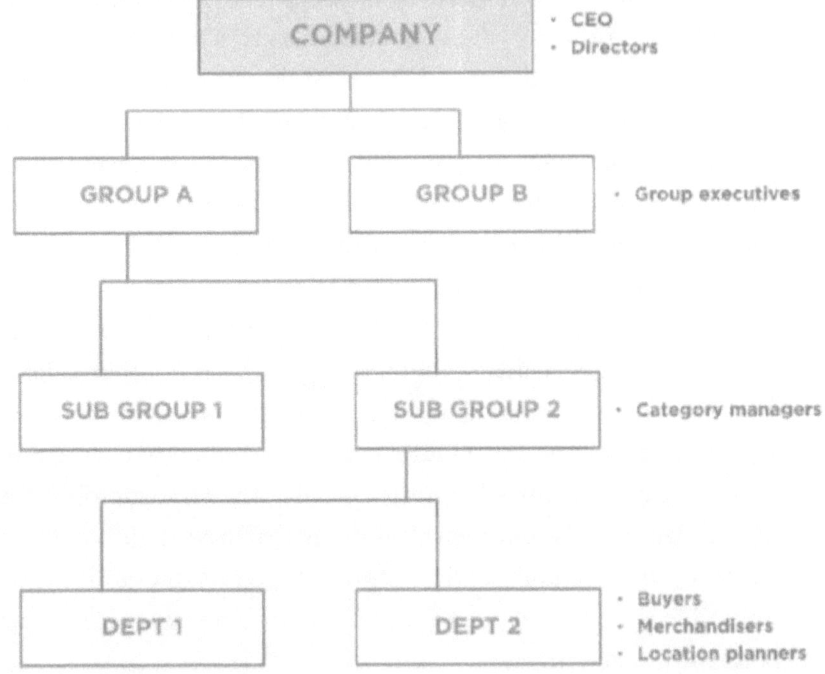

CHALLENGE #16

After focusing on the roles of Merchandisers and Location planners research the role descriptions earlier in the introductory section of the procurement team and comment the following

1. The fundamental difference of the two roles
2. The disadvantages of combining the roles
3. The additional advantages of a separate team of location planners

Customer strategy

Assuming that your customers are all the same is possibly the biggest error that could be made and the crucial part of growing any business is knowing intimately who your customers actually are.

Understanding the profile and lifestyle of the consumer very well is key to determine that the most appropriate product is developed to cater for the relevant customer segments and to ensure that the product information is effectively communicated through an integrated marketing plan and packaging policy.

Various factors have an influence on the profile of customers and knowledge of these will assist in the categorisation of customers and apply the most fitting methodologies that are a prerequisite to best serve them. Generally the typical segmentation of customers is determined by their behavioural needs, psychological characteristics and the environment wherein they exist. The strategic objective is to provide the customer with products that have a combination of integrity, quality and service, represent great value and create an enjoyable shopping experience in a pleasant environment that best suits the target market.

The key factors that influence the customer profiles are

Behavioural influences are those that in the main are habitual and accommodate the personality traits of the customer. The motivating factor for making a purchase can be varied. A consumer may not be too influenced by the on trend level of the product but will possibly prefer to have an offering that will be durable, practical and functional. If these expectations are not met they will no doubt reject the product whereas at the other end of the scale these factors may be of lesser importance.

The potential customer could be more influenced by that which is socially acceptable and reflected in the media such as magazines, television and exhibited by role models like sports stars, actors and professional people who will play an important part of the selection process. The perception of fashion could differ considerably and therefore the fashion retailer will have to rely more and more heavily on practices that will assist in analysing their particular customer's profiles or that which characterises them more accurately.

Other behaviour traits possibly are where purchases are infrequent and will exist based on a need that a shopping experience will be more of a special assignment to acquire appropriate clothing for special occasions such as returning to work, weddings, holidays or sports events.

Buying habits may include the infrequent visit to stores in order to replace the entire wardrobe on a seasonal basis in order to remain relevant and replace those clothes that have reached their performance expiry date.

The satisfaction of psychological needs such as status and image is a strong motivator in the selection of the styles that will help to achieve this objective. Included will be the perceived expectation that needs to be met by the social circle in which the purchaser moves or reflects a level of wealth that is enjoyed.

There might be the natural drive to exploit the best bargains available and some shoppers may even develop a hobby out of pursuing the greatest values available at a maze of factory and value outlets.

Trawling the glitzy malls and frequenting coffee shops and eateries can be the past time that successfully satisfies the social interaction compulsion.

The more down to earth factors that influence the shopping patterns can be the geographical location where the customer resides. As an example is that a definite difference is detected in style preference between the urbanized to those who live in remoter places where the differing demographics have a probable direct relationship to the social economic environment particularly in terms of gender, occupation, age emphasis, household income and life stage.

CASE STUDY

Referring to the overall definition of the CH Clothing Company we are able to compile a customer profile description in terms of the key influences of the overall company as follows

"CH Clothing Company is a respected mass fashion retailer selling mid-price quality product with a broad representation in malls, regional locations, city centres as well as supporting an on line facility offering core basic product supplemented by on trend mid fashion elements to capture a wide cross section of customer profiles"

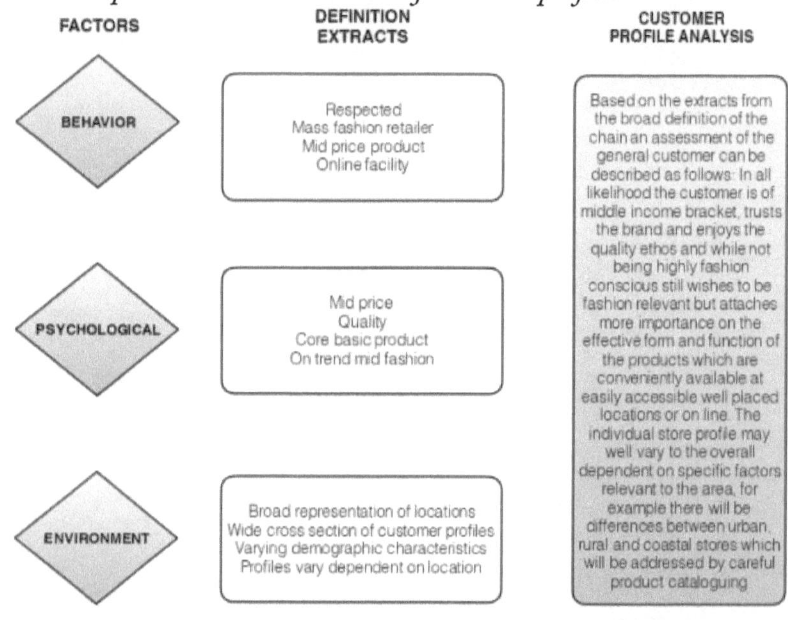

CHALLENGE #17

While there are the technological tools available to analyse the customer profile specific to a particular store a view should be able to be formulated through the simple observation of various elements in and around the store.

Using a hypothetical visit a store based on the observations listed below compile a description of the likely general profile of the store's customers.

1. In the cark park it is noted that out of every ten cars three are Mercedes or BMW, two are SUV types while the rest are Toyotas or Volkswagens.

2. While sitting in a general eatery it is noted that out of ten tables six are eating snack meals such as burgers or toasted sandwiches, two tables are eating steaks or sushi while the other two tables are simply drinking cold drinks.

3. It is noticed that at four out of ten couples are pushing prams.

4. Judging by what clothing is being worn it appears that out of ten people five are conservatively clothed while three others are reasonably trendy while two are wearing high fashion branded attire.

With the advance of till technology and the introduction of loyalty programmes it is now possible to gather a wealth of information that describes purchasing behaviour. The information that is harvested is the details of the product purchase such as style, colour, size, fit and price. The frequency and time of purchase and the relationship to other purchases can be analysed as well as the determination of the average spend per customer in different geographical areas is invaluable in building the profile of the customer base. What is of particular importance is the ability to assess the success of promotional launches and the impact they may have on other products during the time of the promotion.

It is no secret that people are living longer. There are some fundamental factors that need to be considered in terms of the population composition which needs to be taken into account in the longer term. A prime example is the greater number of older people who are still economically active at a much riper age. This is evident especially in the case of those individuals who were born at end of World War II when there was a significant baby boom and those babies are now embarking on their so called twilight years. With improved medical technology, healthier eating and lifestyles together with the explosion of health clubs as well as the trend to extend the years of economic activity has had the effect that the twilight years are going to be somewhat longer than in the past.

Another key factor is that the post war boomers enjoyed the availability of easy credit and a large number have accumulated high levels of debt with the result that when they should have been saving for their retirement years and reducing mortgages instead are landed in the situation that retirement is delayed or even worse some will have to continue working until their last. However, for the baby boomers those that are retiring are now fast approaching their retirement date if not already having experienced it. The impact of this is that there is a significant exodus of talent and work experience out of the market place and as such for those who are on the brink of retirement they are either encouraged to remain in the work place or venture into the consultancy pool.

Forensic auditing studies on mortality rate (SALT Table 1 – 1984-1986} compared in the National English tables for the period 2011 to 2013 showed that the mortality rate improved by 2.5% and 1.9% per annum for men and women respectively. Therefore the assumption can be drawn that a similar improvement going forward is likely to lie at least between these two extremes.

The impact on retailers is the need to make provision to accommodate the active aged in their store design. Store layouts will be required that are easy to shop with minimal confusion, lighting has to be bright and colour corrected to account for failing vision, noise levels need to be reduced to cater for the increased use of hearing aids, product weights must be considered and include an increased carry out service, font sizes need to be larger, shelf heights will have to be such to minimize bending and reaching while packaging should make for easier carrying and opening, queuing philosophies should be reviewed as well as the fitting rooms to permit the comfortable trying on of garments.

At the other end of the scale, the younger generations typically born in the seventies and eighties known as the millennial generation or generation Y are evolving into an extremely different personality to their predecessors and have become legendry in their prolific spending, their brand awareness and because they are technologically advanced this makes them more adventurous. Such characteristics may be evident in the pursuit of their career aspirations as they tend to progress through various places of employment while carving their career at a whim in contrast to their parents who often followed the same occupation for a lifetime. Because these cool, energetic participants are screen junkies they are easily influenced by social media trends and fads. They are therefore able to make informed comparisons and as a result the loyal practice of only shopping at one destination is almost non-existent which places a real test on the retailers to capture a core base market.

Marketing is left with an incredible task to innovate and communicate with this new breed of customer that is arriving on the scene at a rapid pace. Retailers have to start thinking like their customers as in place of window shopping this new breed trawls the internet and stays in contact all the time via the social channels and consequently the retailer need to ramp up their image amongst the channels through financial investment in top class copy writing and superb photographs as well as actively interact on line with their customer. The location of the on line sites should, as with bricks and mortar outlets, be in the best possible space where the greatest exposure to the target customer through the measurement of the number of click troughs is achieved. The offering must be easily found on websites that are advertised forcefully among local advertising vehicles, public relations efforts, promotions and word of mouth.

A popular trend emerging amongst digital enthusiasts is the support for blog sites where the brands are able to speak to an audience in a different light. There is a word of caution in that what they tell the people must be well accepted because should it be met with resistance the consequences could be equally disastrous. Examples exist of some successful fashion blogs that attract thirty thousand hits a day and may have up to two hundred thousand followers on twitter and therefore brands are happy to pay a lot of money to purchase advertising space in these forums. Some brands spend more than fifty percent of their advertising provision on electronic channels and collaborate with bloggers to gain the most editorial exposure. Many designers view the bloggers as their spokespersons as they develop strong relationships with customers by offering fashion tips and advice, the provision of educational material and programmes that help with the customer decision making process as well as at the same time enhancing brand awareness.

Product planning strategy

Once there is a clear understanding of what operational activities are required, the plan of action can be outlined to deliver the strategic objectives and thereby satisfy the goals of the strategy in the most effective way.

What is key in formulating the planning strategy is to set down the clear guidelines in the development of the product mix which will be carefully tailored in the right proportions in order to best serve the customer at the various locations and in terms of styling, colour quantities across the sizes at the most acceptable prices.

For this to be done successfully the overall process of planning follows a set of prescribed activities that make up the mechanics of running the business as well as accommodating the other stakeholder strategies. The steps are a flow of taking in the lessons learnt during the previous season and utilising the learnings as input in the formulation of the strategic goals for the future season.

The goals will give guidance in the preparation of the level of budgets determining the product mix and setting up the range plan from which the orders will be placed. Once production has taken place according to the plan the goods will be allocated to the stores taking into account their specific customer characteristics. Sales will be analysed as they occur and as the performance dictates the forward plans will be reviewed and adjusted appropriately.

Diagrammatically the high level key planning steps can be outlined as follows

Believe it or not the start of planning for a forthcoming season begins with what has happened in the past.

A strategic focus in the assessment of the past performance for the season is to compare the actual vital numbers to that what was expected and understand the deviations whether they were positive or negative. The learnings are imperative in the compilation of a new season's strategy and the setting of targets.

Once there is a clear understanding of what operational activities are required, the plan of action can be outlined to deliver the strategic objectives and thereby satisfy the goals of the strategy in the most effective way.

What is key in formulating the planning strategy is to set down the clear guidelines in the development of the product mix which will be carefully tailored in the right proportions in order to best serve the customer at the various locations and in terms of styling, colour quantities across the sizes at the most acceptable prices.

For this to be done successfully the overall process of planning follows a set of prescribed activities that make up the mechanics of running the business as well as accommodating the other stakeholder strategies. The steps are a flow of taking in the lessons learnt during the previous season and utilising the learnings as input in the formulation of the strategic goals for the future season.

The goals will give guidance in the preparation of the level of budgets determining the product mix and setting up the range plan from which the orders will be placed. Once production has taken place according to the plan the goods will be allocated to the stores taking into account their specific customer characteristics. Sales will be analysed as they occur and as the performance dictates the forward plans will be reviewed and adjusted appropriately.

MERCHANDISE ARITHMETIC

The main purpose of merchandise planning is to forecast sales for the period under review and manage the levels of stock in the correct assortments based on the historical performance and forward trends. Buyers are guided to procure within the parameters of the budget and ensure that the right product is delivered to the right stores in the right quantities of style, colours and size in order to maximise the sales and profit objectives and minimise mark downs. In order that this is done effectively it is important that the numerical planning is done accurately and is able to be measured in line with a set of predetermined criteria.

It is a known fact that things do not always go according to plan so it is equally important to measure the actual performance against what was originally envisaged and recommend corrective action where deviations occur. This may take various forms whether it is buying more of a style if possible, turning off supply or converting styles into those that are more in demand. Allocation quantities need to be reviewed in line with the individual store performances. These actions need to be done as urgently as possible after the analysis is completed.

Key performance indicators

For stakeholders to be able to check whether the performance is on track to achieve the strategic objectives it is measured against a suite of pre-set performance indicators. The most common performance pointers which are assigned targets that will deliver the desired financial requirements, are the following.

Sales
Markdowns

Buying margin

Sales margin

Stock forward cover

Stock annual turn

Return on inventory investment

It is absolutely imperative that these indicators are clearly understood by all members of the retail team both in the head office and stores and what role they play in the support of them. The measures are almost always referred to in financial reports as shareholders utilise these to determine their level of confidence in the company performance.

Business acumen

In order that the profit motives are achieved effectively it is imperative that all team players have an acceptable measure of business acumen. Many decisions made at any level are often of substandard quality through the misinterpretations of basic business formulae and concepts. Clarity through the understanding of retail arithmetic makes life less confusing with less disruption and improved productivity in the generation of profits.

Business acumen can be described as the entrepreneurial ability to improve results through focusing on the customer, applying the knowledge of the business and being aware of the external market environment and competitors.

All vital performance indicators are underpinned by the fundamental building blocks of sales, markdowns, Intake and stock which may be illustrated diagrammatically that highlights the MERCHANT and FINANCIAL kpi's as follows.

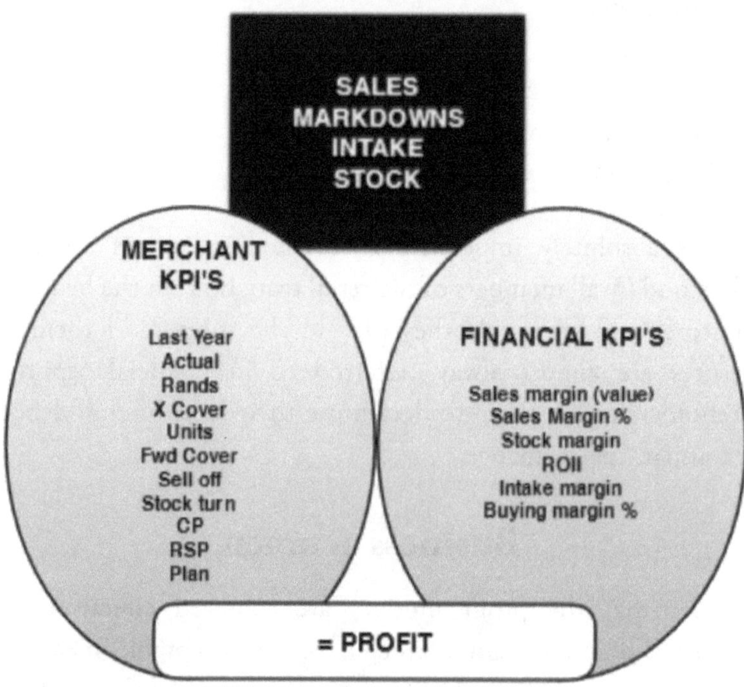

A brief explanation of each one of the key performance indicators as well as how they are derived is outlined as follows.

Sales are recorded and planned in monetary value although reference is frequently made to volumes in order to plan production capacity requirements. The monetary value measurement is expressed as a percentage in relation to another value which is normally against the comparable sales of the previous year or against the budgeted sales for the corresponding current period. The measurement within the stores can also be done such as the takings per square metre to assist in the apportionment of amount of display space deserved by product categories within the departments. Sales per square metre also serve as a benchmark target to which minimum performance is required to assess the viability of carrying particular ranges and is a good measure which can be referenced by the buying teams when probing the sales performance of product in stores. It should be understood that various designs of display equipment such as wall displays, racks and tables are also apportioned varying relative square metreage rates.

Growth percentages compared to other periods are used to identify problems or successes in buying, product flow, inventory levels, merchandising, and advertising assessment. These can be better understood where there is distortion due to changes in the environment such as selling space expansion or store closures, competitive activity and out of the ordinary events.

The calculation of the growth percentage is the method of expressing the difference between two values such as this year and last year sales divided by the total sales for the same period. Alternatively the measurement of growth can also be compared to the set targets which is particularly relevant in the sense that the historical data may be flawed and the fact the business is planned against set targets and should these be deviated from a more accurate corrective adjustment can take place.

$$\text{GROWTH \%} = \frac{TY - LY}{LY} \times 100$$

Assume last year sales was 700 and this year sales are 900. The sales growth would therefore be [(900-700)/900] x 100=22.2%

The desired sales level can also be derived by applying a percentage increase.

Assume a percentage increase of 10% is required against last year and the sales for last year is 700. The required sales budget for this year will therefore be 700 x 1.10=770

It should be noted that in terms of percentage growth a differentiation should be made between overall growth where the total increase of the department includes all products in contrast to a like for like increase which is between identical products from the corresponding season in the previous year and represents a true inflationary measurement.

The common opinion is that the achievement of this measure is the crucial to ensure the delivery of the other key indicators.

Contribution percentage is the way of expressing in monetary or unit value as a percentage that a component represents of the whole the use of this measurement is frequently used to compare performances or to extrapolate in the future planning scenarios at any level of the hierarchy.

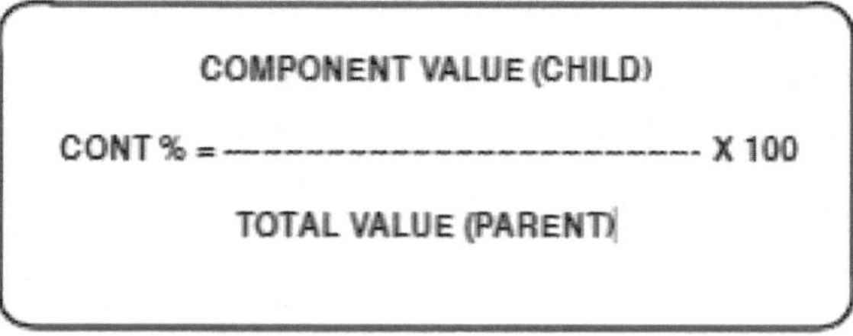

Assume a department (parent) consists of four products (children) a tabular illustration below shows what contribution % the sales of each product represents.

DEPT ABC	SALES	% CONT
PRODUCT A	60 000	24%
PRODUCT B	35 000	14%
PRODUCT C	75 000	30%
PRODUCT D	80 000	32%
TOTAL	250 000	100%

Markdowns are inevitable in some form or other. The requirement to reduce merchandise can be due to various reasons such as sales being below expectation, the need to clear stock due to necessity and allowing the management of the pipeline to facilitate newness to flow through and also to be able to contain stocks within the parameters of the set stock targets. Markdowns need to be provided for by way of a budget in spite of it being difficult to predict the exact nature of the markdown at the lower levels of product.

The markdown value is the monetary value by which the product was reduced.

$$\text{PRICE AT OLD RSP - PRICE AT NET RSP X UNITS} = \text{MARK DOWN VALUE}$$

Markdowns are measured in percentage terms derived by the relationship of the markdown value to the total retail sales for the period.

$$\text{MARKDOWN \% } = \frac{\text{MARKDOWN VALUE}}{\text{ORIGINAL RSP VALUE}} \times 100$$

Assume for the period the value of markdown was 1000 and the corresponding sales were 10000. The markdown percentage would therefore be

(1000/10000) x100=10%

The size of the provision for markdown is dependent on historical data and the acceptable percentage in relation to the original sales budget or a retail selling price. The levels of markdown will vary dependent on the nature of the product.

Typically the more high fashion type product such as ladies tops will have a higher markdown percentage to sales which can be as high as fifteen percent while the very basic product that is sold as a continuity item rather than a single input such as underwear will be much lower and may even only be done routinely to flush older merchandise out of the system. In order to cater for these variances the buying margin policy for the various categories will accordingly reflect these levels of risk.

Product is generally marked down on the go or alternatively the affected goods are removed from display until a planned seasonal sale which may be two or three times per annum. The main reason for higher levels of markdown is most often that the customer rejects the offer through disillusionment or when the most popular colour or size is not available. Fragmentation of ranges inevitably slows the rate of sale and consequently results in displays becoming untidy and disorganised as well as restricting the display space required for new lines. Space constraints often lead to the product being removed from display never to see the light of day again until the major seasonal sale.

Depending on the overall demand for fragmented pockets of stock it may be considered to recall all the odds back to a facility where the goods can be consolidated. New sets of availability are then reported and the goods are redistributed to a limited catalogue of stores that have previously sold the goods at an acceptable level. The risk of this practice is the additional costs which are incurred in handling, transport, repacking, reallocation and redistribution while the goods are still relevant must be such that a profit benefit is still returned. Invariably it is seldom the option that will be selected.

It is not uncommon to pack away seasonal product such as thermal underwear. Winter hosiery, swimwear at the end of the season and bring them back to the display units from storage at the commencement of the next season. The shortcoming is that the stock that is re-introduced is often tatty, discoloured and may even be shop soiled and lacking the crispness of fresh goods. If this practice is done it is advisable to return them to a value add facility where they can be repackaged and correctly price marked for the new season before re-introducing the goods back into the system.

There are various options as how to deal with reductions. The most commonly used one is that where the goods are marked down on a continual basis during the season. This has the downside that it causes a distraction from new ranges and themes as well as can damage the brand integrity in the eye of the customer. The consumers also tend to adjust their buying patterns in the knowledge that the goods will inevitably be cleared at a lower price at some time in the near future and will wait for these occurrences to happen rather than pay the full price. The alternative possibility is to withdraw the affected goods from display until the next specific seasonal sale.

Some chains may have designated stores where sale and distressed goods are combined and sold at reduced prices. Another route that may be followed is to off load the merchandise to jobbers or resellers at very low prices but in both cases this requires added handling as well as the removal of labelling whilst at the same time incurring additional associated costs.

Mark up percentage is described as the percentage of the cost price that is added to the cost price to derive the selling price. The key difference between the mark up and the margin is that the percentage is based on cost while margins are based on sales. It is therefore true to say that a selling price with a 30% margin results in more profit than a selling price with a 30% mark up on the cost price.

$$\text{MARK UP \%} = \frac{\text{SELLING VALUE} - \text{COST VALUE}}{\text{COST VALUE}} \times 100$$

Margins are an indicator of performance relative to certain key measures in the business (usually stock and sales) expressed in monetary terms or as a %. The target margins are set in strategy and KPI's reviews.

Buying margin is the margin at which the goods were purchased and is often referred to as the primary margin. This margin is expressed as a percentage and equates to the selling value less the cost value expressed as a percentage of the selling value.

$$\text{BUY MARGIN \%} = \frac{\text{SELL VAL} - \text{COST VAL}}{\text{SELL VAL}} \times 100$$

Assume that sales budget for the period is 350 000 and the cost value of the goods purchased is 160 000.

The buying margin is therefore 350000–160000=190000

The buying margin percentage equates to [(350000-160000)/350000] x100=54.3%

The margin is a part of the strategic plan and while there is an overall target for the company. The margins at the lower levels will vary and will be largely dependent on the fashionability and volume factor of the product. It may also be strategically different in the sense that a product may be sold at a low or even no margin to gain a competitive advantage and thereby increase market share. As the achievement of the buying or intake margin is critical to the negotiation process it is absolutely essential that it is closely monitored during the procurement process to ensure that the achievement of the overall target margin remains on track.

Sales margin in monetary value is the difference between the actual sales value which is registered at the till and the total cost of the goods sold which includes factors such as markdowns. It should be noted that the cost value of each intake may differ so the cost value will be the weighted combination of the various costs or quantities.

SALES MARGIN (MONETRY) =

SALES - COST OF GOODS SOLD

The margin is expressed as a percentage and refers to the relationship between sales and cost value and the total sales expressed as a percentage.

$$\text{SELL MARGIN \%} = \frac{\text{SALES - COST OF GOODS SOLD}}{\text{SALES}} \times 100$$

* Cost of goods sold = Sales margin

Assume that the sales for the period are 200 000 and the cost of the goods sold (including added costs to the base cost of the garment) are 130 000.

The Sales Margin will therefore be 200000–130000=70000

The Sales Margin % will be (70000/200000) X100=35%

An example of the derivation of the weighted cost value is illustrated in the following diagram

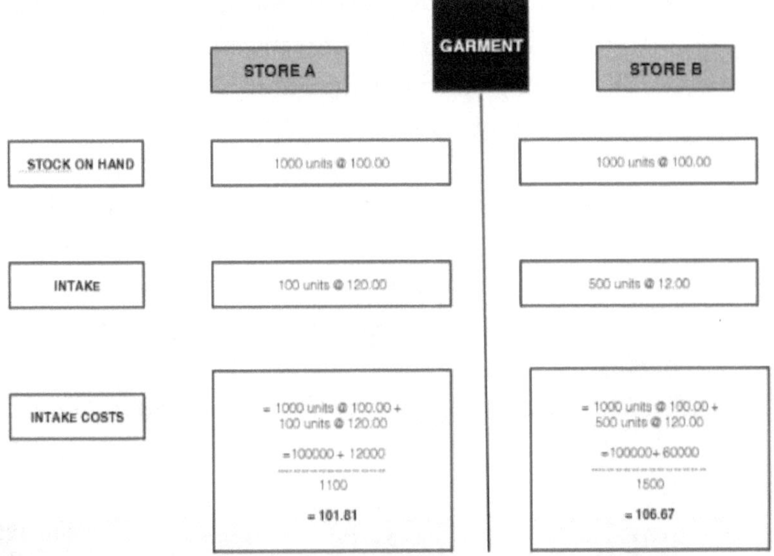

The variance of the anticipated sales volumes that were used to determine the buying margin may well be very different to volume proportions that are actually sold and therefore will ultimately deliver a different aggregated sales margin.

The sales margin target is determined by the intake margin after taking expected markdowns into account and has the same logical relationship between the sales value and cost value expressed as a percentage. The difference however is that the actual sales value which is achieved can be very different. It is therefore key to carefully observe what was expected to happen to what actually happened and make sure that is kept in mind when determining forward predictions.

Other factors that may well influence the accuracy of sales margins may well be instances such as

- Incorrect RSP or cost prices

- Incorrect ticketing
- High returns to manufacturers
- Different shopping patterns to that what was expected in that they may purchase more low margin items
- The turning on or turning off of merchandise which affect the balance of margins

Weighted retail selling prices is where in determining the overall average selling price for a department it takes into account the volumes of each component with varying retail selling prices rather than the straight average calculation using the number of components.

Weighted retail selling prices is best illustrated as follows in the example below

UNITS SOLD	RSP	SALES VALUE	AVERAGE RSP	WEIGHTED AVERAGE RSP
1000	100.00	100 000	(100+150+ 200)	(100000+ 750000+ 500000)
5000	150.00	750 000	----	----
2500	200.00	500 000	3	8500
8500		1 350 000	150.00	158.82

Inflation can only be truly measured by comparing product which is identical or extremely similar from one year to the next and is therefore described as like on like inflation.

Price movement applies to the entire basket of products of a department which may be different in terms of styling, fabric and componentry is included in the determination of the overall change in price across the various pricing categories will indicate the extent by which a departments prices total as an average (including the like for like inflation products) have moved from the one year to the next.

Below is an illustrative diagramme outlining the effect of changing volumes from one year to the next on the overall price movement where a price increase of 10% is applied?

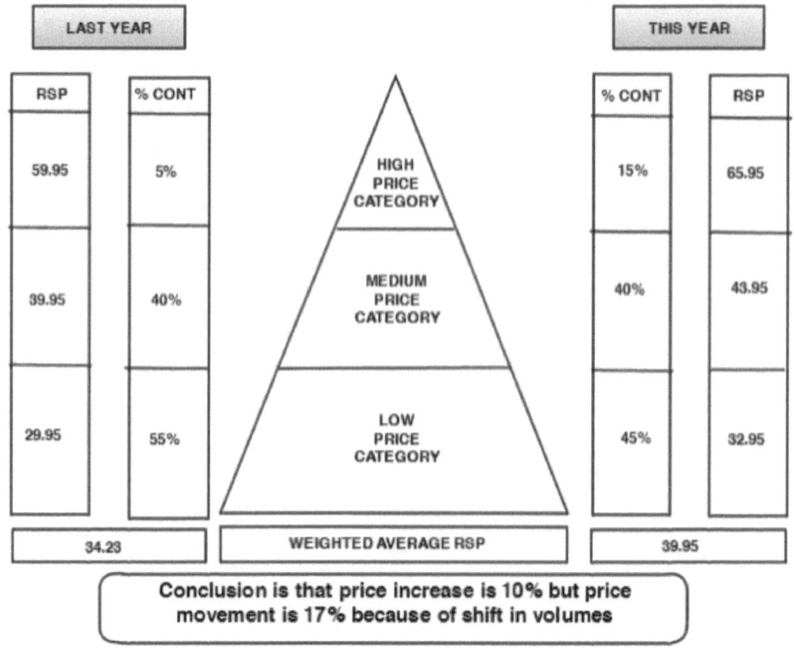

Monetary value compared to unit volume. A critical point to note is that while the average RSP may change significantly and result in an increase above inflation, the net effect would be an increase in margin but the end result would be a reduction in units compared to the previous year and consequently would hamper the ability of the department to service the catalogue as effectively as the previous year. The converse will be experienced where the RSP is reduced assuming the same budget level is maintained.

The qualification needs to be made that the if the end objective is profit in monetary value it stands to reason that in principle budgeted sales are set in financial terms as opposed to unit terms.

As an example assume the following

Last year a product sold 250 000 units per month at 29.95 which would return sales of 7.5 million

If the price is reduced to 24.95 the probability is that the volume per month will increase to 275 000 per month which would deliver a monetary sale of 6.9 million.

The conclusion is that even though the units at the lower RSP increase, the actual revenue is less.

Stock forward cover is the amount of stock required at any one point in time that will permit the forward sales budgets to be achieved. The measurement is typically in weeks and can be expressed as the amount of weeks that is based on the sales plan over the time that it will take for the stock to be exhausted.

Stock levels will essentially be higher or lower over time depending on seasonal trends, promotional launches, markdown activities and holiday events. The fluctuations will be reflected in the sales plans and as a result the inventory level will fall and rise in empathy to the sales plan. The target number of weeks can remain reasonably consistent throughout the year and will really only need to be adjusted where situations deem it necessary such as for factory closures over holiday periods and in the event of build up for new initiative launches such as store openings.

The appropriate number of weeks selected will be determined based on historical data, the strategy intents and the nature of the product. Properties such as fashionability, amount of sizes, lead times from supplier for replenishment, the number of deliveries and turnover of individual stores will have an influence over the number of weeks cover chosen. Commonly the more fashionable the merchandise is, the lesser the number of weeks will be required as the time it is on offer may well be shorter before the next input of new replacement styles in comparison to the basic continuity commodities.

Larger outlets stock tend to sell out at a quicker rate and have greater volumes of sales and therefore are able to survive on less weeks cover compared to the smaller stores with smaller turnovers which demand a less frequent replenishment and consequently require more weeks cover in order that full availability of all colours and sizes are on offer at any one point in time.

The proximity of stores to the replenishment centres will also have an influence on the stockholding requirements and invariably the rural stores far from the distribution points may receive less frequent deliveries which take longer to reach them and subsequently these stores will have to have more weeks cover than their relations in the city centres who are closer to the distribution centres.

The principle, however, remains to keep the forward cover as low as possible in order that the stock will be replaced more regularly and thereby is able to generate profit more frequently.

> WEEKS FORWARD COVER =
>
> CLOSING STOCK - SUM OF FORWARD WEEKS SALES

Assume at a point in time the stock holding is 900

The forward sales per weeks going forward are 150, 200, 130, 100, 120, 110, 90,110,140, and so on...

The number of weeks that the 900 worth of stock will last before running out will be

900= 150+200+130+100+120+110+90

This will therefore represent 7 weeks forward cover of stock required to achieve targeted sales.

The forward cover is a key measurement to determine the stock turn of the business on an annual and seasonal basis needs to take into account

- The amount of stock that can be held on the sales floor at any one point in time
- The amount of stock that can be held at outside storage facilities
- The time that goods are in transit to stores
- The type of merchandise as to whether it is fashion or continuity inputs
- The type of supply chain which may be warehoused or delivered directly ex supplier
- The ability to finance the cost of catalogue
- Any specific risks that may be involved in holding and transit of stock such as shelf life

Times cover is in no way related to forward cover but represents the speed that goods are selling in stores and is reflected in weeks and is seen as a relativity measure between stores in terms of the sales to stock ratios.

The formula to determine the times cover is

$$\frac{\text{OPEN STOCK FOR THE PERIOD}}{\text{AVERAGE SALES FOR THE PERIOD}}$$

Assume the opening stock for January is 2500 in order to calculate the sales to stock ratio for the 4 weeks of January is done as follows
Sales for January = 340+250+190+200 = 980

Average sales = 980/4 = 245
Times cover = 2500/245
= 10.2 weeks

In other words the stock will all be sold out in 10.2 weeks if nothing else is received during the month.

It should be distinguished that that this is seen as a more instantaneous measure to highlight anomalies to alert the need to implement further investigation as it assumes that the rate of sales going forward will be the same as the past.

Stock annual turn is the number of times the stock inventory is sold and replaced in the year. The year is based on a moving 52 actual weeks and therefore does not have a start and end date.

CUMULATIVE SALES FOR THE LAST 52 WEEKS

MOVING AVERAGE STOCK

Each time this happens, profit is generated and therefore the more times this occurs the more times a profit is delivered.

Stock annual turn is usually expressed as the cumulative sales for the previous fifty two weeks divided by the average stock holding for the same period.

Assuming the cumulative sales for the preceding 52 weeks (annual) is 60 000 and the average stock for the period is 15 000 then the stock turn will be 60000/15000 = 4 times.

There is a direct link to stock forward cover value as the lower the number of weeks are, the less the average stock holding will be and as a result the higher the stock turn will be. A point to note about the relationship is that the forward cover can be determined from the stock turn value or vice versa.

$$\text{FORWARD COVER} = \frac{52}{\text{STOCK TURN}}$$

The forward cover can be determined from the stock turn value by dividing the forward cover number of weeks into 52 weeks.

If stock turn is 6 then forward cover will be 52/6 = 8.7 weeks

$$\text{STOCK TURN} = \frac{52}{\text{FORWARD COVER}}$$

Conversely, if forward cover is 9 weeks then stock turn will be 52/9 = 5.8 times

The significance of the non-achievement of the target stock turn can result in the accumulation of higher seasonal stocks which will inevitably be destined for the reduction counters as it will no longer be seasonally relevant and will probably look fatigued and fragmented. The intake of the new seasonal ranges will also be choked in order to remain within the stock parameters. The downside for those retailers who rely on the quicker turn of stock to enable a return which facilitates the payment of goods within the payment terms timeline is that if this is not realised it will have a negative effect on the availability of ready cash or liquidity. The consequence is that the inventory is carried for longer periods of time and the payment of goods before they are sold enforces higher interest charges to finance the holding of goods.

In order to illustrate the effectiveness of the level of stock turn this can be done by the following hypothetical example of playing the one arm bandit gaming machines in the following diagram.

It therefore stands to reason that the higher the stock turn is of a product the more likely it will have a lower margin than a product that has a high margin but turns stock less frequently. This is clearly evidenced by the nature of goods that are marketed.

Diagrammatically the relationship between turn and margin can be illustrated as below

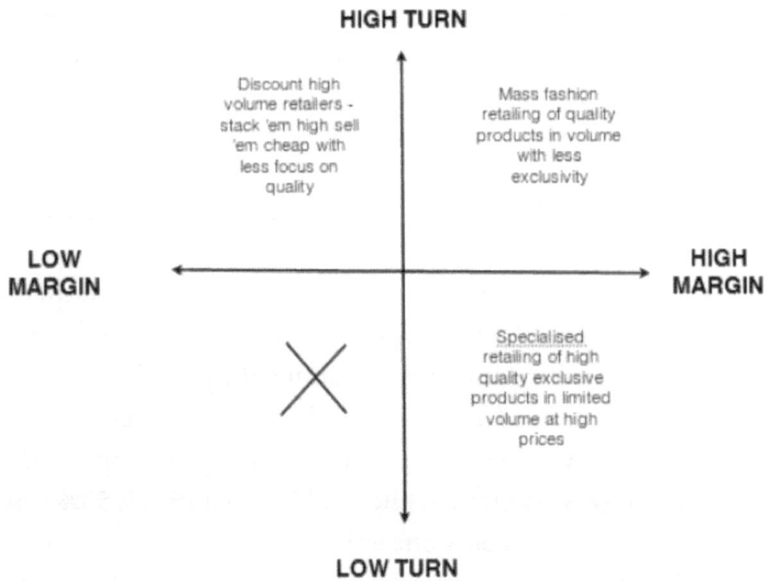

Sell off percentage is defined as the percentage of stock available to be sold within a designated period. The term is also often referred to as the clearance or sell through percentage which indicates how well the stock is being sold.

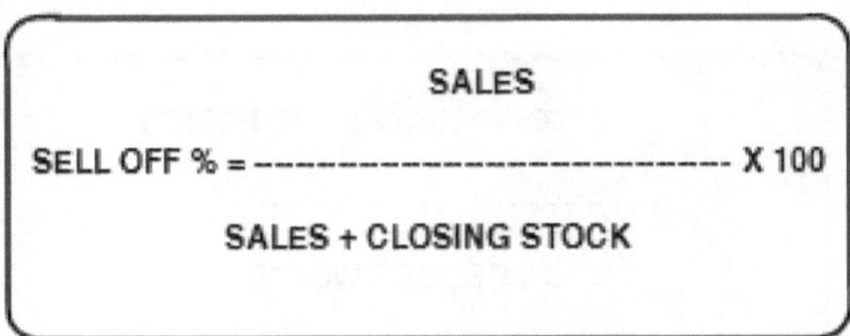

Assume that there are sales for a product for a set period of 40 units which has a closing stock of 160 units at the end of the period.

The resultant sell off % will be 40/ (40+160) x 100 = 20%

While this measurement is glibly used there are pitfalls that need to be avoided to ensure that as a relativity measure apples are not being compared to pears. To avoid this the following set up must be in place:

- The period for the products being compared is exactly the same.
- There must be full availability of the products during the period from the start which means there are no sell outs or any additional or late intake during the period.
- The amount of stock should be considered as low stock levels may deliver a flattering sell off. For example if there are only two units and one is sold the selloff % is 50% which is great but it is only one unit.
- It is therefore a dangerous measure in isolation and each result should be considered with the view of "it depends".

Average per store is a measure which enables the assessment of the number of units being sold per week by store of a department, category or product in relation to other stores and thereby draw conclusions.

$$\frac{\text{TOTAL SALES FOR PERIOD}}{\text{NUMBER OF WEEKS}}$$

Suppositions that may be drawn are

- Are the sales at an acceptable rate to justify the cataloguing of a store?
- Provides a dip stick view of the potential of a product in other stores.
- Allows comparison across groups and stores.
- Provides comparison of actual sales against targets that were bought against.

Shrinkage percentage reflects the percentage of sales lost to shrinkage or wastage and the result is measured against set targets to deem whether or not they are acceptable.

$$\text{SHRINKAGE \%} = \frac{\text{ACTUAL STOCK VALUE} - \text{THEORETICAL STOCK VALUES}}{\text{SALES REVENUE}}$$

The cause of shrinkage is caused by both internal and external factors such as employee theft and paperwork errors and damaged merchandise write offs. External causes are usually pilferage and undetected errors by suppliers.

Return on inventory investment (ROII) is the measure of the amount of return that is received for the investment in stock.

The profit productivity of the stock depends on the number of times the inventory is sold and replaced and the more frequent these spells are the more times it will generate a profit. The relationship of the cumulative monetary sales margin value for the period being measured to the average cost value of stock will deliver the number of times profit was made.

The average cost of the stock is determined by the opening stock at the beginning of the period being measured and is added to the stock values per month which is divided by the number of months.

$$\frac{\text{PROGRESSIVE SALES MARGIN (VALUE)}}{\text{AVERAGE COST OF STOCK}}$$

Accept the period being measured is six months and the total sales margin value is 3000. The opening cost value stock of 1000 added to the stock holdings of each of the six months and divided by the number of months plus 1. This value divided into the total sales margin will deliver the number of times profit was generated.

Average cost of stock = 1000 + (900+800+1100+1200+1000+900) =6900/7=985.7

ROII will be 3000/985.7=3.0

Techniques to improve the return on investments will include

- Run effective promotions regularly

- Reduce the average stock holdings by buying more frequently and weigh up bulk discounts and minimum order quantities very carefully

- At times it is preferable to negotiate longer credit terms with the supplier in order to reduce the stock investment by the sales before payment has to be made

- Consider the viability of offering a product for sale if the return is low

- Set reasonable stock turns for items and work towards achieving an inventory position that returns similar turns for each item in the category

- Remove un acceptable underperforming items from display prior to markdown

CASE STUDY

Given some key data tabulated below which pertains to a basic white shirt in CH Clothing Company's menswear range it can be interrogated and certain deductions are able to be made. (Note that the monetary values are in thousands for the 26 week season)

Men's basic white shirts

		JANUARY				FEBRUARY					MARCH				APRIL					MAY				JUNE			
		1	2	3	4	5	6	7	8	9	10	11	12	13	14	15	16	17	18	19	20	21	22	23	24	25	26
Sales LY	497	7	9	12	16	12	15	17	19	23	19	16	15	17	22	21	25	27	24	21	19	21	25	23	22	24	26
Sales TY	579	10	12	15	20	15	17	20	23	27	22	20	18	19	24	25	28	30	27	24	23	25	29	25	25	27	29
Mark downs	46					5	8	10	6							5	5	6	1								
Open stock		70	80	80	85	83	88	86	90	95	103	98	99	96	95	95	100	110	130	125	132	138	130	132	135	136	135
Close stock		80	80	85	83	88	86	90	95	103	98	99	96	95	95	100	110	130	125	132	138	130	132	135	136	135	140
Cost price	110.00																										
Selling price	199.99																										

CHALLENGE #18

Using the data displayed in the table derive the following measures for the basic white shirt

1. The percentage growth for the 26 weeks

2. The markdown percentage

3. The number of forward weeks cover as at the end of February

4. Dependant on the forward cover derived determine the stock turn value for the year

5. The buying margin percentage

Interdependency of performance indicators

The importance of recognising the interdependence of the performance indicators is paramount.

Should the sales target be under achieved, in all probability the margin targets will not have sufficient sales value to be realised, the stock cover will be higher due to the unsold stock and therefore the stock turn will decrease as will the return on inventory investment.

If the markdowns are higher than originally planned, the margin targets and return on inventory investment will consequently be under achieved.

When the stock sells in different proportions to what was expected and where the products have differential margins, the overall aggregated margin could well deliver a different result to what was anticipated. For example, this phenomenon will occur if sales of loss leading low margin goods exceed budgets and perhaps the higher fashion high margin products sell less than hoped for.

The non-achievement of stock forward cover targets means that the stock annual turns will not be attained and consequently the sales and markdown expectations may or may not be accomplished depending on the severity of the deviation but undoubtedly there will certainly be a resultant impact on the return of inventory investment.

The return on inventory investment will not be realised if any one of the other targets are not achieved.

By means of a matrix the interdependence of the performance indicators may be shown as follows

Note that if the individual performance indicators in the left hand column are not achieved the crosses in the row to the corresponding performance indicators under the relevant headings will also be negatively impacted.

	SALES	MARKDOWNS	BUYING MARGIN	SALES MARGIN	STOCK FORWARD COVER	STOCK ANNUAL TURN	ROII
SALES	X		X	X	X	X	X
MARKDOWNS		X	X	X			X
BUYING MARGIN			X	X			X
SALES MARGIN			X	X			X
STOCK FORWARD COVER	X		X	X	X	X	X
STOCK ANNUAL TURN	X		X	X	X	X	X
ROII	X		X	X	X	X	X

Profit

The success of any business is measured by the value of the profit it delivers. In order that this is reached it should be well understood as to what profit is and in what forms it is expressed.

The vital methods to ensure the achievement of profit targets can be broadly defined as

- Maximising sales
- The careful management of stock commitment to achieve the sales

- Through not over buying or under buying
- Keeping the level of mark down under control within the set targets
- The negotiation of appropriate cost prices
- Concentrating on the management of sales margins as profit is made from sales and not intake
- Focus on the monetary value as it is that what is banked and not the percentage
- The careful management of expenses translates directly into profit.

Gross profit is defined as the amount which is available after the direct costs of product at the point of sale are deducted from the value for which they are sold. The outlays comprise of the cost of the product, warehousing, royalties, packaging origination and samples.

Illustratively the determination of the gross profit can be displayed as follows

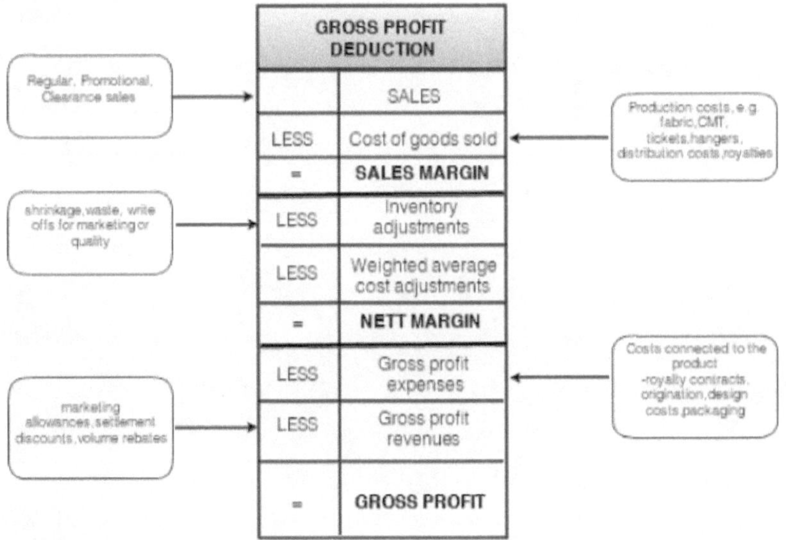

CASE STUDY

From the table of data above the value of the Sales Margin is determined by using the number of units sold which represents the retail sales divided by the selling price which is sell value 579 000 divided by 199.99 equal to 2895 units. The difference of between the sale and cost price is 199.99-110.00 = 89.99 which if multiplied by the 2895 units will deliver a sales margin monetary value of 260,521.00.

CHALLENGE #19

Taking the sales margin of 260,521.00 and given the following extra expenditures and revenues listed below the actual NET PROFIT and GROSS PROFIT needs to determined according to the methodology described above

1. 20,000.00 worth of product is stolen

2. 5,000.00 worth of product are used for advertising shoots

3. 10,000.00 worth is used for design origination costs and packaging.

4. 15,000.00 is recouped from the supplier in the form of settlement discounts

Profit before tax or net profit is the amount left over after the gross profit is reduced by the non-direct product overhead costs such as rent, salaries, transport, packing materials, as well as the unpredictable costs like markdowns, quality returns, spoilage and unforeseen costs like unplanned airfreighting. Revenues in the form of volume incentives and settlement discounts from suppliers will in turn improve the net profit.

The expenses of the business that are not directly linked to the product such as salaries, store costs, cost of support areas like information technology and marketing are apportioned in some way or other to the product, probably through the use of turnover contributions.

Illustratively the determination of the profit before tax can be displayed as follows

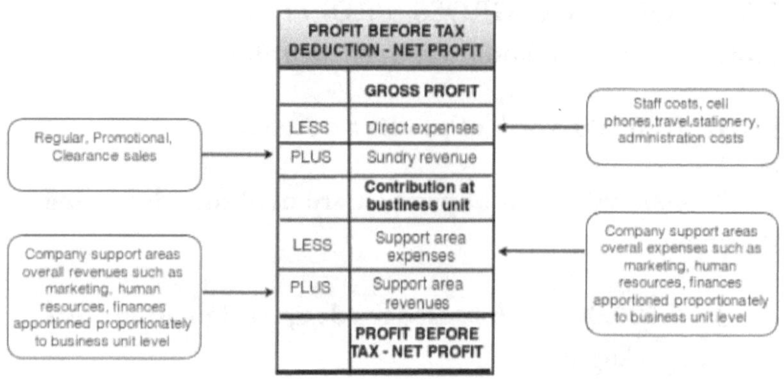

Profit per square metre provides an indication of how much profit an item of merchandise delivers from each square metre of space it occupies and consequently the theory is that the allocation of space allocated to a product is dependent on this measurement.

To achieve the highest profit from the available space can be by taking action on low performing items through promotions, reducing the space allotted or replacing the product. The optimum situation is where all products which have the right space allocation will therefore all deliver the same profit per square metre. As the name suggests, the profit per square metre is calculated by dividing the gross profit of an item by the area of selling it occupies.

$$\text{PR PER SQ MTRE} = \frac{\text{GROSS PROFIT}}{\text{SELLING SQU METRES}}$$

The same principle can be applied by dividing the expenses into the amount of saleable square metreage and therefore the optimum space allocation can also be determined.

Similarly sales per hour and average sales per customer are helpful in terms of staff scheduling and employing staff in functions that are balanced to return an acceptable rate of sale per employee. It should be noted that many or most retailers do not have full time staff members. Therefore to standardise the measurement the number of hours worked is converted to the full time equivalent.

Return on sales is the expression of the profit before tax or net profit expressed as a percentage of sales. A deterioration in this measure from one period to another could indicate problems possibly relative to the pricing policy, excessive markdowns or lack of efficient stock control.

$$\text{ROS} = \frac{\text{PROFIT BEFORE TAX}}{\text{SALES}} \times 100$$

Assume that the profit before tax is 100,000 and the sales for the same period is 500,000 then the return on sales will be (100,000/ 500,000) x 100 = 20%

Break even analysis reflects how much volume must be sold to cover all costs, both fixed and variable before starting to generate a profit. In other words it is that point where there is no profit or no loss.

MASTER DATA MANAGEMENT

A master data management system provides a repository of product information that enables efficient synchronisation among internal retail applications and external stakeholders such as suppliers, warehouses and logistics.

The most common processes comprehended in the master data management solutions are typically source identification, data collection, data transformation, rule administration, error detection and correction, data consolidation and the distribution of data throughout the organisation to ensure consistency and control in the ongoing maintenance and application of this information.

Management of data management is the discipline which is supported by technology that combines elements of data governance, data quality and data integration to ensure that the right data is presented to the right place at the right time.

Without a master data management system in place the result would be the need to perform numerous manual data entry processes across multiple applications. The consequence of this can be product data errors, contractual or purchase order discrepancies, longer lead times and inefficient usage of resources.

The foundation data that resides in the management data management system is static in that it seldom changes and is linked to all peer systems. The information is set up in the background and is held in a central repository and serves as the master of all merchandise and supplier information that is referenced when transactions are done and the data is sent to the relevant systems.

Broadly the information can be categorised to that which relates to the organisation, merchandise hierarchy, suppliers and time hierarchy and within these categories there is reference data which are lower levels pertaining to the various components.

Diagrammatically foundation data may be depicted as follows.

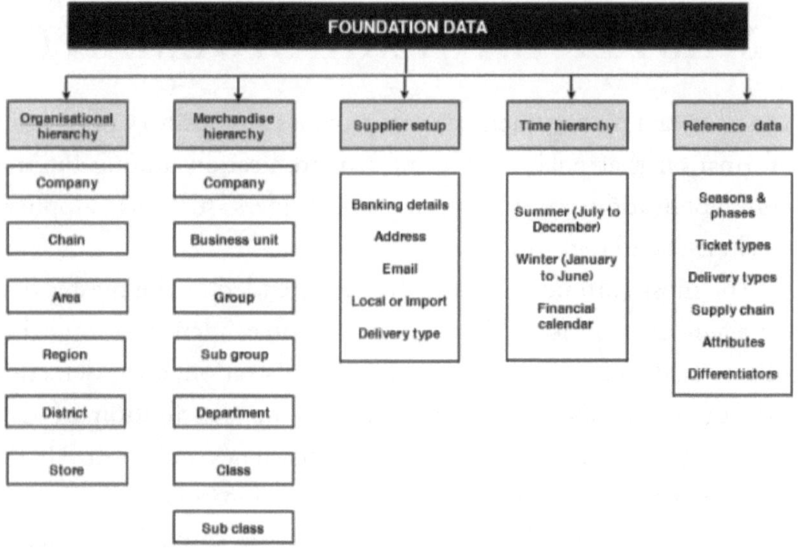

Creation of an item

In the registering of a new region, department, product, class or a new supplier with all their details for a period there will be some options which have to be chosen which reside in the system as reference data which is selected and attached to the object.

The assumption is made that in the following example a new item is being created.

The information that is attached to the item will be as follows

- **Item number – system generated sku number or barcode.**

A stock keeping unit number is assigned to each style colour and size level which enables detailed tracking of sales and stock levels that facilitates effective replenishment.

An example of such a number and associated barcode number will resemble something like

9005173048733 sku (stock keeping unit)

- **Differentiators**

Differentiators as the name implies highlights the distinguishing features that make the item be different to another product. In the creation of an item commences with the process of selecting the type they satisfy and into which group they fall and the lowest level value of the type that is qualified for.

Diagrammatically this concept is illustrated below

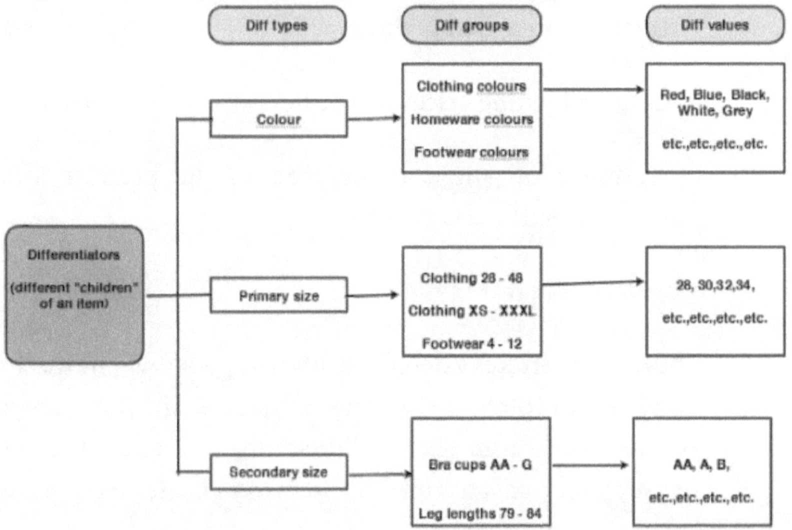

◇ **Attributes**

- User defined attributes attached to items are essential to drive functionality and reporting analysis, some of which may be mandatory and other optional.

- Examples would be whether a product is a continuity or an input product, short sleeves vs. long sleeves, tops vs. bottoms, waisted vs. non waisted

◇ **Seasons**

- Seasonal timing attached being spring/summer or autumn/winter

- Transitional periods between seasons

◇ **Supplier**

- Local vs. imported procurement

- Cost and selling prices will be held at item/supplier level

- Country of origin is attached to the product and displayed on the sew in labels

◇ **Delivery strategy**

The delivery strategy describes how the goods will move through the supply chain to reach the end destination. The delivery strategy will be assigned to a supplier and then inherited to all items created for that supplier to determine how items will be delivered to stores.

- Cross dock supply chain will be where the supplier picks and packs and delivers to a distribution centre which will transport the goods to stores

- Flow through where the supplier delivers in bulk to the distribution centres where the goods will be picked and packed and despatched to stores

- Warehouse where goods are stored awaiting a call off prior to despatch to stores

- Vendor managed inventory where the supplier merchandises the displays in stores and delivers directly to stores

- Direct store delivery where supplier picks and packs the goods and delivers them directly to stores

◈ **Cost price**

- A cost price may be held parent level for the item which will be loaded as the same for all children

- Different cost prices can be attached at children level where applicable

◈ **Selling price**

- Is maintained at item level

- Zone pricing can be the same or different for different regions

- Selling prices can be the same for parent and all children or can differ, for instances larger sizes of an item may be different known as variable pricing

◈ **Ticket type**

- Indicates whether the price ticket should be adhesive or swing ticket

- Separate tickets may need to be attached where a product consists of more than one component such as shoes, children's top and bottom sold as a suit

◇ Units

- Can be the unit of measure such as kg, items or per square metre

- The number of products that are packed together such as a pack of six representing the allocation packs

- Warehouse case packs that indicate the quantities that are stored in a case which must be consistent for stock counting purposes

Once all the mandatory and optional fields within the master data management system is completed the item can be approved that all the information is valid within the system. Transactions can then take place against these items.

The various types of transaction that can be actioned after the item is set up and approved is best illustrated as follows

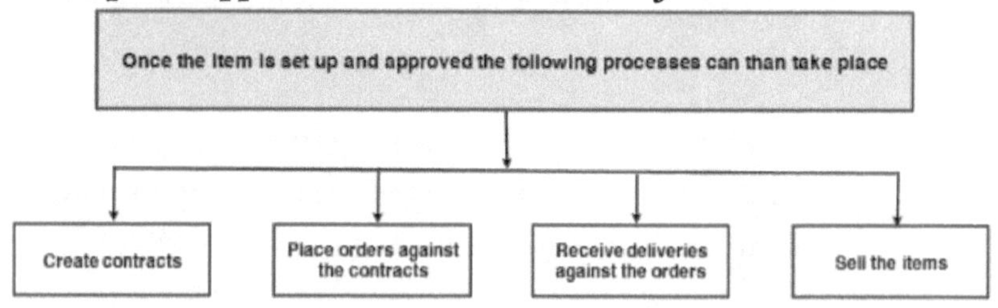

CASE STUDY

From the outline illustrated previously of the Men's Shirts department it is possible to identify some of the key factors of a Master Data Maintenance system.

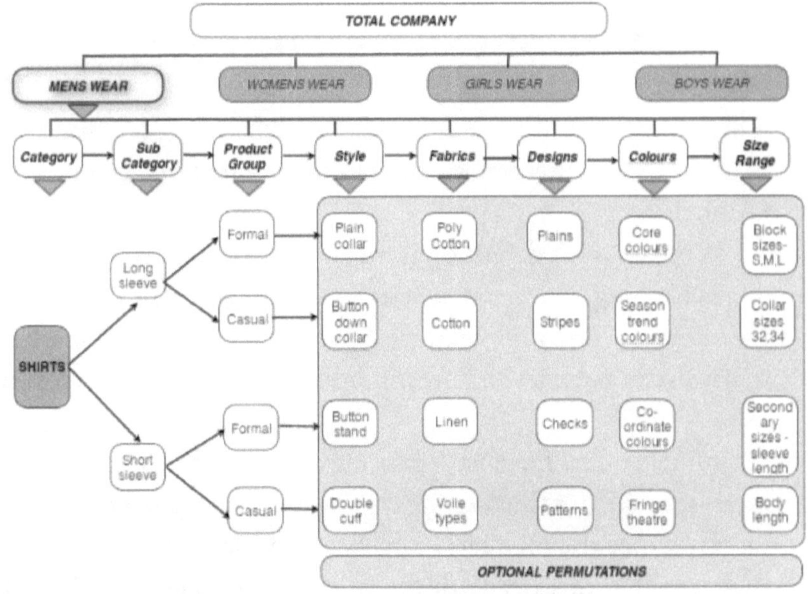

CHALLENGE #20

From the diagramme above identify examples of the following

1. Two organisational hierarchy data specimens
2. Two merchandise hierarchy data specimens
3. Two examples of attributes
4. Three examples of differentiators

MERCHANDISE PLANNING

There is often confusion as to what merchandise planning actually is and varying interpretations are often touted via a multitude of channels.

A broad brush definition is that it is a systematic approach aimed at maximising return on investment, through planning sales and inventory in order to increase profitability. This is done by the maximisation of sales and the minimisation of markdowns and stock outs.

Merchandise financial planning commences by taking a high level approach in the setting of the sales, margin and inventory targets. Once the high level targets are in place the planning teams then are able to cascade down to the lower hierarchical levels of the product at group, category and line level while integrating it at location level across time.

The principle applied is a top down bottom up approach as will be elaborated upon later. Product planning through the hierarchies is mirrored across locations and time which is sometimes referred to as the retail cube.

Illustratively this can be depicted as follows

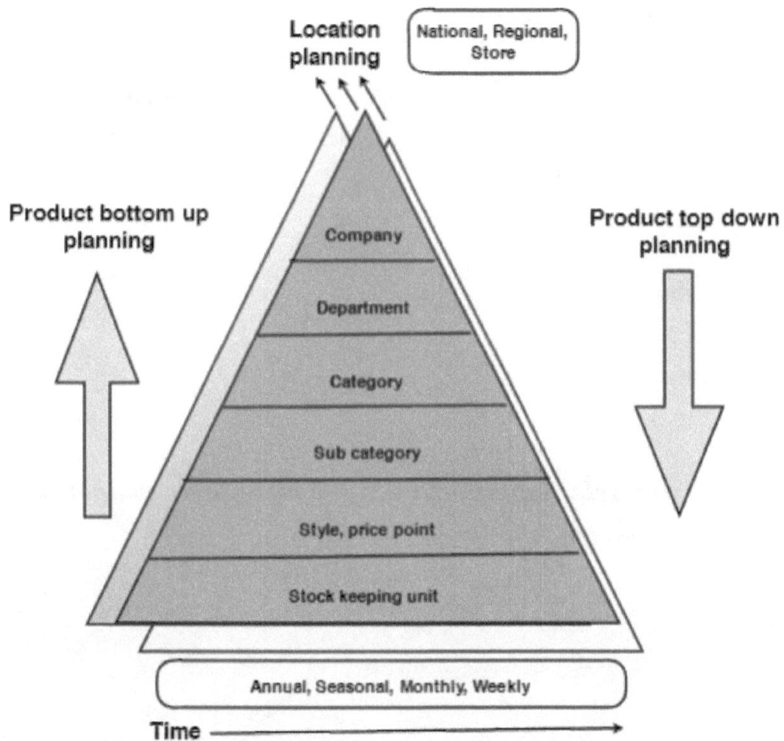

In conjunction with the buyers, designers, sourcing specialists and technologists, the merchandise planner is responsible for the delivery of the departmental strategy to make sure it is aligned to the strategic intent of the company and the group.

The sales forecasting and the planning of the stock levels is done to achieve the sales and margin objectives from departmental level down to the individual product level. Together with the buyer the range planning and building will take place to construct a complete balanced offer of product that satisfies the needs of the target customers.

The intake and orders are carefully controlled to meet the stock requirements as per the plan at any given time while the allocation and distribution of stock is managed in such a way in order to optimise the fulfilment of the customer demands within the selling space available.

The foundation of planning is the manipulation of the components of what is known as the retail balance set which are key to driving out profit.

The balance set components comprise of

- Sales
- Markdowns
- Intake
- Stock

The inter relationship between the balance set components of them can be shown as follows

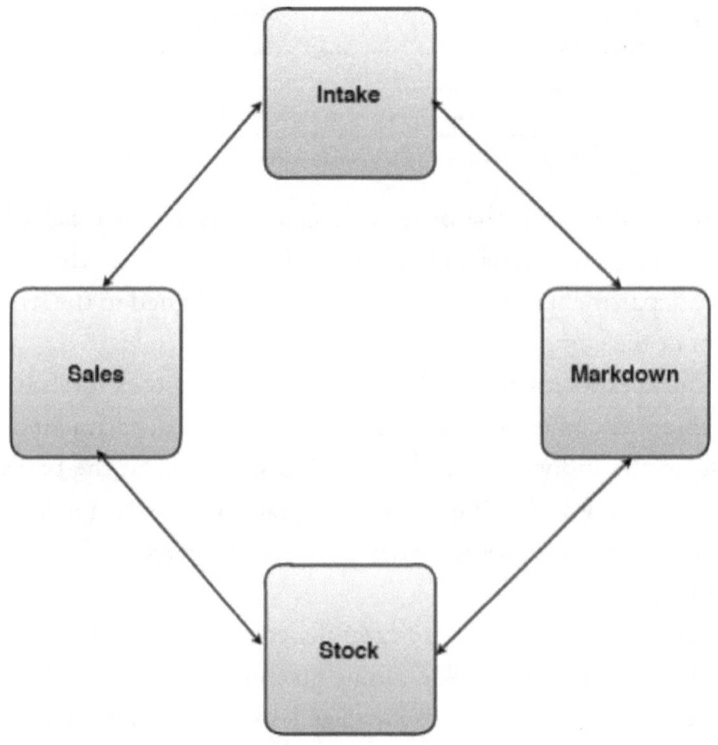

The fundamental calculation rules of the relative components

The common deduction is the necessity to determine how much stock must be bought to meet the planned sales and stock targets or alternatively to consider what the resultant stock levels would be if a pre-determined amount was procured. However the second option is less utilised as invariably the result will be different to that of the original plan.

Assume the components values for a period are

Sales = 1000

Markdowns = 40

Intake = 1240

Closing Stock = 2000

Opening Stock = 1800

Intake = Closing stock plus sales and markdown less opening stock

(2000+1000+40)-1800 = 1240

Closing Stock = Opening Stock less Sales and Markdowns plus Intake

(1800-1000-40)+1240 = 2000

Basic steps of planning process

The principles of planning outlined below is affectionately referred to by some retailers as WISSI which stands for the weekly sales, stock and intake plan. This process has been adopted in some format or other by many merchants worldwide and forms the basis of the logic in technical planning packages which are marketed by a number of software developers. The basic principles are also key to the integration of the planning function with suites of other operational packages such as allocation systems, buying range planning, critical path management, warehousing and distribution applications.

CASE STUDY

Using the data matrix of CH Clothing Company it is able to be demonstrated how to determine what the Intake value will be for the 26 week season using the process above

Men's basic white shirts

		JANUARY				FEBRUARY					MARCH				APRIL				MAY					JUNE		
		1	2	3	4	5	6	7	8	9	10	11	12	13	14	15	16	17	18	19	20	21	22	23	24	25	26
Sales LY	497	7	9	12	16	12	15	17	19	23	19	16	15	17	22	21	25	27	24	21	19	21	25	23	22	24	26
Sales TY	579	10	12	15	20	15	17	20	23	27	22	20	18	19	24	25	28	30	27	24	23	25	29	25	25	27	29
Mark downs	46					5	8	10	6							5	5	6	1								
Open stock		70	80	80	85	83	88	86	90	95	103	98	99	96	95	95	100	110	130	125	132	138	130	132	135	136	135
Close stock		80	80	85	83	88	86	90	95	103	98	99	96	95	95	100	110	130	125	132	138	130	132	135	136	135	140
Cost price	110.00																										
Selling price	199.99																										

CHALLENGE #21

Referring to the matrix above determine the intake value for the 26 week period

The sequence of steps to determine an intake plan is portrayed as follows

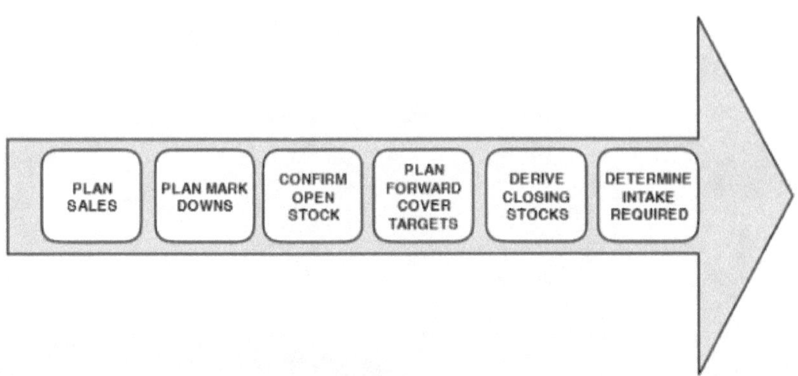

Plan sales involves the forecasting of sales across time, usually for a six monthly season by month by week in a shape that resembles past history and accounts for any strategic intent such as new product launches, store openings, competitive activity and special events like significant world sports happenings and environmental initiatives. It needs to be recognised that some occasions take place at different times from year to year such as Easter and Eid and should be provided for accordingly.

Statistical methods of sales forecasting commonly use the exponential smoothing of trends or weighted moving average options in simple models which are relatively easy to use. For more complex scenarios such as with the introduction of new categories or catering for products with erratic sales it is likely that the predictions will include a safety stock factor to cater for the unexpected. In such cases some companies utilise experts or rely on advanced software to assist in the analysis and formulation of expected patterns.

It should be noted that the combination of the individual product life cycles are overlaid across time to accumulate the formation of the upper level sales pattern.

The traditional life cycle of a product may be illustrated as follows

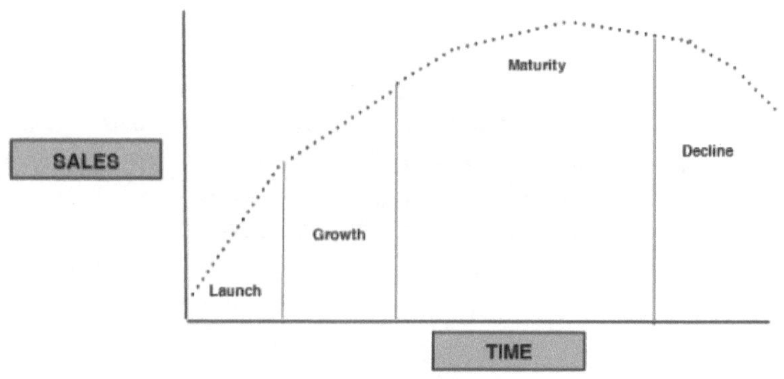

Plan markdowns is required as it is inevitable that not all goods will sell as expected which means that the clearance of oddments is necessary in order to facilitate the flow of newness and other promotional activities as well as relieve any space constraints.

The level of provision for markdowns that is set is influenced by historical trends and the characteristics of the product. The higher the fashionability of the category, the greater is the risk and therefore for such products a higher markdown allowance is necessary. The converse applies for basic continuity product. While it is usually quite easy to accurately predict the amount of acceptable markdown at the higher departmental level, the markdown value contribution of individual line products can differ considerably to expectations.

Traditional types of markdown are the typical end of season cleanouts where there is an aggressive campaign to remove the unwanted product to provide for the introduction of a new seasons launch or for a promotional product sale as part of a strategic intent.

The argument exists that although the regular sell off of products attracts more feet in the store and stimulates the sale of regular priced goods while freeing up space for new launches the customer soon understands the strategy and adapts buying patterns.in order to benefit from the inevitable reduction.

There are a number of innovative promotional approaches that are taking hold in order to stimulate not only sales but also generate some other spin offs.

A classic example is the American tradition of the Black Friday thanksgiving sale which takes place on the first Friday after Thanksgiving which almost all types of retailers participate in with some really aggressive discounts. These are eagerly supported by all customers who are happy to participate in the mayhem of crowds who storm the shops and websites in search of big bargains. This phenomenon has begun to be adopted by a number of countries in spite of it not being part of their culture but does serve as an opportunity to build some hype for their business when customers are very receptive to spending their money.

There are however pros and cons in the participation of such a promotion. Some of the pros are the generation of shopper enthusiasm for the business, with the right offers it is an opportunity to expose the business to new customers who may be willing to return, it is also a chance to rid the store of older, slower selling inventory that would inevitably have to be marked down. On the downside such severe promotions may lead to potential customers holding back on full price purchases for the weeks before until the designate date arrives. It is not uncommon that some retailers place a blanket discount on all goods for the specific day which although increases the flow of feet significantly it is logical that the best sellers will still sell at a greater rate than less wanted product with the result that there will be a shortage of the most wanted product and the store is left with the most unpopular product on offer in the run up to the peak trading period of the holidays. There is also the need to ensure that your logistical infrastructure is able to accommodate with the rush effectively and that the website is robust enough to serve all the additional traffic as if this is not the case it is likely that the brand could be damaged.

The sell through plan of a sale depends on the intended time the affected goods are placed on offer with scheduled phases of further intermittent reductions and a final liquidation at the end of the period. The general trend that exists as a rule of thumb is that most of the fashion and brand retailers sell fifty to sixty percent of their stock at full price while the rest of the merchandise is sold at discounts of thirty to fifty percent eroding approximately twenty percent of margin while the balance is virtually written off.

Illustratively the markdown activity with probable examples of periods and percentage cuts can be represented as follows.

The progressive phases of markdown sales

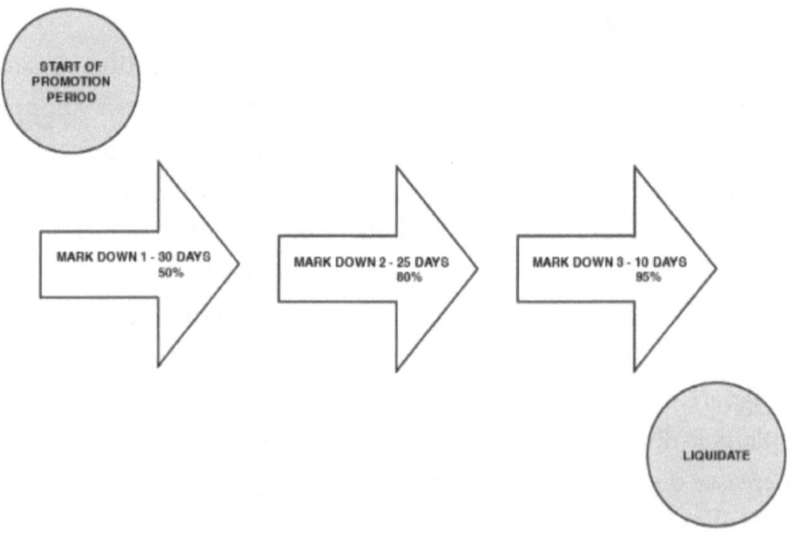

Planned promotions should always have a structured post mortem assessment. The framework of the analysis could possibly be done by measuring by how much sales improve for a set period after the promotional launch compared to the level of sales prior to the campaign.

A selection of similar products can be earmarked as control items to which an evaluation can be made in terms of the uplift in sales experienced versus the sales of the control items as well as what the effect of possible substitution purchases were during the same period. Based on these findings the conclusion may be drawn as to the success and viability in terms of increase in profit and market penetration.

Consideration should be given to the space constraints in tight metreage stores to accommodate aggressive promotions. If the volumes and number of customer choices are too great, it may result in the operational efficiencies of the store being compromised and will result in the layout becoming disconnected from the strategic intent. In these instances it may be considered to transfer some or all of the reduced stock to larger stores.

Confirm opening stock. The starting point for stock represents the actual value of closing stock in the previous period. This has to be recognised as the value affects the required intake particularly in the early part of the new season and may well also have an impact on the level of planned markdown that subsequently may need to be reviewed.

In the illustration below the planned opening stock for week 1 is 7000 more than the actual open stock of 70000 and therefore the intake will have to increase by 7000 to keep in line with the planned closing stock of 79000

	TOTAL SEASON	WK 1
OPEN STOCK	77 000	77 000
SALES	370 000	10 000
MARKDOWN	700	
INTAKE	376 700	12 000
FWD COVER		6
CLOSING STOCK	83 000	79 000

Plan forward cover targets based on the acceptable number of weeks that are strategically agreed for the various categories of products which will aid the achievement of the approved stock turn.

	TOTAL SEASON	MONTH 1				MO[N]	
		WK 1	WK 2	WK 3	WK 4	WK 5	WK 6
OPEN STOCK	77 000	77 000	79 000	82 000	81 000	81 000	88 000
SALES	370 000	10 000	12 000	14 000	14 000	12 000	13 000

In wk 1 the planned open stock is 77000

The fwd wks cover is set at 6

Adding up the sales for the fwd 6 weeks gives a required opening stock of 77000 in wk 1

FWD COVER		6	6	6	6	6	6

Derive closing stock values using the number of weeks forward cover at the end of each month and apply them to the weekly sales plan going forward.

Determine the intake required through the balanced set calculation of closing stock plus sales and markdown less opening stock for each month and the total season.

It should be noted that the weekly sales into the early part of the next season should be taken into account in order to calculate the closing stock targets to meet the forward cover requirements.

In the construction of the simplified model of the intake plan below a flat forward cover of six weeks has been selected for ease of illustration. In reality it may change in the event of special happenings such as factory closures over holiday periods when the routine distribution is disrupted or there is stock build up requirement for new initiative launches, packaging change overs, catalogue adjustments and new store openings.

A representative example of the intake plan

	TOTAL SEASON	MONTH 1				MONTH 2				MONTH 3				
		WK 1	WK 2	WK 3	WK 4	WK 5	WK 6	WK 7	WK 8	WK 9	WK 10	WK 11	WK 12	WK 13
OPEN STOCK	77 000	77 000	79 000	82 000	81 000	81 000	88 000	96 000	98 000	98 000	99 000	98 000	91 000	83 000
SALES	370 000	10 000	12 000	14 000	14 000	12 000	13 000	14 000	15 000	13 000	14 000	19 000	21 000	16 000
MARKDOWN	700				700									
INTAKE	376 700	12 000	15 000	11 000	14 700	19 000	21 000	16 000	15 000	14 000	13 000	12 000	13 000	15 000
FWD COVER		6	6	6	6	6	6	6	6	6	6	6	6	6
CLOSING STOCK	83 000	79 000	82 000	81 000	81 000	88 000	96 000	98 000	98 000	99 000	98 000	91 000	83 000	82 000

	TOTAL SEASON	MONTH 4				MONTH 5				MONTH 6				
		WK 14	WK 15	WK 16	WK 17	WK 18	WK 19	WK 20	WK 21	WK 22	WK 23	WK 24	WK 25	WK 26
OPEN STOCK	77 000	82 000	83 000	84 000	85 000	86 000	87 000	87 000	85 000	83 000	83 000	85 000	85 000	83 000
SALES	370 000	15 000	14 000	13 000	12 000	13 000	15 000	16 000	15 000	14 000	13 000	14 000	15 000	14 000
MARKDOWN	700													
INTAKE	376 700	16 000	15 000	14 000	13 000	14 000	15 000	14 000	13 000	14 000	15 000	14 000	13 000	14 000
FWD COVER		6	6	6	6	6	6	6	6	6	6	6	6	6
CLOSING STOCK	83 000	83 000	84 000	85 000	86 000	87 000	87 000	85 000	83 000	83 000	85 000	85 000	83 000	83 000

Monthly financial planning

As part of the preparation of the intake plan it is good practice to present a basic month by month financial plan for the department. This will enable all the department month by month plans to be rolled up to group level and then all groups can be consolidated to total company level. A clear picture of the financial requirements to run the business is thereby provided to senior management and enables the arrangements for the liquidity of funds necessary for each month.

The merchandise financial plan facilitates the high level plan for the total organisation through the accumulation of all the lower level plans. Through this the organisations traditional open to buy requirement across the planning calendar across time can be determined.

Using the values from the intake plan above the financial planning summary will look as follows

DEPARTMENTAL MONTHLY FINANCIAL SUMMARY

	OPEN STOCK	SALES	MARKDOWN	INTAKE	CLOSE STOCK
MONTH 1	77 000	50 000	700	54 700	81 000
MONTH 2	81 000	54 000		71 000	98 000
MONTH 3	98 000	83 000		67 000	82 000
MONTH 4	82 000	54 000		46 200	85 000
MONTH 5	85 000	59 000		70 000	83 000
MONTH 6	83 000	56 000		56 000	83 000

The determination of intake required is applicable at any product hierarchy level. The highest platform would be for the total company which then flows down to group and department. Thereafter it can be drilled down to product level and subsequently to colour and size.

The same holds true for location planning from total company through to regional and store level.

CASE STUDY

The table below reflects the financial plan for CH Clothing Company for the period January to June.

TOTAL COMPANY FINANCIAL PLAN					
'000	OPEN STOCK	SALES	MARK DOWN	INTAKE	CLOSE STOCK
January	580	670		790	700
February	700	830	250	1240	860
March	860	700		630	790
April	790	890	150	1330	1080
May	1080	1060	30	1110	1100
June	1100	880		780	1000
Total Season					

CHALLENGE #22

With reference to the table above determine the values that should be reflected in the row for the total season.

1. Open Stock
2. Sales
3. Markdown
4. Intake
5. Close Stock

The principle of top down planning and bottom up verification is key to accurate forecasting. Experience shows that should planning be done from bottom up with a consolidation to a higher level, it is inevitable that the original overall top level plan will be exceeded.

If each line is considered in isolation, the reality of the influencing factors such as late deliveries, unforeseen obstacles and events are discounted and will therefore invariably deliver a much more optimistic plan. The added danger of a bottom up approach could possibly result in uncertainty or mistrust of the strategy and therefore plans with excessive percentage increases on last year should be challenged and be given careful consideration and validation.

A point to remember is that budgets cannot be banked and it seems to be a natural tendency of human nature to be optimistic and endeavour to justify higher budget levels. It is important to remain as realistic as possible in the setting of the financial plan levels.

The challenge of chasing products where performance is above expectation is far more pleasurable than frantically switching off production and suffering the consequences of over commitments which may be in the form of completed product or raw materials. The threat of suppliers having to work shorter hours or needing to retrench production staff can also become a real possibility.

Plans should be realistic in terms of the transition from a preceding season into a new season. Formulating budgets in isolation comes with the dogged assumption that the errors of the previous season will not be repeated nor will there be any misjudgements going forward. The expectation is also that the benefits which will be enjoyed through new initiatives and products are over and above current levels of performance. The reality is however that this does not happen from day one when at midnight of the last day of the previous season the mediocre level of sales will instantly transform into a higher optimistic level of performance almost as if a message was shot off to all customers to tell them to start buying more.

Another common trap is that during the formulation of the strategy and operational plan the desires are considered to be a given and it is assumed without doubt that it is going to happen. A common example is the want to generate higher levels of profit which may be done through the adjustment of the margin policy upwards and inevitably selling prices as well. It is presumed that the change will be happily accepted by customers and intake plans are then put in place to meet the revised targets. The unfortunate inevitability is that the changeover does not happen immediately from day one of the new season as it takes a time for customers to digest and possibly modify buying habits. Consequently disillusionment amongst the retail team reigns which results in strategy and sales plans being questioned and a resultant panic plan to rectify the situation is implemented at an early stage.

During the trading period the actual values will differ to the planned expectations and the anticipated values need to be substituted with the actual. The plan going forward consequently needs to be adjusted based on a different opening stock, changed markdown value and therefore requires that the intake value to be adjusted in order to bring the plan back in line.

Where performance is not up to standard, the product mix of the intake going forward may still remain well-matched to the plan in terms of any new coordinated ranges and seasonal launches. In order to ensure that this is done effectively it could be necessary to consider other options whereby stock levels may be allowed to drift above planned levels for a time and to be gradually brought back in line to realistic targets.

A worthy practice is to permit for spare open to buy right up to the latest point in time before committing in contract form. Such a tactic will facilitate the pursuit of the better selling lines or being able to absorb growing overstocks thus maintaining tighter stock controls and avoiding possible financial disaster.

Integration of hierarchy level plans

Product plans from a company level down to individual product group by week need to be integrated with the location planning hierarchy in order that the stores are stocked with the most appropriate assortment of product to effectively satisfy the customer needs.

The same principle applies in location plans that the higher hierarchical levels are considered to be the most accurate to lay down the parameters to which plans from the lower levels are balanced back to.

The integration of plans is illustrated below

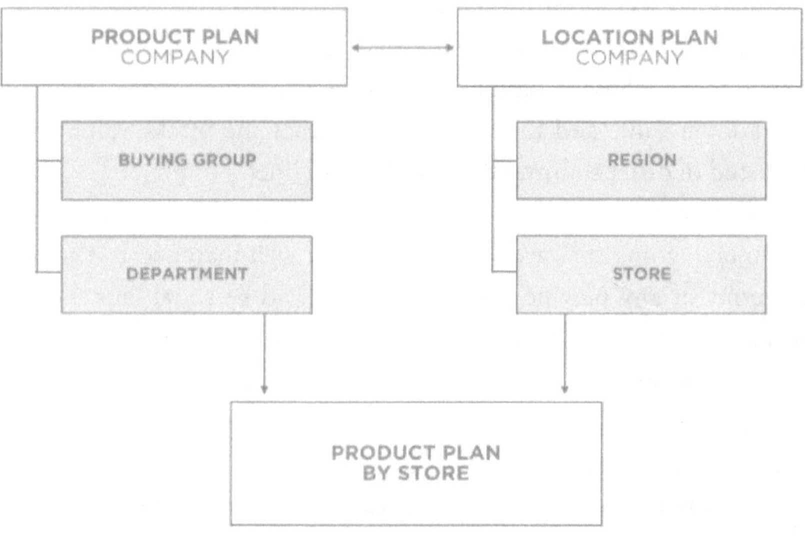

CASE STUDY

CH Clothing Company has a total monetary sales value of 5,030,000 for the season. Replicating the illustration above we are able to determine the product plan by store assuming the following.

◈ *The Product and Location plan is the same at 5,030,000 for the total company.*

◈ *The Buying group is Menswear which is 20% of the total company.*

◈ *The department is the Men's shirts department which represents 8% of the Menswear group.*

◈ *The Region being examined is region 1 which is 15% of the total Company Location plan.*

◈ *Within the region Store A has been selected which is 5% of the region 1.*

◈ *The shirts department in Store A will be therefore 8% of the total store.*

CHALLENGE #23

Knowing the above it is possible to determine the various values of the Product plan combined to the Location plan. Based on this provide the following monetary values.

1. The value of Menswear Group.
2. The value of Menswear in Region 1.
3. The value of the Men's Shirts department.
4. The value of Store A in Region 1.
5. The value of Men's Shirts department in Store A.

Location plans

In setting up the location plans it is important to be aware of what products are going to which stores and be sure that they are in suitable proportions and quantities that will best service the unique customer profiles that are applicable to the individual stores. The store profile or personality will be influenced predominantly by the surrounding economic factors, lifestyles and cultural demographics. A common technique to consider is to cluster similar profile stores into specific groupings so that they all carry like catalogues of products which will assist in the efficiency of planning and achieve a comparable handwriting across the chain.

A logical way to define the accurate range of product types as well as give guidance to the quantities for the right places is through the drafting of a matrix which indicates the correct kind of products that are to be destined to different groups of stores. In principle there is a base selection of product that would go to all stores and thereafter selected products which will be earmarked for specific store profile groups dependent on factors such as sales budgets, space constraints, layout plans, price sensitivity and fashion demands. The main purpose is to ensure that a store receives the correct width of range based on the store's unique characteristics and future expected performance.

A simple example of such a matrix could look as follows.

DEPARTMENT XYZ	STORE PROFILE Group A	STORE PROFILE Group B	STORE PROFILE Group C	STORE PROFILE Group D	STORE PROFILE Group E
PRODUCT 1	X	X	X	X	X
PRODUCT 2	X	X	X	X	X
PRODUCT 3	X	X	X	X	X
PRODUCT 4	X	X	X	X	X
PRODUCT 5	X	X	X	X	X
PRODUCT 6	X	X	X		
PRODUCT 7	X	X	X	X	
PRODUCT 8	X	X			
PRODUCT 9	X	X			X
PRODUCT 10	X				

Realistic sales plans by subclass for each store are put in place which eventually rolls up to the location plan at a total department level which provides a guideline for the number of choices that should be planned for each store grouping.

New stores or stores with partial sales history are also planned in the location plans taking into account like profile stores, like turnovers, the store opening date and the overall location planned sales and the stores average unit sales by style.

The location plan delivers the store sales plans by subclass over time, the store groupings by subclass down to style level over time.

Once the store plans are completed and are rolled up to the total location plan the requirement is that they need to be reconciled to the department merchandise plan at corporate subclass level which enables the department strategic intent to be taken into account and provide a sales shape across time to ensure store and product growths are planned similarly.

An underlying standard which needs to be understood is that planning is a constantly changing iterative process that requires continual pre-season and in-season review dependent on customers, competitors and suppliers behaving differently to what was anticipated. Other factors may be renovations, store format changes, modernisations, revamps etc. that have to be taken into account in the location plan.

A point of consideration that should never be ignored once again is the eighty twenty rule, also known as the Pareto principle where it is acknowledged that eighty percent of the result is delivered by twenty percent of the effort or participants.

In the context of stores it is probable that twenty percent of the stores deliver eighty percent of the sales and deserve the proportionate dedication of energy and focus, as does the thick middle sizes such as medium and large and therefore should always be in stock. Core base colours such as white, black, naturals and greys also contribute largely to the sales and should always be evident in volume. It is clear that certain styling features will likewise guarantee the bulk of sales and should be finalised first and certain peak trading periods such as holidays or special events will contribute largely to the total seasonal sales and must be managed very carefully in terms of production planning and delivery scheduling.

It should be qualified that it is not necessarily exactly a ratio of eighty versus twenty as in certain cases it could be a ninety to ten or seventy to thirty relationship but nevertheless the principle still holds true.

Sophisticated merchandise planning applications

Many retailers are still reliant on basic spreadsheets or outdated planning applications to conduct business.

The use of sophisticated, high technical retail planning solutions without doubt bring with it a number of benefits enabling the retailer to have a competitive advantage with a greater level of efficiency.

Some of the major benefits is that there is a far greater degree of accuracy with one version of the truth as data is integrated across a number of systems which eliminates the continual disputes trying to agree which systems data is correct. The converse, however, also exists in that if the data is wrong from the source it is wrong everywhere.

Various consistent views can be created with spreadsheet capabilities that are able to be rolled up or down through and reconciled across all hierarchies which includes historical data. These features accommodate forecasting and hind sighting capabilities as well as facilitate collaboration with other platforms such as logistics.

Data is seamlessly linked across all plans and is particularly beneficial to planning and action of assortment and allocation plans which can facilitate flexible "what if" planning.

A vital requirement is that such systems must be user friendly and easy to use which allows the planner to complete tasks more quickly. The danger exists that if this requirement is not met the mastering of the system becomes the prime objective of the user rather than the focus on true merchanting.

MERCHANDISE ASSORTMENT PLANNING

The assortment of product carried in a retailer's store at any point in time is defined by the types of product on offer. The primary goal of effective assortment planning is to specify a mix of product that will maximise the sales and gross margin.

There are a variety of issues that have to be considered to make a proper determination and the decision making processes subject to several different conditions. These conditions may include issues such as a limited budget for purchase of products, restricted available shelf space for displaying products, seasonal items, holiday selling cycles and a variety of other miscellaneous constraints.

Assortment planning needs to take into account the typical profiles that the retailer is servicing. The seasonal introduction of new products, brands and trends based on continually changing consumer tastes. This frequently necessitates buyers and designers to consult with trend forecasting companies and other sources to assist.

In essence the SKU's or stock keeping units that that exist are segmented into categories such as menswear and thereafter into sub categories such as men's casualwear and thereafter into departments, product groups down to products which are defined by style, colour and size which is the fundamental SKU level.

It is critical that the assortment plan reflects the appropriate mix in terms of width and depth of product mix where the continuity and newness of products is a balance by which the consumers are adequately catered for.

The range summary is required to establish a broad framework. It consists of the initial drafting of a matrix of the mix of product to give guidance of the construction of the range plan which is the range strategy forming part of the department strategy. The source of inputs for the range strategy is the information in the existing range plan, the group strategy and budgets as well as lessons learnt during the previous season.,

A guideline of the number of customer choices in each sub class of product with no volumes attached, the catalogue of stores the customer choices will service over the various time phases will be reflected in the range summary.

The example of a range strategy in the form of a tick sheet is depicted as follows

SKIRTS	Product type	Jan.	Feb.	Mar.	Apr.	May	June
Style 1	Cont	x	x	x	x	x	x
Style 2	Volume	x	x	x			
Style 3	Volume				x	x	x
Style 4	Volume	x	x	x			
Style 5	Volume				x	x	x
Style 6	Input	x					
Style 7	Input		x				
Style 8	Input			x			
Style 9	Input				x		
Style 10	Input					x	
Style 11	Input						x
No of options		4	4	4	4	4	4

The number of styles in total is 11 but equates to 4 per time period for this specific selection of stores

Once the framework is in place the process of forming the content of the range in terms of the attributes and theme of the range has to be constructed.

The main players in this process are the designers, buyers and technologists.

Design briefs are made up of significant trend and brand information which are constructed by the design team that include information such as anticipated key silhouettes within the assortments and colour themes, fabric types, print influences and technical direction which will be distributed to buying, planning, technology and sourcing teams.

The brief takes the form of a presentation with the use of story boards and flow charts with description of the themes.

Design concept workshops are set up with relevant stakeholders that may or may not include suppliers with appropriate samples, materials and artwork out of which seasonal concept story boards will evolve by department or brand that will depict the expected themes, key looks for the season, colour palettes, styles and fabric types that will be dominant

A simple example of a typical story board ladies fashion highlighting looks, colour pallette, fabrics and themes is illustrated below

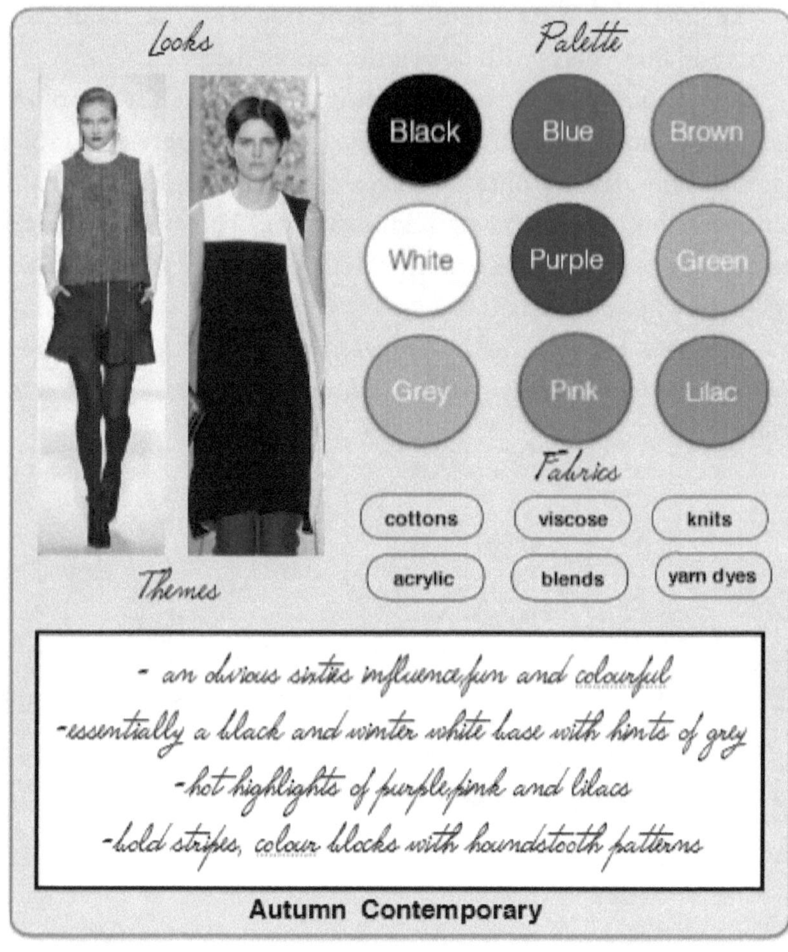

After the design brief is completed and is signed off by the senior management team, buying, design and trend teams commence the conducting of product workshops.

Trends, Insights and Fads

Trends and insights indicate as to where your brand currently is and ideally where it should be. They are used to guide your decision making and help in the formulation of the strategy until the whole picture evolves.

The trend can be best described as the general direction such as consumer buying behaviour is developing and is changing, it therefore has no beginning and has no end as it provides indicators in the development of the brand.

Trends are driven by attributes such as a specific look, a lifestyle, a colour, fabric, style, a shape or innovation. It is crucial that a trend is accepted by the target customer in that they need to understand and embrace the trend as well as the fact that the style can be adapted for mass appeal. The trend must be able to be accommodated in the existing price structure and have an acceptable amount of risk that will blend into the overall range. It is therefore really important that to minimise the risk that the trends have to be identified as those that have staying power and have the potential of becoming profitable and that the strategy can be adapted in order that they are in accordance with emerging trend data so as to match the customers' needs , wants and desires.

It is important to note that trends are not necessarily continually on an increment, some explode and become relevant while others disappear. They are also not created in isolation as they are influenced by social and environmental factors which will have an effect on various industries, individuals, companies' products and services which makes the harvesting of accurate data paramount.

An insight differs in that it comprises of accurate understanding and intuitive analysis of the person or thing that is served. In other words it is the "why", and 'what if" and so it therefore depends on creative thinking and analysis.

There is often confusion in the distinction as to what is a trend and that which is a fad. To distinguish between the two, a trend is a popular general direction which takes longer to build than a fad and lasts longer for which there is a bigger demand. The fad generally has a smaller demand and seldom migrates into the mainstream and characteristically generates a very high rate of interest for a very short period of time and is often just a flash in the pan. To draw a comparison belted waists for dresses may be seen as a trend for an entire season or longer but "oncies" all in one fleece garments for men were a fad that did not last very long.

It is therefore understandable that the implementation of trends, insights and fads can be considerably complex but eventually the objective through the integration of the three elements is to through being innovation and steady management to provide a nimble, agile and flexible business plans, marketing strategies, brand development, and organisational structures within a constantly changing operational environment.

Product workshops aim to build a balanced assortment for the season which is aligned to the strategies as set down and meet the range summary.

In these workshops the following will take place

- Samples, artwork and prototypes will be reviewed and approved or rejected

- The colour palettes will be set across the customer segmentations, core continuity products and fashion assortments

- The continuity, core and input items will be confirmed

- Gaps or outstanding items will be identified for which appropriate designs need to sourced

The volumes per customer choice at sub class level is provided by the planning arm and the buyer will decide which product will be assigned to the choice option.

The responsibilities of the main participants in the product workshop is illustrated as follows

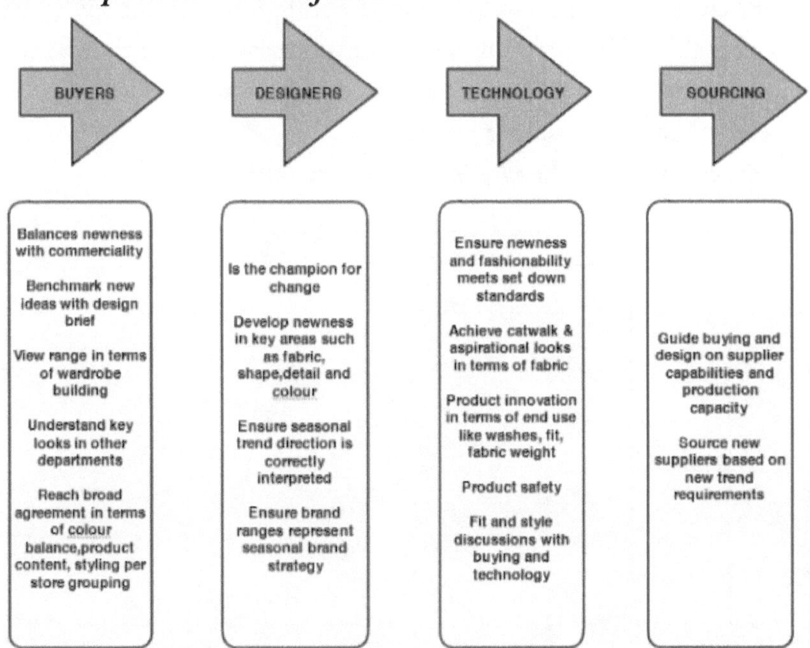

Suppliers are briefed and will submit appropriate samples according to the design brief pack for consideration in terms of the requirements that have emerged out of the product workshops. If the submissions are successful the samples will be finalised and accepted.

After the products are finalised, the formal contractual procurement process will commence.

Department line sales summary

Prior to the building of the range or buying plan there must be an indication of the expected item sales in money value and units as well as the relative proportion splits across the range for the various store catalogues with the relative variances between this year and last year for the sales value, units and price which will all serve as the preliminary basis for discussion and provide the guidance for the formulation of the intake and range plan.

Price moves highlight whether the inflationary indications are at acceptable levels particularly where products are identical to the previous year and the like for like percentage move is at least in line or is less than the consumer price index.

An example of a line by line summary is as follows

PROD NO	DESCRIPTION	STORE CATALOGUE	SELLING PRICE			SALES '000			SALES UNITS		
			LY	TY	% inc/dec	LY	TY	% inc/dec	LY	TY	% inc/dec
	PROD GROUP 1										
1001	Style ABCD	All	95.00	99.99	5.2%	680 000	730 000	6.7%	7 158	7 300	2.0%
2001	Style ABCE	All	125.00	129.99	4.0%	500 000	550 000	10.0%	4 000	4 231	5.7%
	PROD GROUP 2										
1002	Style ABCF	All	175.00	180.00	2.9%	299 000	350 000	17.0%	1 708	1 944	13.8%
2002	Style ABCG	All	175.00	180.00	2.9%	345 000	400 000	15.9%	1 971	2 222	12.8%
3001	Style ABCH	All	175.00	180.00	2.9%	365 000	390 000	6.8%	2 085	2 027	9.7%
TOTAL DEPARTMENT			129.40	136.53	5.5%	2 189 000	2 420 000	10.6%	16 922	17 724	4.7%

The construction of a range plan may commence once the financial targets are available

CASE STUDY

Referring to the range description of the shirt department as below

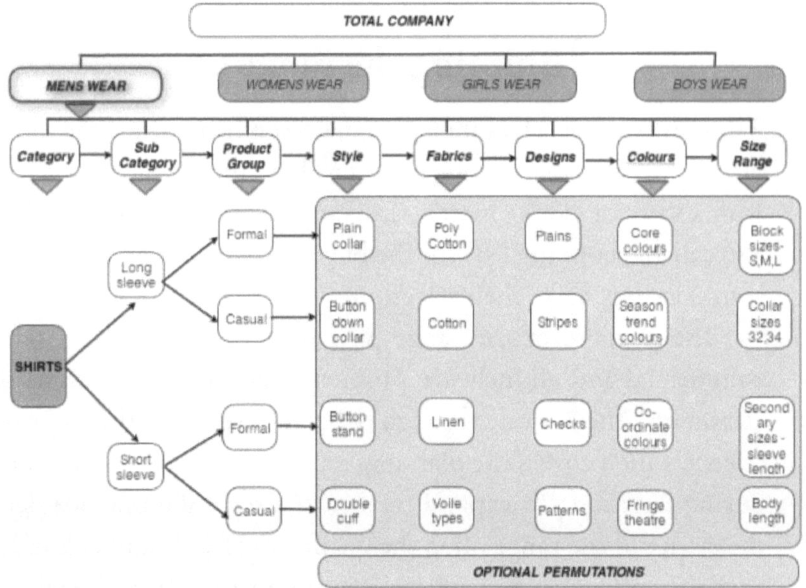

A possible example of a simple line by line budget summary will likely reflect the following

DEPARMENTAL SALES SUMMARY

Prod No	Description	Store Catalogue	Selling Price			Sales '000			Sales Units		
			LY	TY	% inc/dec	LY	TY	% inc/dec	LY	TY	% inc/dec
Category	Long sleeve										
Sub Group	Formal L/S										
1001	Plains/self pattern	All	150.00	160.00	6.7%	174 100	200 000	14.9%	1 161	1250	7.7%
Sub Group	Casual L/S										
1002	Prints/checks	All	180.00	199.00	10.6%	124 094	150 000	20.9%	689	754	9.3%
Category	Short sleeve										
Sub Group	Formal S/S										
2001	Plains/self pattern	All	140.00	150.00	7.1%	74 611	85 000	13.9%	533	567	6.3%
Sub Group	Casual S/S										
2002	Prints/checks	All	160.00	170.00	6.3%	124 195	150 000	20.8%	776	882	13.7%
TOTAL SHIRTS DEPARTMENT			157.32	169.43	7.7%	497 000	585 000	17.7%	3 159	3453	9.3%

CHALLENGE #24

The following needs to be explained

1. The selling price in the total row are not rounded and do not resemble those at line level. Why is this?

2. While the LY sales match those in the previous shirts department matrix the TY sales do not match. Why is this?

Building the range plan

The construction of a range plan may commence once the financial targets are available through the product and store plans together with a store catalogue matrix. The range plan enables the drafting of a so called "shopping list" for the buying team to be able to fill in the blanks as they make their selections.

The purpose of the range plan is to ensure that the offer of commercial and all-inclusive product ranges meet the needs of all customers. This is done through the combination of the elements of science which covers the planning aspect and art that represents the buying function. To expand further, the scientific practice delivers the clarity of the range offer, the quantities of style and colour levels with the correct pricing policies that support structured cataloguing which meet the varying customer profile pools. The artistic involvement delivers beautiful product and style in categories offering real choice in a way that they are easy to shop. The determination to achieve a successful balanced combination will assist in the potential maximisation of sales and profit as well as undoubtedly help to grow market share.

The philosophies of building a range is the procedure of analysing the historical sales of product categories as well as heeding the lessons learnt from previous seasons and being guided by the strategic definitions. Modifications to the current range structures could be done to compensate for missed opportunities, lost sales through uncommon adversities which should be accounted for as is the need to cater for inflated sales as a result of upcoming out of the norm special events.

Stages Of building the range

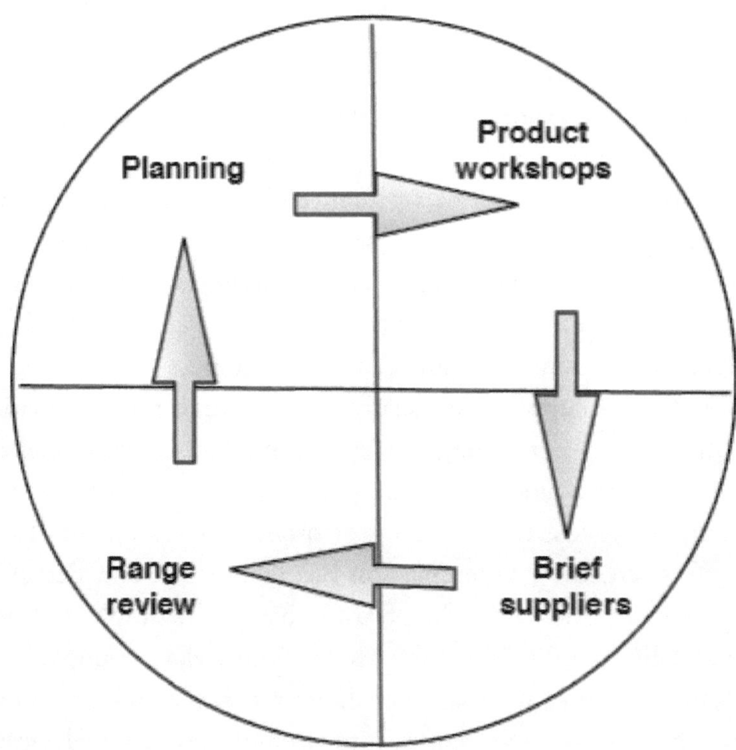

Planning begins with the range strategy document or matrix tick sheet which covers the customer choices across the period in time such as the season for six months for both the spring/summer and autumn/winter periods.

This stage is completed by the buyer and planner with reference to the group and departmental strategy.

Buyers give consideration to the historical sales, lessons learnt, customer and market shifts to determine the ideal flow of products to accommodate the continuity and input lines utilising the understanding of actual sales, customer needs and marketing plan.

Planners consider the history and lessons learnt, strategy, budgets, volumes, and the frequency of newness and catalogue shifts.

The buyers and planners then agree a final version of the range plan within the parameters of the intake budget.

Product workshops are conducted to identify the continuity items which represent the building blocks of the department, the highlighting of those products which can be seen as those that will take the department to new levels that prevent the ranges becoming stagnant, incorporating the new fashion trends which potentially could result in new shifts and ensure an appropriate level of balance between newness and traditional continuity items.

Briefing of suppliers is usually done through the compilation of a briefing pack containing quality information which enables the supplier to clearly understand the thinking of the department and get it right the first time in terms of product development. To do this effectively, the communication has to be clear and details of components, fabrics and styling features have to be simply specified. A good habit to utilise is to reference previous styles or samples.

Range reviews or final workshops are the conclusion point where the product selected is compared to the original agreed concepts and strategies to decide whether or not any changes need to be made. A cross check needs to be done to make sure that the competitive or sales environment have not altered in any significant way and plans must to be adjusted accordingly. The sequencing of the range and volumes is confirmed to ensure that all end uses are catered for, that products do not compete with each other and the categories are balanced. Lastly the range should be built from bottom up across the various groupings of stores to determine how the product will be represented across the entire chain.

The right product at the right time in the right place in the right quantities and the influences that affect these attributes is illustrated below

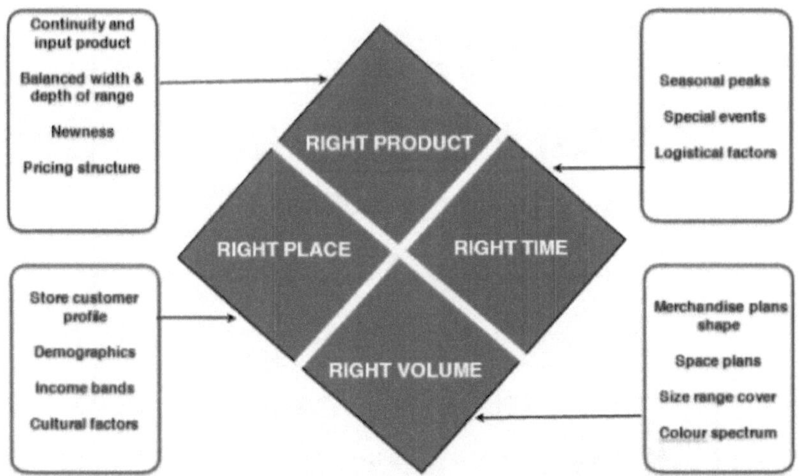

A balance of the right product mix between the basic range types and the fashion inputs has to be determined. The large volume items should be the first focus to ensure that the relevant high money takers are looked after adequately. Second is the necessity to correctly identify the characteristics of fashion forward goods for each product category in order that they best meet the respective store groupings customer profiles and reflect good relative value in comparison to other internal or external products.

The end goal is best summarised by the well-worn quote of having the right product at the right time in the right place in the right quantities.

A simple range plan model based on the guidelines reflected in the departmental line summary above is illustrated on the next page.

Product Group	Style	Colour	Stores	Cont /input	Cost price	Sell price	Intake margin	Intake sell value	Intake units	Week 1	Week 2	Week 3	Week 4	Week 5	Week 6	Week 7	Week 8	Week 9	Week 10	Week 11	Week 12
				Department XYZ Range Plan						Month 1				Month 2				Month 3			
1	1001	White	All	Cont	46.99	99.99	53%	350000	2500	150	175	200	225	125	175	200	275	150	200	200	175
		Black	All	Cont	46.99	99.99	53%	200000	2000	120	140	160	180	100	140	180	220	120	160	180	140
		Blue	Grp A,B,C	Cont	46.99	99.99	53%	160000	1600	96	112	128	144	80	112	128	176	96	128	128	112
		Purple	Grp A,B	Cont	46.99	99.99	53%	120000	1200	72	84	96	108	60	84	96	132	72	96	96	84
	2001	Beige	All	Cont	63.69	129.99	51%	300000	2308	138	162	185	208	115	162	185	254	156	185	185	162
		White	All	Cont	63.69	129.99	51%	250000	1923	115	135	154	173	96	135	154	212	115	154	154	135
		Green	Grp A	Cont	63.69	129.99	51%	100000	768	46	46	54	61	38	54	61	84	46	61	61	54
Product group 1				Intake units					12300	758	861	981	1107	615	861	981	1353	738	984	984	861
				Intake selling value				1380000		82800	95600	110400	124200	69000	96600	110400	151800	82800	110400	110900	96600
				Merchandise intake plan				1380500		82930	96635	110440	124245	69025	96635	110440	151855	82830	110440	110440	96635
2	1003	Purple	All	Input	82.81	180	54%	190000	833	706		125									
		Yellow	All	Input	82.81	180	54%	120000	667	567		100									
		Orange	Grp A,B	Input	82.81	180	54%	80000	444	378		67									
	2002	Pink	All	Input	82.81	180	54%	170000	944					803		142					
		Brown	All	Input	82.81	180	54%	140000	778					661		117					
		Black	Grp A,B	Input	82.81	180	54%	100000	556					472		83					
	3001	Green	All	Input	82.81	180	54%	190000	1056									897		158	
		White	All	Input	82.81	180	54%	170000	944									803		142	
		Grey	Grp A,B	Input	82.81	180	54%	130000	722									614		108	
Product group 2				Intake units					6944	1853		392		1936		342		3314		408	
				Intake selling value				1250000		297500		52500		348500		61500		416500		73500	
				Merchandise intake plan				1250100		297800		52400		348700		61600		416400		73400	
3	1003	Purpl	All	Input	103.42	220	53%	190000	682	580		102									
		Yellow	All	Input	103.42	220	53%	170000	773	657		116									
		Orange	Grp A,B	Input	103.42	220	53%	120000	546	464		82									
	2003	Pink	All	Input	103.42	220	53%	170000	773					657		116					
		Brown	All	Input	103.42	220	53%	190000	864					734		130					
		Black	Grp A,B	Input	103.42	220	53%	130000	591					502		89					
	3002	Green	All	Input	103.42	220	53%	180000	808									685		123	
		White	All	Input	103.42	220	53%	170000	783									667		116	
		Grey	Grp A,B	Input	103.42	220	53%	130000	591									502		89	
Product group 3				Intake units					6411	1701		300		1893		335		1854		328	
				Intake selling value				1410000		374220		65000		416500		73500		408000		72000	
				Merchandise intake plan				1410100		374010		65920		416800		73450		408020		72100	
Total Dept XYZ				Intake units					25655	4292	861	1573	1107	4444	861	1658	1353	4906	984	1720	
				Intake selling value				4040000		754520	96600	227900	124200	834000	96600	245400	151800	907500	110400	255800	
				Merchandise intake plan				4040700		754440	96635	228760	124245	834525	96635	245490	151855	907250	110440	156544	

For clarification of the range plan section A provides all the key data of the product in terms of product group in terms of the department's product group, style, colour, sore catalogue, whether the style is a fashion input or is a replenishment continuity line, the cost and selling price as well the resultant intake margin. The total intake value and intake units represents the "buy".

The intake value and unit buy is summarised at the product group and total level with a comparison to the merchandise intake plan which delivers the alignment status between the assortment plan and the merchandise financial plan.

Section A

Department XYZ Range Plan

Product Group	Style	Colour	Stores	Cont /Input	Cost price	Sell price	Intake margin	Intake sell value	Intake units
1	1001	White	All	Cont	46.99	99.99	53%	250000	2500
		Black	All	Cont	46.99	99.99	53%	200000	2000
		Blue	Grp A,B,C	Cont	46.99	99.99	53%	160000	1600
		Purple	Grp A,B	Cont	46.99	99.99	53%	120000	1200
	2001	Beige	All	Cont	63.69	129.99	51%	300000	2308
		White	All	Cont	63.69	129.99	51%	250000	1923
		Green	Grp A	Cont	63.69	129.99	51%	100000	768
Product group 1	Intake units								12300
	Intake selling value							1380000	
	Merchandise intake plan							1380500	
2	1002	Purple	All	Input	82.81	180	54%	150000	833
		Yellow	All	Input	82.81	180	54%	120000	667
		Orange	Grp A,B	Input	82.81	180	54%	80000	444
	2002	Pink	All	Input	82.81	180	54%	170000	944
		Brown	All	Input	82.81	180	54%	140000	778
		Black	Grp A,B	Input	82.81	180	54%	100000	556
	3001	Green	All	Input	82.81	180	54%	190000	1056
		White	All	Input	82.81	180	54%	170000	944
		Grey	Grp A,B	Input	82.81	180	54%	130000	722
Product group 2	Intake units								6944
	Intake selling value							1250000	
	Merchandise intake plan							1250100	
3	1003	Purpl	All	Input	103.42	220	53%	150000	682
		Yellow	All	Input	103.42	220	53%	170000	773
		Orange	Grp A,B	Input	103.42	220	53%	120000	546
	2003	Pink	All	Input	103.42	220	53%	170000	773
		Brown	All	Input	103.42	220	53%	190000	864
		Black	Grp A,B	Input	103.42	220	53%	130000	591
	3002	Green	All	Input	103.42	220	53%	180000	808
		White	All	Input	103.42	220	53%	170000	783
		Grey	Grp A,B	Input	103.42	220	53%	130000	591
Product group 3	Intake units								6411
	Intake selling value							1410000	
	Merchandise intake plan							1410100	
Total Dept XYZ	Intake units								25655
	Intake selling value							4040000	
	Merchandise intake plan							4040700	

Section B represents the monthly and weekly intake required across time in the same or similar shape as the merchandise intake plan in units per style in units which represent the quantities that will be required to be contracted and reflected on the production plans of the relevant suppliers.

The total values are summarised in units, intake value and relationship to the financial merchandise intake plan by month and week

Section B

Month 1				Month 2				Month 3				
week 1	week 2	week 3	week 4	week 5	week 6	week 7	week 8	week 9	week 10	week 11	week 12	week 13
150	175	200	225	125	175	200	275	150	200	200	175	250
120	140	160	180	100	140	160	220	120	160	160	140	200
96	112	128	144	80	112	128	176	96	128	128	112	160
72	84	96	108	60	84	96	132	72	96	96	84	120
138	162	185	208	115	162	185	254	138	185	185	162	231
115	135	154	173	96	135	154	212	115	154	154	135	192
46	46	54	61	38	54	61	84	46	61	61	54	77
738	861	981	1107	615	861	981	1353	738	984	984	861	1230
82800	96600	110400	124200	69000	96600	110400	151800	82800	110400	110400	96600	138000
82830	96635	110440	124245	69025	96635	110440	151855	82830	110440	11044	96635	138050
708		125										
567		100										
378		67										
				803		142						
				661		117						
				472		83						
								897		158		
								803		142		
								614		108		
1853		292		1936		342		2314		409		
297500		52500		348500		61500		416500		73500		
297600		52400		348700		61600		416400		73400		
580		102										
657		116										
464		82										
				657		116						
				734		130						
				502		89						
								685		123		
								657		116		
								502		89		
1701		300		1893		335		1854		328		
374220		65000		416500		73500		409000		72000		
374010		65920		416900		73450		409020		72100		
4292	861	1573	1107	4444	861	1658	1353	4906	984	1720		
754520	96600	227900	124200	834000	96600	245400	151800	907300	110400	255900		
754440	96635	228780	124245	834525	96635	245490	151855	907250	110440	156644		

The model assumes the following.

The plan is for a department that has one continuity product group and two product groups for input fashion styles.

The catalogue makes a provision to keep in line with the product and location matrix plan.

The shape of intake across time is regulated as per the shape reflected in the merchandise sales plan.

The period being planned is for three months of a six month season.

The merchandise intake plan row is included for a direct comparison to the merchandise plan intake values for easy reconciliation to ensure that the planned buy is in line with the financial intention.

The intake margin column enables the continual monitor to ensure that the target intake margin is on track with that as deemed to be in the strategy.

The closing stock is determined using the weeks forward cover and therefore takes into account the sales values of the first few weeks in the next phase in order to calculate the closing stocks towards the latter part of the season.

The volumes of the inputs are those that are required to service the catalogue and be on offer for sale until replenished by the next style input. As in the example it is wise to keep a second smaller input to replenish initial sales as some stores will sell out quicker or slower than expected. If the full quantity is put in all at once there could be a situation where there will be pockets of stock left over which will increase the potential of mark downs while on the other hand probable sales will be lost in those stores that are depleted of stock.

The offer for sales time period is determined by the frequency of inputs. In the example above the inputs are the monthly themes and the sales period that are attributed to each style will be for six weeks after which any leftover stocks will be destined for the reduced counters or racks.

Volume and choice balance

The creation of the initial range plan reflects the quantities that have to be bought at item level by colour, in the correct size ranges, at the target mark-ups and retail selling prices. It is essential that the monetary buying amounts of the plan are aligned to the merchandise plan intake values.

The buying plan should reflect the strategy which guarantees the correct amount of selection within the stock parameters while still providing the right spread of products in the required quantities that will best serve the target customer in both style, form and function at any point in time of the season.

During the construction of the plan, the principle that needs to be adhered to is that the merchandise plan must guide the buy with the customer top of mind. Lessons learnt from previous seasons need to be analysed and equally applied to both the basic continuity lines as well as the high end fashion products. Fundamentally it is also important to get the right balance of the correct number of choices in quantities that enable the guarantee of basic lines in depth without impeding the introduction of newness.

It happens often that too much emphasis is placed on the fringe or peripheral lines, or there is excessive similarity in characteristics and price offerings that can disrupt the balance. The emotional wishes of the buying team and suppliers can also have an influence on a distorted balance being achieved and should be guarded against.

The range plan which represents the assortment of products developed within specific categories must represent the organisation of the business and therefore should be balanced across the width and depth of the structure.

The width represents how broad the choice of product is while the depth represents the quantities required to cover the number of sizes and colours including the amount of price points within the product categories. It is probably easier for niche retailers that focus on a narrower customer segment of the market to best be able to serve the both the depth and width demands of their market.

The difficulties that retailers are faced with in striking the right balance of width and depth of ranges is that of presenting real customer choice while at same time optimising the return on investment. In other words, there is the need to attract customers by maintaining a level of newness and fashionability without compromising the traditional or core customers and especially the high volume sellers. It is therefore critical that the buyer has a clear vision of the marketing position and understands the target customer though continuous research which provides the confidence to determine as to what should or should not be kept in the range.

The other challenge of having a too broad choice of styles is that the decision making process becomes an effort to select a product and diminishes the pleasure of the shopping experience.

The volume and choice balance emphasis that the customer expects to find new styles in their size in a variety of colours can be illustrated as follows.

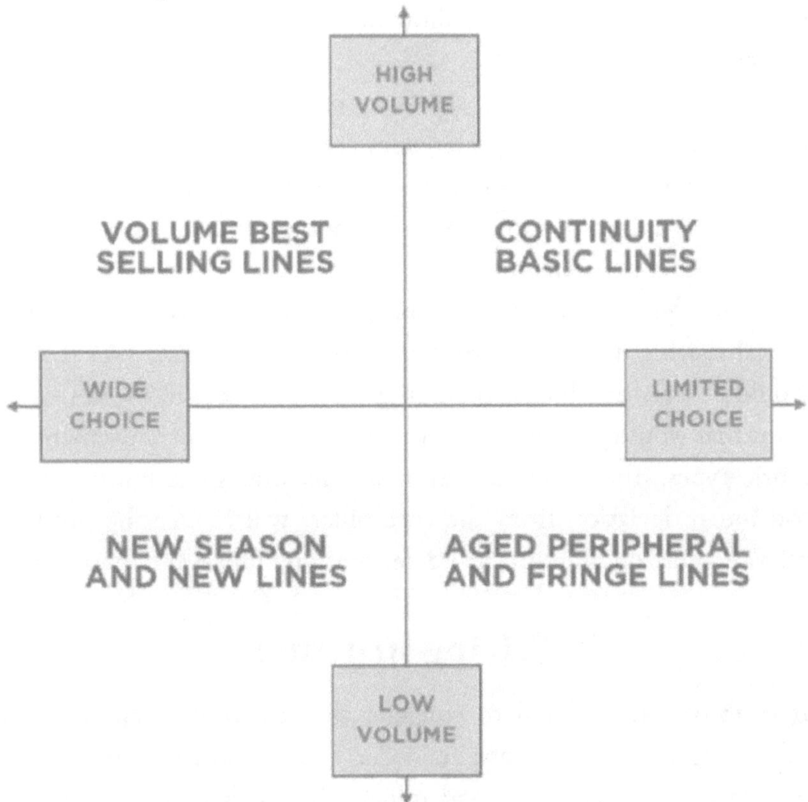

Style and shape proportions

The styles that will make up the range structure are dictated by history, the strategy guidelines and direction provided by the design or trend teams.

If one considers the thought process of a customer when a selection is being made, the first feature that she will be attracted to is the style. If the style does not meet the required taste level it will be ignored. The criteria that will influence this choice may not necessarily be the level of fashionability but also the practicality of the garment in meeting the required functionality, examples of which are sleeve lengths, belted or unbelted waists, lengths, neckline or any other feature that will allow the customer to feel comfortable and confident to wear.

Multiple choices form the basis of range plan structure and ensure that all customer preferences are catered for. Another need that has to be provided for is the availability of styling and colours that can be easily coordinated with other product styles within the same or other departments.

Consideration also needs to be given to the cross co-ordination of fashionable items being supported by core product. An example would be a fashion blouse including the core shades in the design or print that would go happily with a basic core skirt in complimentary fabric types. The implementation of this strategy is important as too much deviation from the core pillars will reduce the product relevance and could result in a deterioration of market penetration.

Pricing structure

It is absolutely essential to consider the structure or architecture of pricing across the range in order that a consistent balance is maintained between the good value, mid and luxury price points. Added to this is the controlling of the price movement from one season to the next. The rate of increases or decreases need to be measured on a like for like basis whereby the change in price of identical products is compared to an acceptable overall rate such as the consumer price index while still maintaining the margin targets. Other products should also represent good value in comparison to similar products in the market place.

The philosophy and pricing strategy of the retailer will dictate the balance of price groups dependent on the customer segments that they serve. Probable examples would be where a discount value chain will have about ninety percent of product in the low value band while the middle price type of retailer will have possibly forty percent low price goods with the bulk of products falling into the mid-price range at about fifty five percent. Top end luxury retailers will commonly have in excess of ninety percent of prices falling in the high price range.

A pitfall that needs to be avoided is a scenario where critical price points are maintained through harsh negotiation tactics for more than one or two seasons as it could happen that it will eventually reach a point that without an increase it may become no longer viable for the supplier to manufacture. A decision to then move the price to a realistic level could result in the customer resisting the purchase as a result of the perception that the price is excessive in relation to the previous season. Credibility may also be lost as there may be great difficulty in justifying the narrower gap difference between other products within the range and they in turn could be interpreted to represent poor value.

Extreme deep cut promotions may have a similar impact and the danger exists that the balance of the margins may become distorted. An overall anticipated intake margin is based on planned quantities but in reality is rapidly lessened where repetitive turn-ons of the lower margin product takes place.

A factor that must be considered is the effect of the price movement on unit volumes and whether or not the reduced quantities will still service the store catalogue sufficiently to maintain good continuity. If this is not the case it may require the rationalisation of the number of customer choices offered or a restriction of the store catalogue for the product.

A tactic that retailers frequently resort to in terms of a psychological influence is the selection of the number of price points as well as the pricing terminology. For this reason price points such as 99.99 presents a better perception of value than if the product was marked 100.00. This technique however must be handled with caution as for high ticketed items it is better to present 300.00 rather than 299.00 as this may deliver a message of perceived deviousness. In terms of the gaps between price points, the wider they are among the product groups the better is the value perception. In cases where the customer is bombarded with too many price options it becomes increasingly difficult to assess the value variance between products.

Retailers sometimes apply regional pricing where the income status of customers differ. The result is that customers in the poorer areas enjoy a discount that is subsidised by those in the more affluent areas. Similarly there are unscrupulous retailers who launch a product at an unrealistic high price and after a short period reduce it to a price that delivers a normal margin but is promoted aggressively as great value. These practices once exposed are not well received by consumers and become great topics of discussion on social media.

Colour range

The second determining feature of the product that will influence the purchasing decision will be the colour. Colour is the first element of newness and trend direction that is displayed. Many season's ranges can fail through poor interpretation of the seasonal colour trend. How the colour themes are flowed across the seasons is important as is the harmony that exists with not only the colours within each individual product range but also with the overall look of the store. The visual impact is important in that it transmits a subliminal message to the customer through a fine balance of fashion colours to those that the customer prefers.

Core colours should be banked first even though they may not always be the most exciting. A wise retailer once said "white is a business" and this certainly holds true for black, grey, navy, beige and brown year in and year out. The trending themes such as lilacs, pinks, yellows are more often than not linked to the prevailing trends and will dictate the seasonal themes from month to month. There is a place for the high risk edgy colours such funky pinks, shocking purples and burnt oranges as they provide the theatre even though they may not deliver the best returns.

In order to achieve the best variety it is important to ensure that the planned colour spectrum is reflected as a whole by assigning different colours across the diverse styles in the range with the overall proportions meeting the targets of the strategic intent.

Examining the table below it is evident that the plan is not aligned to the strategic target and therefore a revisit to the proportions will be required to bring them in line with the objective.

NUMBER	COLOUR	UNITS	LY	UNITS PLANNED	TY	TY TARGET
1	White	250	19%	356	25%	28%
2	Black	430	33%	356	25%	25%
3	Stone	130	10%	178	13%	15%
4	Khaki	200	15%	178	13%	12%
5	Red	250	19%	178	13%	10%
6	Pink	40	3%	178	13%	10%
	TOTAL	1 300	100%	1 424	100%	100%

Size architecture

As has been highlighted previously, the first attractor to the customer is the style and then colour but the reality remains that the choice will only be complete if the size is available in the wanted style and colour. For this reason many retailers will display their offerings by size so as to minimize the frustration that results when the size is not available in the desired style and colour.

The need to minimise the non-availability of particular sizes is the main reason as to why special attention should be paid to the careful planning and analysis of size profiles.

It is logical that stores have differing size profiles which are driven by the local demographics, shopping patterns and cultural preferences. For this reason the product groupings and styling features need to be carefully assessed. Typical examples would be that possibly in the rural areas customers may be genetically of a larger stature than their counterparts in the cities and could also have a more conservative attitude than the adventurous city slickers. Religious beliefs may also have an influence where certain parts of the body such as arms need to be covered.

As with the top down and bottom up merchandise planning principle we need to determine the overall national size curve for a department, product category and product in order to place the full combined order with the supplier.

Similarly the accumulated store size profiles have to be derived and aligned with the product size profile in order that allocations can meet both the product and store needs.

The size analysis for small, medium and large emphasis size stores will require differing size ratios for each group.

By way of illustration

The department requires total of 6200 units. Based on historical and trend analysis the target size ratio will represent.

	SMALL	MEDIUM	LARGE	X-LARGE
TOTAL ORDER	1 000	1 500	2 500	1 200
SIZE RATIO %	16%	24%	40%	20%

There are three product styles which may or may not be ordered from the same supplier but each will be in the form of a separate order or contract. Because of the different characteristics of each style, the size ratio requirements may be different.

The quantities in the table below will reflect these separate style orders

STYLE	SMALL	MEDIUM	LARGE	X-LARGE
STYLE A (basic for average customer)	300	500	600	400
% RATIO	17%	28%	33%	22%
STYLE B (larger for fuller figure)	200	600	1 100	800
% RATIO	8%	22%	40%	30%
STYLE C (petite high fashion style)	600	900	400	200
% RATIO	29%	43%	19%	9%
TOTAL	1 100	2 000	2 100	1 400
% RATIO	17%	30%	32%	21%

It is not uncommon in women's sizing designed to fit diverse body shapes to carry different descriptive names. Such variations include the height of a person dependent on the torso or back length, whether the bust, waist and hips are straighter which is usually more relevant to teenagers or curvier for mostly adult women.

Examples of such descriptive categories are commonly misses sizes, junior sizes, women's or plus sizes, petite, junior petite and the like.

In order to cater for the varying size silhouettes of individual stores the relevant size ratios pertaining to the particular stores have to be applied. A practical way of doing this can be done by grouping stores with similar size profiles together and utilise these groupings for planned allocations.

A simple working example is outlined below.

Style A – Basic for average customer

Total units are 1800 units

Assume that the total proportions for the store groupings are

Small size emphasis stores 25% 440 units

Medium size emphasis stores 55% 990 units

Large size emphasis stores 20% 370 units

Based on historical analysis and trend assessment assume that size % splits across the size range for the various store size profiles will be as follows.

Small Medium Large X-Large

Small size emphasis stores 22% 27% 32% 19%

Medium size emphasis stores 15% 31% 32% 22%

Large size emphasis stores 13% 21% 37% 29%

The results displayed in the table below reflects in what proportions the total ordered quantity of 1800 will be allocated to meet the size profiles of the individual stores.

	SMALL	MEDIUM	LARGE	X-LARGE
SMALL EMPHASIS STORES	97	119	140	85
SIZE RATIO	22%	27%	32%	19%
MEDIUM EMPHASIS STORES	153	305	320	209
SIZE RATIO	15%	31%	32%	22%
LARGE EMPHASIS STORES	50	76	140	106
SIZE RATIO	13%	21%	37%	29%
TOTAL	300	500	600	379
SIZE RATIO	17%	28%	33%	22%

A typical overall size curve can be illustrated using a Bell type curve

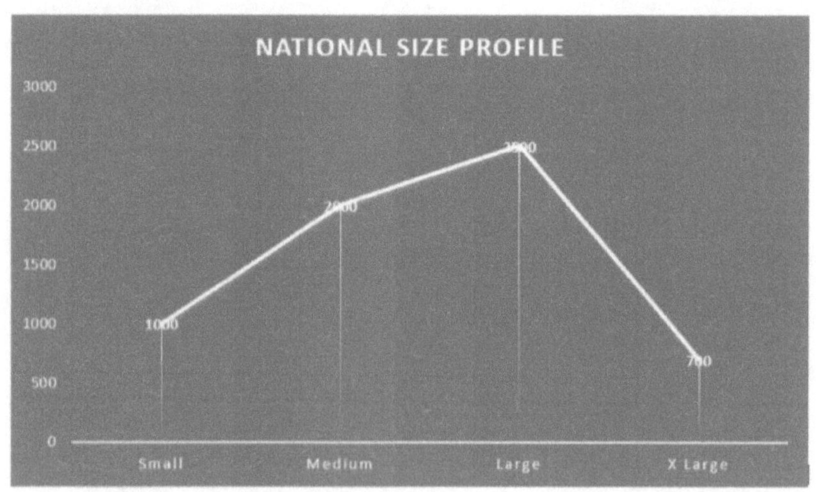

While the above represents the overall size curve this will have to be equivalent to the sum of the individual product categories size curves.

For simplicity we can assume that this overall curve is made up of three product types which are a basic type with medium size emphasis, a style for the fuller figure and a high fashion smaller size emphasis requirement. These in turn need to service stores that are size small emphasis, size medium emphasis and size large emphasis profiles.

In conclusion a check list should be drafted which confirms that all the deliverables expected from the range plan are adequately covered. These would include the confirmation of the presence of key looks and trends for the season, that all the end use options are available for the customer, that the range has a look of freshness, the assortment includes the expect to find products and does not contain any duplications.

Validation is required to ensure that the strategic intents of the product group, supplier, sourcing team and designers have been met and lastly that the margin target is achieved.

The use of trials

The trusted use of trial quantities which can be put into stores prior to the season may be intended to test attributes such as styling, colours, prints, fabrics, fashion looks, technical or innovative direction or even a value added feature such as a detachable hood in order to gauge the potential of a market.

The trial must also be specific as to what is being tested and it is not advisable to combine different features at the same time. For example, if the purpose is to test a colour, it should be done in a tried and tested style rather than using a new concept style. If this is not done, it could lead to a confused result as to whether it was the style that was successful or was it because of the colour that sales were disappointing.

In order to get a realistic reading of the potential of an untested product it is important to utilise the stores that represent the target market across the chain rather than simply using the larger stores in an environment where there is all likelihood of selling. It is preferred to use a selected cross section of stores and compare performance against similar control styles in the same stores and then extrapolate the results to all stores in the intended catalogue to determine the overall sales potential of the trial product.

Where open to buy is restricted, which is almost always the case, a recommended tactic is to hive off an amount upfront which will allow the freedom to experiment at any time and potentially grow a high volume line.

Range presentations

It is only natural that before the final go-ahead to commit to production is given that the intended range for the forthcoming season is presented to the senior management of a retail organisation in order to get their views, buy in and sign off as a combined decision making unit.

Prior to the commencement of the season it is normal that the design team briefs management and buying groups of key looks, colour themes and other relevant trends for the forthcoming season, while the post seasonal analysis is presented by the commercial team of the buying groups to highlight some of the key lessons learnt from the previous season's trading. The commercial arm will also get approval of proposed budget levels and strategy intents from senior management to ensure that all are aligned in thinking before going ahead with the planning process and the range build.

The range presentations can take on varying formats but in the main the end objective remains the same in that all stakeholders must be comfortable with the selections and strategies to maximise the sales and profit potential.

The attendees who would participate would normally be senior management and the representatives of the relevant buying teams being the category managers, buyers, merchandisers, technologists, location planners, allocators, marketing team, store representatives, members of the design team and supply chain or logistical team members all of whom may well make contributions where appropriate.

Typical contributions are where the technologists may describe new innovations, the garment technologists or sourcing specialists could discuss supplier issues and describe new suppliers. A store representative will add comment as to possibly the practicality of styling based on what they have gleaned through their interaction with customers. Location planners will confirm that the quantities being purchased are sufficient to serve the designated catalogue or will accommodate the volumes required for planned promotions as outlined by marketing.

The agenda is usually commenced with an overall summary by the category manager of the strategy which will refer to supplier sourcing, technological developments, pricing policies, key looks and themes and lessons learnt from the previous year which have been taken on board.

The presentation of the numbers side of the department is done by the merchandiser using the line by line department summary as a point of reference. The main points that are highlighted will be the budget levels emphasising the performance in comparison to last year as well as the proportions of each product category with special attention being given to the splits between the automatic replenishment type product and the more fashionable input lines which will carry the newness and represent the more exciting part of the range.

It is usually with regard to this that some form of clarification may be required where levels tend to deviate from the norm. An example of this may well be reflected in increases that are excessive but are justified possibly by a new initiative or increase in store catalogue that is being introduced. What must be guarded against is that the level of increase of the continuity lines tends to be set more conservatively as the assumption is made that they can grow to a level which will be greater than the budget because the raw material requirement is placed ahead of time. The temptation is thereby to free up funds to enable the introduction or addition of the more fashionable product which will not be as easy to turn on. Technically if thought is applied to this practice, it is nothing else but a disguised form of over buying.

Another point needs to be made with reference to the practice of funding the input fashion lines from the surplus created by the conservative budgeting of continuity lines. If this tactic is employed it will result in the distortion of the buying margin. The reality is that the continuity lines will probably sell at higher levels than budgeted but as they carry more conservative margins the actual overall margin will be less than that which was presented.

Other aspects that will be referred to be the unit increases in relation to last year and comments will be made about the overall increase or decrease in percentage terms and differentiation will be made between the like for like product price movements which should be referenced to the current consumer price index.

The profit margins will be discussed to ensure that the profit objectives are met taking into account the levels of mark downs planned and confirming the reality of these amounts based on historical performance.

The attribute splits need to be confirmed such as short sleeves versus long sleeves, collar versus non-collar, tops compared to bottoms, colour ratios, size characteristics, woven versus knitted goods, the fabric type splits and the like.

While the number part of the meeting is often seen as the dull and boring bit with very little exciting exposure to the actual product it nevertheless remains probably the most important part of setting the business end foundation and should be given the attention to detail that is deserved.

Once the numbers have been agreed and all team members are comfortable, the buyer will proceed to present the product that is going to make up the range which is going to deliver the budgetary objectives. The most convenient way is to first display the continuity product that will flow through for the entire season and then drop in the monthly inputs which will emphasise the themes in terms of styling and colour for each relevant month. It is also important to check that the specific looks tie in with the other department's complementary product to ensure themes are aligned.

The products display the detail pertaining to the garment on an attached card such as the quantity being purchased, the catalogue of the stores that they are destined for, the selling price and margin and colours with corresponding swatches. Where possible the product should be in the actual material and make up that will be representative of what will be seen in stores. It may have to be that for product which is earmarked for a latter part of the seasons that CAD boards will have to suffice.

In the presentation of the range by month a recommended tactic would be to build the look by store catalogue where the smaller stores range will be displayed first and ticked off and then followed by what the next band of stores will receive until the full range which the flagship stores will carry is displayed. In this way the range across the full chain can be envisaged and attendees are not misled into thinking that the look of the entire range is going to all stores.

As with other meetings the conclusions should be noted, actions listed with time deadlines attached and an accountability component included. This note should be circulated to all attendees and kept on file to serve as a point of reference should there be disagreement when the actual goods reach the sales floor and they are not remembered as the same that was signed off.

Responsibilities of key presenters at a product and planning review

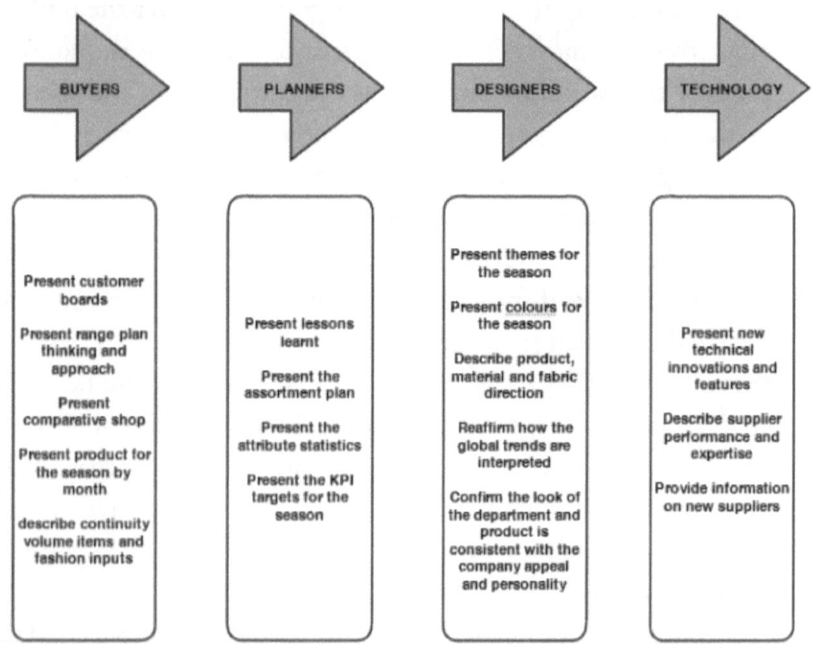

Store range profiling

The differing customer profiles of individual stores is not limited to the size profiles but requires a skilled knowledge of the stores in order that complete customer needs are optimally serviced.

In the main the responsibility rests with the planner while in some organisations there may be dedicated location planners who will study the key attributes of stores in conjunction with the sales and management staff within the stores. This is often a point that is overlooked as it is easy to be too defensive as to the reasons why certain products have not performed to expectation. An objective separate view from those who interact at the coalface with the customer places the reality of the situation in perspective.

Not all stores will be able to stock everything and the catalogues need to flex to best meet the demand for the customer that is served by the particular store.

What is important to note is that the sum of the location plans from individual store to total company need to be in line with the total merchandise plans which are reconciled to the overall buy.

In terms of the forward cover requirements of stores they are dependent on the rate of turnover that the stores enjoy. In principle the high turnover larger stores will tend to have lower forward covers as they need less stock in relation to the volume of sales to maintain effective levels of display whereas at the other end of the scale the smaller low turnover stores which require more stock in relation to their sales to maintain the availability of all sizes and colours all of the time and thus will be replenished less frequently. The typical relationship would be that the larger stores will require in the region of five weeks forward cover whereas the smaller stores may need ten weeks of forward sales to present full availability to the customers. For this reason and the physical constraints it is likely that the smaller stores will carry a lesser number of styles in the catalogue in comparison to the larger units.

The catalogue of the store will be influenced by the demographics, income bands and cultural factors. The process that the location planner will follow when assessing a store is firstly to review the sales levels of the various categories of product and examine those areas where there have been unacceptable levels of markdown and probe the reasons why this has occurred which may result in a decision to remove certain categories. Conversely missed opportunities need to be identified and action plans drafted to ensure that these are optimised going forward.

It is unlikely that the sales shape across time for every store is going to match that of the overall company. A prime example is a coastal resort store will experience seasonal peak sales during holiday periods while they will be extremely conservative outside these times or conversely stores will experience depressed sales in university towns where there is an exodus of students during the holiday period.

The frequently recommended approach is to plan each store as if it is your only store. This is however easier said than done particularly where some chains may have hundreds of stores. In many cases the control of stocks at micro level can be extremely time consuming and complex but the use of technical software packages have made it possible to accurately measure sales performance and determine stock requirements to the finest detail based on historical sales patterns.

New stores need to be reviewed as the sales shape may be distorted by the initial opening hype or the fact that it may have been only partially open for the period under review. A common approach that is adopted to plan the range selection for new or refurbished stores is to mirror them to a similar profile store and base the quantities on a comparable turnover size store.

Where sales are disappointingly low it might require the de-cataloguing of certain lines or certain sizes of a specific offering in order to minimise markdowns without disappointing a large section of customers and enabling the freeing up of more space to expose good performing ranges more forcefully.

A scenario could exist where stores require a wider assortment of product in lesser quantities. The obvious influencing factors in the main will be space constraints, the changing demographics of the town, the store may have been modernized or a new mall may have opened or closed all of which would justify a wider assortment.

The effective utilisation of space in a store is determined by the percentage sales contribution of each product category. Strategically this may be deviated from, examples of which are where a possible focus is required on a new range launch or because of a younger customer age demographic who have more children will inspire a thrust to aggressively feature children's ranges. In principle these deviations must be carefully considered so that the other product groupings are not placed in danger of being stifled entirely.

The measurement of space is translated into facings or opportunities for the customers to choose from with relevant appropriate values attached for shelves, rails, pegs, table displays in conjunction with the equipment positioning. In other words, a rail in the darkest back corner of the store will carry less value to that on the entry aisle at the front door of the store which enjoys the greatest traffic flow. The placement of total departments will follow the same principle where the highest turnover departments will enjoy the more prominent positioning with greater exposure.

The layout of the store should facilitate a journey through the store from one area to another interlaced with coordinated displays suggesting to the customer options to consider for a complete wardrobe option including apparel, accessories and impulse products before they reach the pay points. Layouts that are static straight up and down rows fail to entice customers to other areas of the store.

STOCK MANAGEMENT

The efficient management of stock is frequently neglected. The inclination is to believe that the more sold, the greater is the profit. While this is true, without the careful management of stock holdings the profit benefit can easily be eradicated. There are a number of reasons for this but it cannot be emphasized enough that constant attention is required to ensure that potential profits are not quickly eroded either through sell outs or overstocks.

The first sign of poor sales of a style is often optimistically justified by assuming that things will get better and the conclusion is too easily arrived at that it is merely a temporary setback. Good examples are thinking that the weather is not quite right, a big event has occupied the customer's minds, and the customer does not understand the product or a competitor had a killer sale at the same time. Inevitably this procrastination of corrective behaviour results in the point of no return being reached and by the time reality sets in, the consequent punishment in the form of higher markdowns could be the result.

Another common trap is that when sales are sluggish to throw more stock at the problem. Store management often justify poor performance by routinely stating that they do not have enough stock. However, upon examination, it is found more often than not that this is not the case and more intense probing needs to be conducted.

Stockholdings must be kept as tight as possible and where essential, the rationalisation through the elimination of fringe sizes and colours or whole ranges from the store catalogue will keep forward covers to a minimum and improve stock turns.

Promotional activity in whatever form that is appropriate can also help to alleviate the situation. Such price cuts or offers must be meaningful and albeit at lower margins, the removal of stock allows the inflow of newer fresh socks together with the freeing up of display area and does not force the banishment of goods to storage possibly never to see the light of day again until the major clearance sales.

Contingency plans should be put in place such as turning off production of slow selling styles, converting the style into more successful shapes and if the problem lies with the colour or fabrication it is better to take the write down on fabric rather than in garment form.

In this day and age where the accuracy of stock data bases is reliant on the efficiency of the information technology systems, the correct labelling of product is absolutely essential so that the precise data is captured which is critical for the effective replenishment of the product.

Pilferage, shop spoilage, customer returns of poor quality products, incorrect stock counts, visual display garments and goodwill donations are part and parcel of the retail environment and such product is rendered unsaleable but remains on the stock records which then distorts the replenishment needs. Stock adjustments are normally done by store staff and as a result the human error factor is very real as well as the manipulation of records is tempting to guarantee a flattering lower shrinkage result.

The more basic continuity lines that are on display for long periods of time are most susceptible to stock inaccuracies. A revealing sign of such a situation may be where stocks are reflected week after week but do not have any corresponding sales on performance documents. The impact of these false positive records is often evident that when sales slowdown of such a style and a new injection of goods with a different stock keeping record suddenly delivers a much improved sales performance.

Some retailers apply a technique of stock ageing where goods are date coded and after a reasonable period of time a particular date code can be considered as phantom or odds and ends and are flushed out by deleting them from the stock record data base.

Fashion input styles may also be date coded and are flagged for price reduction at a point in time when the styles or colours are no longer relevant to the prevailing trends or themes. For this reason the incorporation of date codes in the barcode assists in the correct rotation of stock whereby the older dated stock is sold first but this requires well controlled stock rotation disciplines in warehouses and stores.

The converse situation where the stocks are supposedly non-existent is not as serious as it may still be available for sale. The real impact is dependent on the size of the error as the non-existence of records of stock will attract a need to be replaced and could lead to potential overstocks.

The maintenance of accurate stock data is dependent largely on the well regimented stock takes as in spite of the belief that continual cyclical counts will keep physical stocks in line with theoretical records. The truth is that often these deliver greater inaccuracies as they are not as disciplined and often misplaced stocks, duplicate displays and soiled goods are excluded from counts. Added to this regular stock counts come with extra costs and the value of the product may not warrant the additional effort whereas the more expensive product may well need to be strictly controlled.

Other points where the accuracy of stock records are in jeopardy are at the point where the goods are received. The accurate receipt of product from the supplier at the warehouse needs to be well controlled as if, for example, the goods have the incorrect SKU ticket the receipt will automatically reflect against the wrong product in the scanning process. The withdrawal of stock from warehouse shelves and subsequently is picked and packed for store delivery has to be correctly recorded in order that the balances remain credible.

The receipt by the store is usually done at face value in order that the flow of goods to the sales floor is continuous. This heightens the possibility of pilferage in transit in spite of various preventative security measures. There is also the risk of incorrect documentation or suspect manipulation during the hand over processes.

Where disputes between the stores and the warehouse or distribution centre do arise the settlement of the claim tends to linger on as neither party wish to take on a negative mark against their shrinkage results with the result that final resolution often does not happen.

System errors or incorrect information is very real in the transmission of data between platforms which can go undetected until such stage that the all ills are blamed on "the system" which generates a mistrust which is not easily challenged or disproved but even worse, decisions and adjustments are made using incorrect data.

TECHNOLOGY

Up to now the focus has been on the planning and buying infrastructure required to procure product and ensure the efficiencies that will enable the maximization of the profit opportunities. However this will not be entirely possible unless the product is as close to perfect in terms of meeting predetermined quality standards, the addition of new or innovative features, is safe and meets the ever changing social and global needs. These are the factors or pillars that underpin the very reason for the existence of technology.

Quality

A product achieves a high standard of quality if it presents well on display, fits well, wears well, washes well, is fit for purpose, offers value for money, is free from any defects, insufficiencies and is unhampered from deviance to standards.

The activities need to ensure that the product meets the stated design, technical tolerances, fit, and fabric and colour specifications. This is often easier said than done. Supplier capabilities must be freely available to achieve this as well as the fact that unclear communications of expectations and standards may result in specifications not being met due to time and cost pressures.

Innovation

In order that the offering remains competitive it is imperative that new features or attributes are implemented constantly. For this to happen it requires the continual investment in new, improved ways of developing and producing product or materials. Innovation may be related to the fabric, components, treatments, end product attributes, packaging or sources of supply.

Inventive construction can add value the garment in terms of form and function such as adjustable waistbands for improved comfort. The secure lock stitching of buttons and other small items on children's garments which reduce the possibility of them being swallowed. The use of especially engineered interlinings which have more resilience enable garments to be totally machine washable, for example in the case of men's suits.

Social and environmental responsibilities

In the modern day and age most people are very aware of the responsibilities that suppliers are required to meet in order to keep the world as sustainable as possible.

The use of organic fabrics like cotton that is derived from organically grown crops, the unsavoury practice of child labour in production process, the structures in place for the removal of chemical wastes and many others are issues which are continually challenged.

The evolution of production units in China initially did not see environmental awareness as a primary focus as they were more concerned with survival but as they have developed, the treatment of waste and use of electricity has become a more important factor to be considered and the laying down of guidelines and regulations have become the norm. Although the Chinese have become environmentally sensitive and implement environment protection measures there is still the tendency to focus more on the protection of personal health. The situation is in the process of slowly improving to protect other environmental factors largely due to the improved education standards of younger management.

The key points of attention for sustainable environment awareness is the measurement and constantly improving efforts to reduce electricity consumption with the reduction of energy targets in place and the use of solar panel technology or even something as simple as the siting of administration desks next to windows. The same applies to the reduced use of water and where possible the practice to use recycled water has been introduced.

Safety

The safety of the customer must always be paramount as there are volumes of examples of where people have been injured or worse due to unsafe or defective product. Technology should constantly strive to meet the highest standards of safety in their products as well as that of the plants in which they are manufactured and the logistical process that is followed in order to get the product to market. Where required, the customer should be fully informed of particular risks inherent to the products.

If supplier's products do not conform to safety regulations they are subject to risks particularly where the required certificates are not available to show that they have met the obligatory regulations. The standards should be documented on laboratory test reports and supported by the pre-production samples either completed by the retailer's technologists or an accredited independent third party external laboratory. In some of the large trusted suppliers there may be internal specialists who self-regulate this process but this may present a challenge where there is a broad range of product categories being manufactured.

Fabric Technology

In the buying arena an integral part of the role is a pre requisite knowledge of textiles and the beginning to end production process associated with garment creation. With a good understanding of fabrics the product appeal, value and innovation aspects can be maximised and the most appropriate material can be identified for a product that will deliver the required performance to best meet the end user requirements and expectations. The briefing and negotiating process with suppliers is also able to be conducted with greater authority and credibility.

Ongoing development of new fabrics is reliant on inputs from various sources such as that of designers, buyers, suppliers, mills, yarn providers as well as the dyestuff and chemical suppliers. A healthy interaction between the main players permit the fabric innovation decisions to be made earlier and consequentially enable quicker product development.

The understanding of fabrics enables the buying arm to maximise product appeal, develop innovative product, select the most suitable fabric for the product type which delivers the best performance for the end user and exceeds their expectations.

The production process using fibres converted to yarns together with processing through to the finished product can be outlined as follows

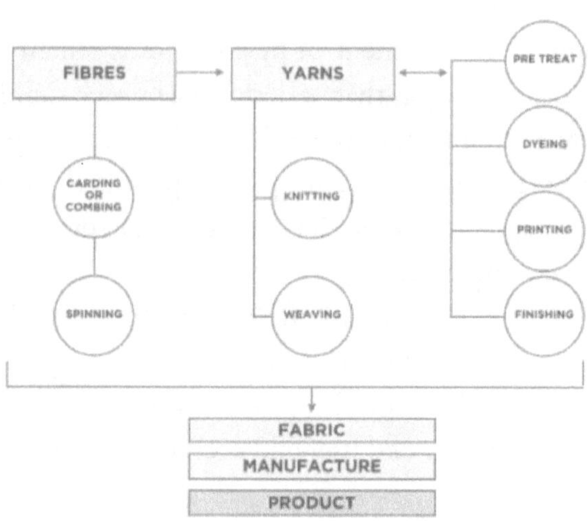

Fibres

The essential requirements for fibres to be spun into yarns is that it must be at least five millimetres in length and should be flexible and strong enough. Other inherent properties should include elasticity, fineness, uniformity, durability and a measure of lustre.

Fibres are either natural which tend to be predisposed to irregularities or synthetic that are more consistent and easier to control. Through the blending of both types in varying proportions it is possible to achieve a bit of the best of both worlds.

The continual developments of new and blends of fibres have transformed the performance of many fabrics particularly in terms of the form, function, safety and fashionability. Typical examples of this is the reduction of creasing and the evolvement of easy care properties.

Staple fibres which are of defined lengths are used for the construction of both natural and synthetic yarns whereas man-made filament fibres are extruded from natural gases and oil and stretched into continuous strands to manufacture synthetic yarns.

The properties of fibres vary dependent on the source.

◇ Natural fibres such as cotton absorb moisture well but need to be well prepared to counteract shrinkage, stretching, fading or being eaten by fish moths.

◇ Mercerised cotton has super aesthetics and handle and enables the achievement of deeper shades.

◇ Synthetic polyester has good easy to care properties, does not shrink or stretch and is economical but is not very absorbent.

◇ Acrylic is seen as a cheaper wool alternative which is moth proof but is prone to pilling.

◇ Viscose delivers a higher lustre with a soother softer handle.

◇ A blended combination of yarns from natural and synthetic parents take on the characteristics of both and the extent to which this is achieved is dependent on the combined proportions.

The different types of fibres that can be converted into yarns can be illustrated as follows

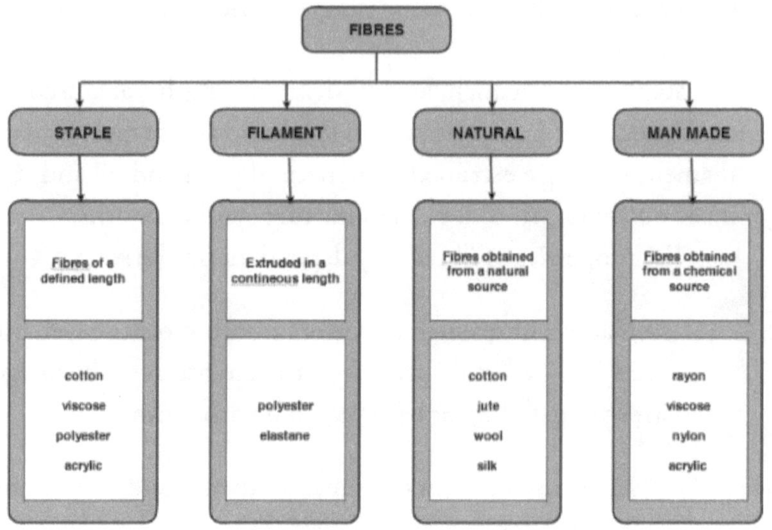

Yarns

Yarn is a continuous length of twisted or interlocked fibres which are used in the production of textiles, crocheting, knitting, weaving, embroidery, and rope making. There are two types being staple yarns that are spun from natural fibres and filament yarns which are derived from synthetic fibres.

Spinning of yarns may be of the same fibre or can be a blend of natural and synthetic fibres in varying proportions. The properties of warmth, lightness, durability or softness of handle can be achieved to a higher or lesser degree through the varying of the ratios in the blending in order to best utilise the positive characteristics of each fibre. An example is the polyester and cotton blend where the original cotton characteristics of softness and breathability are retained whilst the polyester offers the strength, wrinkle and mildew resistance.

Cotton yarns can either be combed whereby during the process a stronger and more luxurious yarn is created and the hairy surplus of the fibre is removed in comparison to carded yarns which have less body and are more hairy.

The different types of yarns, methodology of manufacture and properties are illustrated below

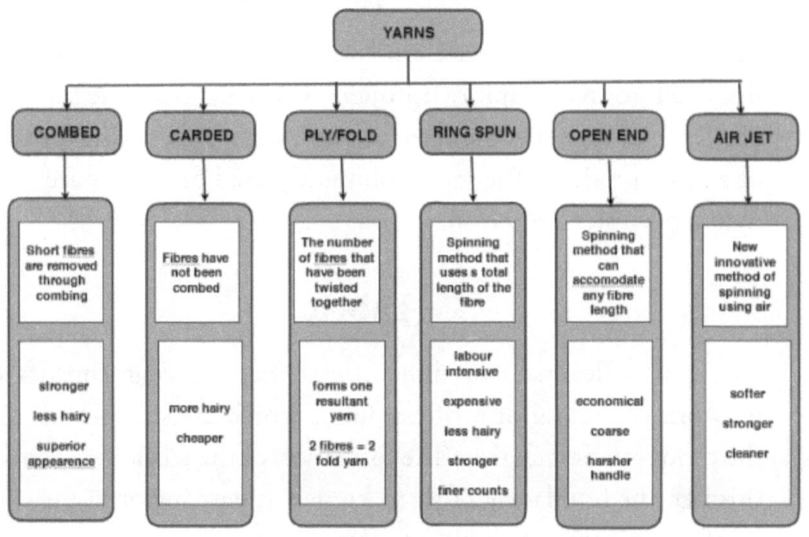

Yarn counts

Yarn count is a numerical measurement of the fineness of the yarn that denotes the relationship of the weight and length of yarn. As a rule, the finer the count, the more expensive is the fabric and it will be lighter if compared to like constructions with subjectively nicer handle and drape.

CASE STUDY

The cotton (80%)/polyester (20%) blend formal shirt of CH Clothing Company has the characteristics of being more luxurious than that in the rest of the market place.

CHALLENGE #25

Make comment about the yarn best utilised in terms of

1. The type and advantage of the yarn.

2. The treatment and advantage of the yarn.
3. The count and the advantage of the yarn.

Sewing threads

Sewing threads are special kinds of yarn that are engineered and designed to pass rapidly through a sewing machine needle to efficiently form a stitch and to function without breaking for the life of a sewn product. The most commonly used fine fibres are cotton, nylon, polyester and rayon.

Fabric

Fabric is a flexible two dimensional material that consists of a network of natural or artificial fibres which are suitable for use in the production of clothes. The formation of the fabric is constructed through the interlacing of yarns known as weaving or in the case of knitting, it is the interloping of yarns.

Fabric blends are created to best utilise the positive characteristics of each fibre and the different fibres that are blended are usually natural and manmade fibres. For example a polyester cotton blend will retain the soft breathable properties of the cotton while polyester adds the strength, wrinkle free and mildew resistant features.

Fabric weight

The standard global measurement of fabric weight is grams per square metre (gsm). Factors that can influence the weight is the combination of yarns, yarn counts, knitting gauges, weaves and any finishes that are applied.

Knitted fabrics

Knitting is where the raw materials in the form of yarn are knitted into unfinished material commonly known as greige fabric. This is done by the use of needles that intermesh the yarn into loops. The weight of the fabric will be dependent of the yarn count as well as the gauge of the yarn. The foremost types of knitted fabrics are single jersey, ribs, interlock and fleece.

The machines that knit can either be circular or flat in setup.

Circular machines do weft knitting which is where the yarns run horizontally across the width the fabric with the needles moving either collectively or individually to form loops.

Weft knitting configuration where the needles are laid across the needles in the weft or width of the fabric

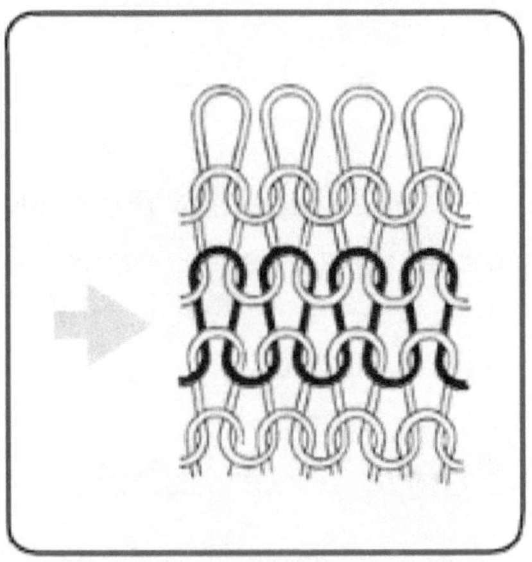

Flat knitting machines do warp knitting where the yarns run vertically through the length of the fabric and all the needles are used collectively to form the loops.

Warp knitting configuration where the yarns are laid across the length or the warp of the fabric. The loop structure is usually formed across two three needles.

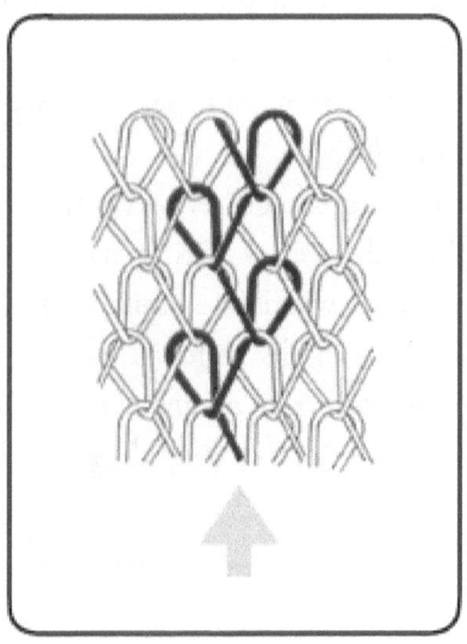

The gauge of the fabric is determined by the number of needles per inch and therefore the higher the number of needles the finer will be the fabric such as single jersey will the fewer the number of needles will deliver fabric such as knitwear.

Single Jersey fabrics

The common construction of single jersey fabrics is 24-28 gauge and have a weight of approximately 120-200 gsm. Single jersey is mostly used for products such as t-shirts, sleepwear, leggings and bedding.

The advantage is that it can be blended with other fabrics, such as elastane, has comfort as well as stretch, drapes well and is great value. The downsides are that it is prone to shrinkage and if blended with polyester it is likely to pill and have less absorbency.

Rib fabrics

The feature of ribbed fabric is that it displays plain and purl stitches along the course on both sides of the fabric and consists of alternating raised and depressed wales.

The characteristics of rib fabrics are that it offers better fit support, is warm as it traps air in the structure and drapes better than woven fabrics. However the finished fabric is generally more expensive than single jersey, has higher shrinkage than woven and because of the ridge structure it is difficult to print on. The finishing of the cuffs and waist bands need to be combined with elastane to function effectively. The fabric is commonly used for t-shirts and styled tops.

Interlock fabrics

Interlock fabrics are knitted on circular machines and the structure looks the same on the back and front of the fabric. It is a typical winter fabric and is commonly used for tracksuits and sleepwear.

The pros of interlock is that it is warmer than single jersey and is also heavier which gives it better thermal properties. It can be combined with viloft or Lycra and has better drape than woven material. The cons are that it shrinks more than woven, is unstable during processing and has poor recovery which is illustrated for example where garments may bag at the knees or stretch inconsistently.

Warp knits versus weft knits

Warp knits offer better stability with less shrinkage than wefts and commonly use synthetic yarns. They have a vertical stripe and are commonly used for swimwear, lace, mesh and net material.

Weft knits are used more often with natural fibres and have more stretch than warp knits. Stripes are horizontal and more often than not are used for t-shirts, fleece, underwear, sleepwear or tights.

Generally knitted garments are predominantly more casual, comfortable to wear and always stretchy, easy to wash, often wrinkle free and relatively inexpensive. Unfortunately they lack crispness and are not as dressy as woven, can shrink, stretch and lose shape and therefore can quickly look shabby and unflattering.

CASE STUDY

CH Clothing Company has less knitted options of tops than woven fabric shirts in the formal area.

CHALLENGE #26

Name three reasons as to why preference is given to woven fabrics instead of knitted products in the formal shirt area.

Woven fabrics

There are two main types of woven fabrics, namely plain or twill. Other woven fabrics include satins, sateen, dobby and jacquards.

The crisscross configuration of the warp and weft yarns to form the woven fabric is illustrated below
   Plain weaves

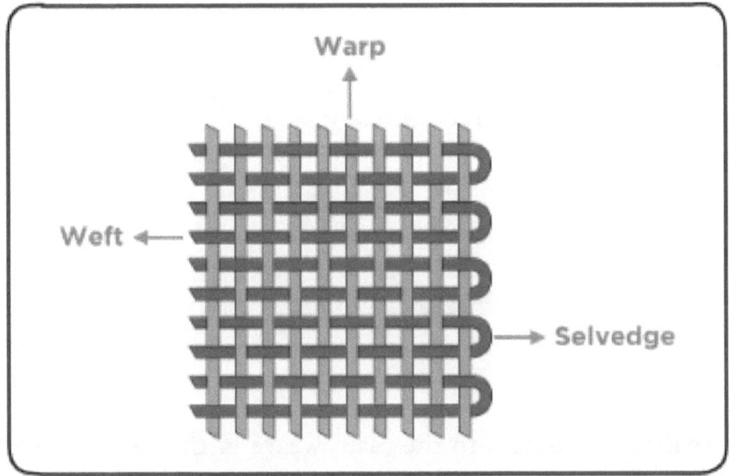

Plain weave is the most basic woven fabric where the warp and the weft are so aligned that they form a simple crisscross pattern such as in poplin, shirting and canvas where the thickness of the yarn determines the characteristic of the fabric. Plain weaves are mostly seen in shirts, shorts, sheeting and tablecloths.

While they are more affordable than other weaves and are generally more stable than knits but there can be a tendency for seam slippage or poor tear strength with lighter weights.
   Twill weaves

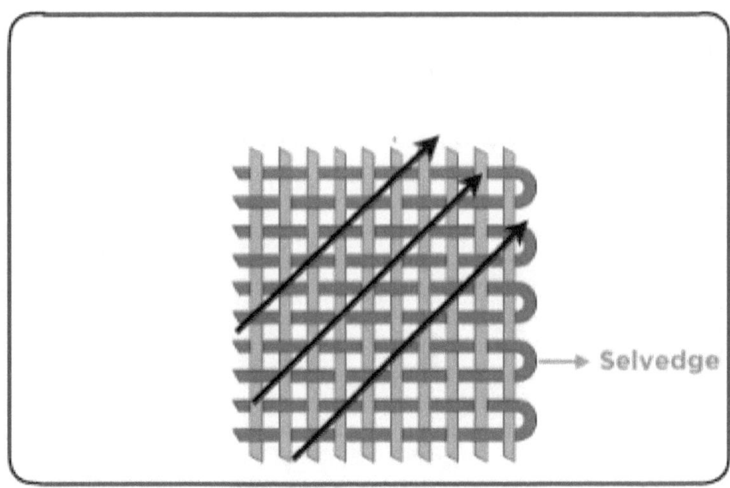

The twill weave differs to the plain weave in that the weft thread passes over one or more warp threads and then under one or more and so on. This type of weave is commonly used for chino trousers, denims, jackets, curtains and cushions.

Twill weaves have a defined face and more drape than plain weaves but are more prone to seam slippage.

Satins and sateen have a high lustre or shine where the satins utilise synthetic yarns, usually polyester, which can be either knitted or woven whereas sateen is made from natural short staple yarns such as cotton. The beauty of both satin and sateen is that they have a great visual appeal with a luxurious handle and is cool to wear. The downside is that they are difficult to manufacture and are prone to seam slippage and require appropriate machinery and needles.

Jacquard and dobby weaves are constructions that give special weave effects or surface interest where jacquard is more expensive to manufacture than dobby and is used to create complex design effects on the fabric surface such as that for jackets, curtains or table cloths. Dobby designs are simple weave effects and usually are used for shirting, bedding and tablecloths.

Overall woven fabrics appear crisper, are smarter, look pristine and seldom shrink or lose shape. They are, however, relatively more expensive than knits, not as soft and do not stretch which can make the garment feel restrictive in terms of comfort. Washing is more arduous or requires dry cleaning and the fabric wrinkles more easily.

While the warp yarns run lengthwise in the fabric and the weft yarns run across the width the fabric the fabric also has a face and a back with the face side having a better appearance which usually forms the outside of the garment.

CASE STUDY

The shirt department will use in the main woven fabrics which will be plain, yarn dyed designs, printed or self-pattern.

CHALLENGE #27

1. In the main what type of weaves will be used for plain, yarn dyed or printed garments?

2. What typical weave will be used in the surface interest garments?

Processing options

Greige fabrics require additional processing prior to being able to be made into a garment. Options such as pre-treatment, dying, printing and finishing are applied in order to improve the appearance, the handle, the addition of colour and patterns as well as the manual finishing such as brushing, and suedeing after the fabric after weaving or knitting is complete.

Pre-treatment

Pre-treatment consists of any process that is applied prior to any dying and printing is commenced. Typical pre- treatment includes the following.

Desizing is a chemical process to remove starch and oil from fabric.

Scouring is a washing process to remove impurities.

Bleaching consists of a chemical process to remove fibrous material such as cotton husk sand make the fabric whiter before dying, particularly for lighter colours.

Pre-heat setting stabilizes synthetic fabrics or fabrics containing spandex prior to dying.

Bio-polishing uses enzymes to remove hairiness, reduce pilling, improve appearance and enhance drape and handle.

Mercerizing is a chemical process whereby the use of a combination of caustic soda together with tension on cotton fabric to achieve brighter, more vibrant colours with a crisper smooth handle.

Dyeing

Dyeing colours fabrics though the dyeing of yarns, fibres or fabrics. The amount of dye required is dependent on the depth of the shade and the weight of the fabric requiring a mixture of water, dye, and an auxiliary such as salt or acid in order to facilitate the process.

The costs of dying varies dependent on the petro chemical market status, the depth or brightness of the shade required, the quality of dyestuffs utilised that meets the standards of light fastness, wash fastness and the environmental factors that need to be adhered to.

Continuous dying is where the fabric is fed continually through the dying machine and is usually the method applied for dying woven materials or garments such as chinos and sheeting. The advantage of this method of dyeing is that it is more cost effective for larger orders, accommodates crease free fabric and is a relatively quick process. However the negative is that there is relatively high wastage during the start-up and sampling process. Shades may also vary from one end of the fabric to the other through uneven penetration of dyestuffs and the handle tends to be quite harsh in relation to discontinuous dyeing processes.

Discontinuous dying is a stop start process whereby fixed quantity of fabric is dyed at one time in batches. Care needs to be taken to ensure that there is accurate colour matching between batches. This form of dyeing is used mainly for knitted fabrics where the fabric is allowed to shrink or stretch as there is less tension in comparison to woven fabrics. The process is cost effective for both large and small quantities and is commonly used for the dyeing of yarns where each yarn is dyed prior to weaving, for piece dyeing where the fabric is weaved before dyeing and completed garment dyeing.

Yarn dyeing has the advantage of better handling, aesthetics, and enables appealing crisp design in comparison to print especially for stripes and checks which can be equally attractive on both sides of the fabric. The downside is that it requires a considerable higher stock investments as each yarn needs to be dyed a different colour and minimum quantities usually apply. The manufacture of fabric is time intensive and requires a longer lead time and the fabric is not only more expensive than piece dyed fabric there is also a limited choice of colour especially from the East.

Piece dyeing has the advantage of having a shorter lead time than yarn dyeing and colour decisions can be taken later and deliver a softer handle. Disadvantage however is that it takes longer than continuous dyeing and the shade variations have to be carefully handled.

Garment dyeing is ideal for making colour decisions as close to the need as possible and tactics are developed whereby the base colours are held in stock and a quantity of undyed garments are held in readiness to dye in the ratios that the market dictates. Garments are usually informal and the colour and handle is very casual. Shrinkage is a factor that must be managed in the dyeing process and ensure that the end product is shrink free. Due to the fact that the batches are smaller and the process is slower the costs are generally higher with an added high reject rate as it is difficult to manage colour consistency across batches.

Printing

Textile printing is best described as the process of applying colour on fabric in definite patterns or designs which is not dissimilar to dyeing except that the colours are restricted to specific design requirements and is normally on only one side of the fabric.

There are certain considerations that need to be taken into account like the fact that the fabric needs to be prepared for printing through washing to remove excess starch and acids, the fabric must be absorbent as well as the need to ensure that the fabric is spun in order to safeguard that the surface is suitable for printing through the elimination of free fibres leaving the fabric as smooth as possible.

The correct choice of design is critical to the success of the print execution with regular communication between buying and the supplier or print provider in order that the expectations are met.

Cost of the printing is influenced by the size of the print where the bigger the panel or transfer print the more expensive it will be. The more colours that are utilised the more screens will be required and therefore the more costly it will be. The same principle applies to the greater the cover and special effects will add to the price.

The quality of the print is monitored by ensuring the registration is perfect through the accurate alignment of the screens, the coverage or thickness of the print paste is consistent to avoid variation of shades, the absence of short hairs or fibrillation will deliver smoother fabric and therefore higher standards. Other pitfalls that need to be avoided is the grinning through of the base fabric through the print design, or the cracking of the print deign when the material is stretched.

The performance of bulk testing such as wash, rub and light fastness after completion of the process is required to uphold standards.

As is the case with dyeing, there is two types of printing being discontinuous and continuous printing.

Discontinuous printing is in the form of panel and transfer printing.

Panel printing is in the case where the print is added to a panel or the garment and is typically used for t-shirts, sleep shirts and tracksuits.

The techniques of panel printing takes the following methods.

- **Spot colour printing** where solid areas of colour is applied for example used for character prints which are cheaper and quicker to reproduce.

- **Index printing** uses more tones to create more colours giving greater dimension which comes at a greater cost.

- **Simulated photographic printing** is the reproduction of photographs onto darker base ground colours which takes longer and is expensive.

- **The use of four colours, cyan, magenta, yellow and black for printing** enables the reproduction of photographs on lighter base fabrics.

- **Digital printing** is limited to size constraints and is relatively expensive.

- **Simulated printing** is utilised where the design resembles special effects such as embroidery or applique at a much reduced cost than the real effect.

- **High density printing** gives a three dimensional effect to the print where certain parts are raised. The downside is that it a slow process and is very expensive as specialised screens are required.

- **Spray effects** is where colours are sprayed onto the fabric and is typically used on denim and can be used in conjunction with a print making it quite costly.

Products that are used for panel prints are those that are water based for mostly lighter grounds, where chemical plastisol is used on darker grounds and gives a stiffer handle. Special effects are created whereby the fibre is dissolved leaving the polyester to be displayed but requires additional was treatment. Flocking delivers a velvet effect, while puff printing produces a raised three dimensional effect. Gel adds to a glossy effect and glitter delivers a shiny, sparkling effect.

Transfer printing follows the same process as panel printing except that the printing is applied to paper which is in turn applied to the garment, usually for logos, smaller prints on underwear and t-shirts during production through the use of a heat press. It is therefore more suitable for smaller prints. Transfer printing is also more cost effective and has the advantage that it does not have to be out sourced to an external printer.

Continuous printing is mostly rotary, flatbed or sublimation paper printing.

Rotary printing is the most common form of continuous printing through the use of roller screens where the ink is squeezed through the screens to form the design and is suitable for high volume runs. The number of screens is dependent on the complexity of designs, the number of tones, colours, effects and the machine capability in terms of the number of heads. It should be noted that the clarity and registration is more superior to flatbed machines.

Sublimation printing uses a continuous roll of paper which is applied to moving fabric via heat application and pressure through a two-step process whereby the paper is printed and then transferred onto the fabric. Rotary printing generates high definition but is restricted to polyester as it cannot be utilised for cotton bases and dyestuffs are used instead of inks.

The main techniques used in all types of continuous printing is commonly pigment, dispersive and reactive printing.

Pigment printing technique sits on top of woven or knitted fabric of any fibre type, and is the cheapest and most commonly available. It can be used together with reactive type of printing which produces a washed down casual look but runs the risk of creating a stiffer surface handle.

Sublimation and disperse printing techniques are achieved through a chemical process whereby dyestuff alters from solid form to gas through the application of heat and used to transfer a dyestuff into a polyester fibre either off paper in the case of sublimation printing or out of a direct paste for disperse printing. The advantages of this process is that it delivers a superior handle, is quicker than conventional printing, and is suitable for small production runs. Bright colours, with good colour fastness and easy care properties are characteristic but unfortunately it is more expensive than pigment and is restricted to polyester.

Reactive printing techniques can only be used on 100% cotton and viscose mostly for garments such as dresses, tops, sleepwear, underwear and leggings. That have better handle, stretch, absorbency, comfort and better seam appearance but is more expensive than pigment printing.

Finishing

Finishing, either chemical or mechanical is any process that is performed on yarn, fabric or product to improve the look, feel and performance.

This is done through the drying and stabilisation of fabric or the application of chemical finishes in order to soften in order to improve the sewability of the fabric, reduce creasing, prevention of microbial growth, prevention of seam slippage, make shower proof or manage the moisture which makes synthetics more comfortable to wear.

Mechanical finishes is that such as brushing or suedeing to provide a unique surface to the fabric that is good to handle. Sanforising reduces shrinkage on woven fabrics while compacting reduces shrinkage on knitted fabrics. Felting or milling is applied to woollen fabrics which creates a felt feel such as that used for melton jackets. Calendaring provides a shiny smooth surface while cropping reduces pilling through the reduction of the formation of hairy balls.

CASE STUDY

For some specific garments CH Clothing Company use various finishes to improve the performance of their products.

CHALLENGE #28

Describe three chemical finishes and three mechanical finishes that will be used on the following

1. **Three chemical finishing on woven products such as shirts or trousers**
2. **Three manual finishing on knitted products such as jerseys or tracksuits**

Denim is characterised by the yarn treatment where the inner core of the yarn is undyed while the outer core is the darker indigo dyed which lends to the fading properties as the outer core progressively gets exposed to the wear and tear. The harsh yarns are typically open end with the softer inner core being smoother combed yarn. Slub is purposely spun to look irregular with thick and thin places.

Denim fabric consists of blends with cotton generally blended with elastane to give stretch, polyester to give an element of shine, or all three yarns to provide stretch and shine. Fabrics are typically constructed as a plain or twill weave in weights of five to six ounces for shirting or bottoms at seven to fourteen ounces depending on seasonality.

The colour of the indigo varies from light to dark dependent on the amount of dye or the number of dips. The use of sulphur on top or bottom either gives black blue or blue black colouration.

Various washes are conducted in order to create different characteristics. These will include desize washes to remove the starch that has been applied for weaving, stone washing is very aggressive using a pumice stone to give distressed finish however enzyme washes are not as damaging as stone washing but the finish simulates that of stone wash. Bleach washing fades out the denim while sand blasting with a sand gun to cause abrasion while hand sanding creates a more gentle form of abrasion which will cause whiskers at the edges to give an aged look. Other types of washes are used to create creases or folds by using resins, snow washing is done with stones soaked in bleach which creates marble wash look. Tinting effects are created by lightly overdyeing the fabric such as a tea stain or orange tint effect.

Testing requirements

In order to uphold customer satisfaction certain key quality standards need to be maintained through the testing of elements of the fabrics. The tests performed can be separated into wet and dry processes.

Wet testing consists of stability tests that check the shrinkage of the fabric which does not impair the fit, the shape and the comfort of the garment, spirality tests measures the extent of side seam skewing after the garment has been washed. Wash tests determine if there is an unacceptable loss or bleeding of colour that will stain other garments in the wash load. Related to this would be the effect of leaving the garments damp in the wash such as cross staining of other products. Perspiration tests determine the potential of cross staining or discolouration of garments when exposed to perspiration. Light tests measure the effect of exposure to sun while chlorine and salt water testing checks for any reaction such as fading and cross staining to swimming pool or sea water.

Dry testing takes the form of abrasion testing to test for resistance to wear such as the knees of children's bottom garments. Pilling tests assess the susceptibility to little balls of fibres being formed on knitted and woven garments, tear strength tests measure the resistance to ripping of woven fabrics while tensile strength tests measure the amount of force required to rip or tear the fabric. Weight of fabric tests are performed to make sure the fabric is within the grams per square metre parameters of the specifications. Burst tests measure that can be applied on the fabric for example in the elbow area while the fabric slippage tests measure to what degree the seams can absorb pressure. Stretch and recovery tests ensure that the elastane properties perform as expected, dry rub tests measure the effect of the abrasion of two fabrics that are light and dark in colour, for example a pair of jeans and a white blouse.

CASE STUDY

The philosophy of the CH Clothing Company is strictly one that the products that they sell are of high quality that they fully meet the customer's expectation of form and function.

CHALLENGE #29

Describe what the following tests are applied to achieve

Abrasion test
1. Tensile test
2. Stability test
3. Weight of fabric test
4. Wash test
5. Spirality test
6. Fabric slippage test
7. Perspiration test
8. Light test
9. Pilling test

PRODUCTION

During production it is important that the most suitable fabric is utilised to ensure the best performance of the product for the intended end use. What is equally significant is the specifications of all the components, make up and fit criteria and that benchmark quality tolerances or allowances are set to safeguard that the product meets all the form and function requirements. The responsibility for this aspect lies with garment technology and quality control.

Innovative garment construction is an integral part of the task of a garment technologist and many examples exist of creative inventions that have changed products to better serve the form and function of the garment. Examples include the modification of waist bands either by the inclusion of elastic which helps retain the shape of the waist or the waist ease design which provides for and adjustable waist bands that promote the comfort of the outerwear garment. Lingerie has also seen significant changes such as reinforced midriff panels in corsetry that enable smoother contour to seamless on sides of undergarments and the exclusion of elastic from leg opens which results in no visible panty lines under the outerwear garment. Bra technology is a science on its own and classic examples are the push up bra where especially designed foam profiles allow for better presentation of the cleavage, detachable straps facilitate the wearing of shoulder free and halter neck garments. Enhanced cup designs provide for smoother contour bras while the use of smart foam moulds perfectly and deliver the best vehicle for the ever popular t-shirt bra. A vast amount of work has been done in transforming traditionally dry cleanable products to being easy care and machine washable. This is achieved through the engineering of fabrics and components with durable fibres that are resilient and hard wearing.

A large part of the garment technology function is to match the technical capabilities and skills of the manufacturer to best benefit from commercial opportunities that may exist. Coupled to this would be the effective re-engineering of garments to capitalise on the cost saving aspect without the downgrading of the quality or performance of the product. The same objective can be strived for through the coaching and consulting with suppliers to review existing processes to improve efficiencies and achieve continuous improvement in fit and function of garments.

For these reasons regular manufacturer quality audits need to be conducted at both the assessment stage prior to production and also at any other time as deemed necessary in order to identify and prioritise any production risks as soon as possible. Such audits may take place in the movement of production to more appropriate suppliers, review existing suppliers that may be producing new kinds of products, ensure that the correct level of quality assurance exists where volumes have been increased significantly, the production of product for strategically critical launches or promotions involving marketing initiatives.

In order to minimise the risks that may negatively influence production it is best to identify production risks upfront, being completely aware as to exactly where goods are being produced or outsourced, that the critical path of management is closely monitored and managed and that a production schedule is easily visible and up to date with items being prioritised.

An example of a typical factory layout can be illustrated as follows which facilitates the free flow of material and operations in a structured way that alleviates the risk of congestion or bottle necks.

A simple example of the factory layout and flow

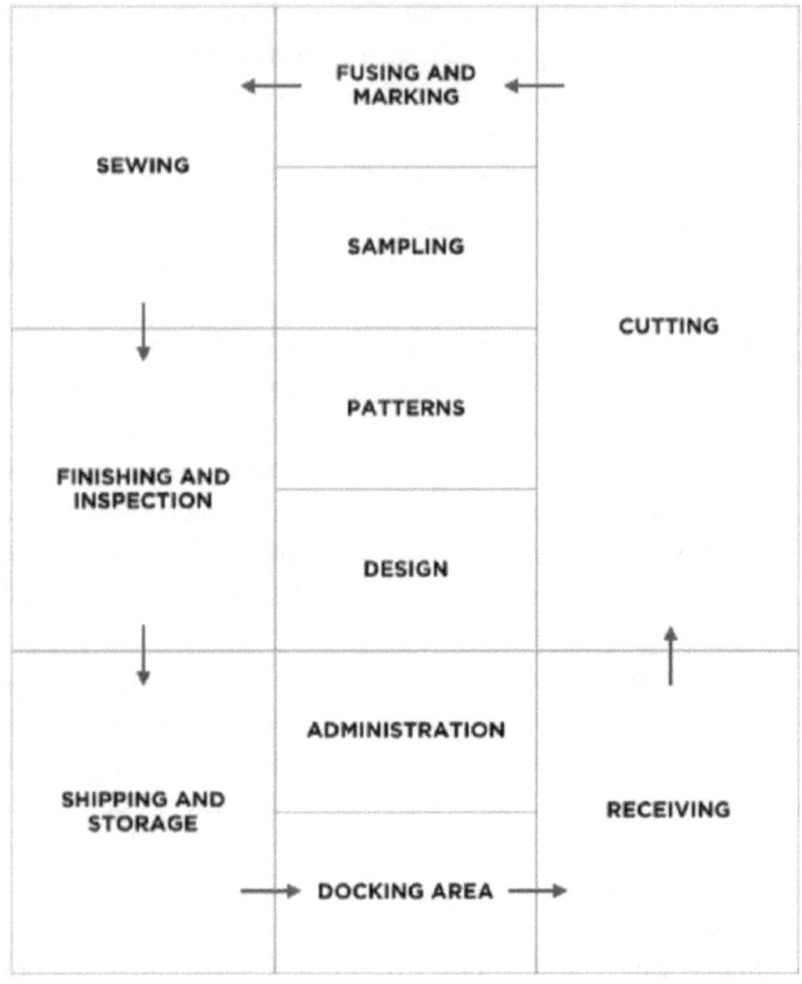

Manufacturing process

The process that is followed in the manufacture of a garment from beginning to end can be depicted as follows which is accommodated by the free flow factory design.

Drawing or sketch

An image of the concept for the garment is prepared to assist the pattern maker in understanding the style details required when constructing the patterns.

Basic block

A standard block with correct proportions is outlined by the pattern maker which is then used to construct a working pattern to be utilised by the sewing unit. The use of dummies in constructing the pattern provide an accurate base from which to work with clear direction in terms of fit and reduces the time spent on guess work. Patterns can be generated manually or computerised.

The stages of a blouse pattern development process may be illustrated as follows

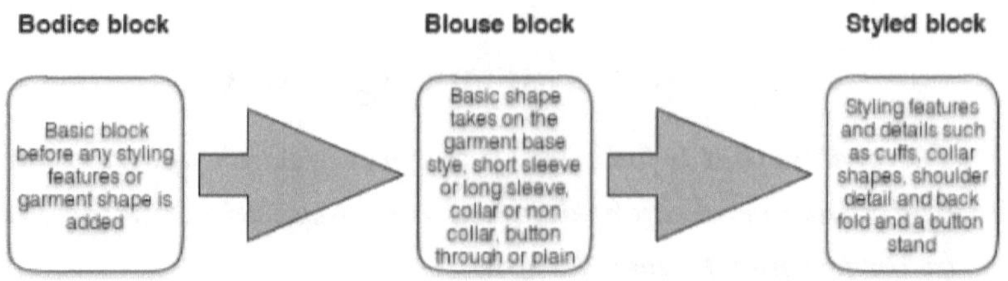

The benefits of standard blocks ensures the consistency of fit across different styles and particularly across different suppliers. It serves as a common base for pattern makers to work from, for example arm holes balance remain correct before any styling features are added, the shoulder slope remains the same across different styles and the minimum body over tolerances are set in place.

The pattern tolerances and allowances that need to be established are

- Over body tolerance is built into the fit of the garments to allow for movement within the size parameters.

- Shrinkage allowance is generally added to the width and length of the pattern which can vary according to the type of fabric and provision for any processing that takes place such as garment washing.

- Printing allowance is accommodated dependent on the size of the print, method of printing such as panel printing where extra allowance is added to the length and width of the pattern to accommodate shrinkage during the curing process.

Working pattern

Sample machinists require a base to create a garment which is presented in the form of a working pattern and may or may not be modified during the sampling process.

Sample making

The concept or representative idea is created from a working pattern to be assembled into garment form. This may not necessarily be done using the intended fabric in order to save costs but are primarily used to analyse the pattern fit and design. The sample is then reviewed by a panel of designers, pattern makers and sewing specialists who can recommend changes.

Costing

The fundamental cost structure is determined based on the fabric usage and the time taken to produce the garment known as the labour minute rating.

Production pattern

The final perfect pattern evolves from the working pattern and is used in bulk production. There are various tolerances and allowances that are accommodated for during the pattern make. Examples may be the over body tolerance which is built into the fit of the garment to allow ease of movement within the size parameters, a shrinkage allowance which is added to the pattern piece in the width and the length accommodates fabric shrinkage during printing.

Grading

The provision for the size spread is done by a pattern grader who creates patterns in different sizes by scaling the sample size, which is usually a middle size production pattern up or down. This may be done manually or by a computer. Production samples of the graded pattern samples are made and tested for fit and serve as a point of reference.

Marker making

Markers or the cutting plan are printed or drawn as an outline of the pattern parts onto paper that is the same width and length of the fabric which is positioned on top of the lay and held in place by weights. This is an essential step in the manufacture process as it serves as a guide for the operator during the cutting procedure. The function can be done manually or utilising a computerised marker package. Manual marking is time consuming, subject to errors such as overlapping poor definition and the accuracies are dependent on the operator's skill levels. The computerised process on the other hand is accurate, quicker, and determines the optimum usage of fabric. It can also be retained on record for future reference.

An illustration of the marking of patterns on the fabric lay on the cutting table

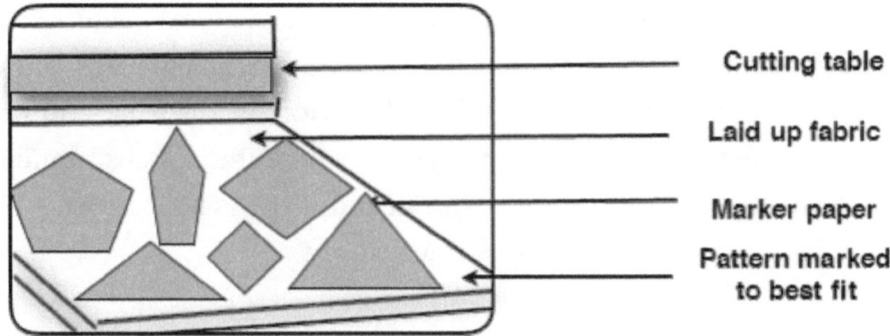

The rating or consumption is the actual amount of fabric required to cut a specific garment and the adequacy of a marker is the percentage of the fabric that is covered by the cut patterns. The less unused fabric which is not covered by the patterns, the higher is the efficiency as it should be remembered that the waste is still included in the cost of the garment. Other factors that influence the efficiency of fabric usage is different pile directions or one way characteristics, stripes or checks that need to match, border prints, size ratios and the number of units.

Some of the quality defects that need to be watched out for during the spreading operation is possible missing pattern parts, patterns facing the incorrect direction on napped fabrics such as velvets and those with different pile ways, mismatched stripes and checks, different fabric grains or where the line definition is poor.

Fabric spread

In order to prepare for the cutting process the fabric is spread out on tables. The extent of the lay will be calculated according to the marker and the number of lays which determines the lay height to meet the order plan of a specific contract. It is important that the fabric is inspected prior to and during spreading where it is confirmed that it meets the buyers requirements, does not shrink during steaming or fusing, bow or skew and is free from defects. It is also is measured to ensure that the fabric meets the specifications.

This operation can be done either manually where the fabric is stared at the end of the table and the roll is moved backwards while the width edges are aligned, is free of tension and wrinkle. Automatic spreading is done utilising a machine where the operator stands on a platform while the fabric is spread and is then cut at the start of the table and then returns to lay the next ply.

Cutting

In preparation for cutting the fabric has to be withdrawn from a storage area where the fabric is stored in a cool environment off the floor in shelves or on palettes out of the way of direct sunlight which can cause discolouration of fabric.

The amount of fabric required is calculated by the ratings as achieved by the markers and before cutting can commence it has to be relaxed for twenty four hours.

The height of the lay should be such that it allows the easy manoeuvring of straight blades through the lay and preventing the possibility for the lay to shift in spite of weights being used to keep the paper markers in place.

During the laying process which may be done manually or by the utilisation of an automated spreader of the fabric it is important that the different dye lots are separated in order to avoid colour variations in the sewing process. The lays should not be too high otherwise the fabric may move during the cutting and a maximum height of eighteen centimetres is recommended.

In terms of laying up one way fabrics such as corduroys, stripes or checks this has to be done manually for matching.

Fusing is used commonly for collars, cuffs, facings, garment panels and waistbands utilising a machine that applies heat and pressure for the operation.

Where products need to be processed, for example garment washing, the quantities are set up in smaller lays to enable completed garments to be sent to the processor in manageable quantities.

The most common cutting process is done using a powered cutting machine suitable for the type of cloth. Portable straight blade machines are used for bigger garment components which has a vertical blade that reciprocates up and down and corners and curves can be cut accurately. The depth of the lay is dependent on the length of the blade and pieces cut from the lay will be identical. The portable round blade machine is however only able to cut in straight lines or very gentle curves. Such machines are very popular as they are fast and light.

Stationery or fixed cutters such as the band knife contains a narrow, sharp endless blade and the fabric is pushed against the blade by hand where there is an air cushion below the pile to facilitate easy movement while following the markers.so that corners, tight curves and pointed incisions are cut precisely.

Other types of stationery cutters are the servo cutter which combines vertical cutting and a band knife into one machine with an overhead servo machine with adjustable speed and a knife that is suspended perpendicularly on a swivel arm. Metal die cutting where the die is placed on top of the material and is pressed through the fabric is mainly used for leathers coated and laminated materials.

Smaller parts such as collars and cuffs are cut using a band knife machine. For safety assurance it is imperative that metal gloves are worn when operating these machines

As technology has progressed in the modern age the cutting operation driven by computerized programmes have become more popular. This new technology lays the fabric on an air suction table which prevents movement of the lay which is uniform without excessive stretching and because is automated it requires fewer people, is much faster than the conventional cutting process and more accurate and therefore in the long term becomes cost efficient.

Other methods of stationery cutting is the use of plasma cutting which is the use of high temperature high velocity gas jets but does come with higher engineering and costs. Water jet cutting is achieved by high velocity of water in the form of a thin stream that tears the fires on impact and is best suited to fabric such as leather and plastic. The disadvantages that exist is the inconsistency, wet edges and high equipment costs.

Defects in the cutting process may consist of frayed, ragged or serrated edges and precision of patterns that eliminate over or under cutting.

Bundling

It is important that dye lots are be separated to avoid colour variations on panels when garments are sewn and therefore the cut panels are sorted into complete garments by size and separate dye lots. The grouping of these cut sections are numbered and then bundled ready to be sent to the sewing section.

Sewing

After the sorted bundles are received they can be stitched. For example, the sleeves, bodice and collars are assembled and stitched together to complete the final form of the garment.

It is important that certain elements are compatible with the fabric such as the stich type, machine with correct attachments and folders, needle type, seam and thread widths, all of which will contribute towards the appearance, functionality and cost of the garment.

As important is the operator skill levels that are necessary in terms of the core competence required with the appropriate experience in regard to abilities such as manual dexterity, finger dexterity, near vision, colour discrimination and the attention to detail.

In the sign off of the garment construction standards the guidelines that need to be followed are those dictated by the fittings, the pre-production samples and the final production samples.

The most common stitch types are:

Lock stitch which is used mainly in visible areas such as top stitching and on collars as well as for the insertion of zips.

Over locking stitches are utilised to cover raw edges of exposed seams.

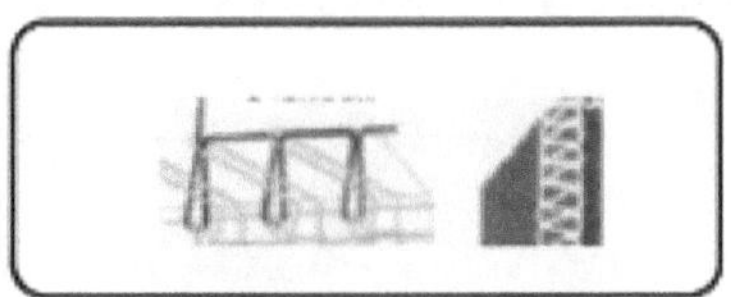

Safety stitches which are predominantly used for the joining seams mostly for woven and denim fabrics.

Mock safety stitches are also used for the joining of seams but mainly for knitted fabrics.

Chain stitch close seams of mainly woven and denim products.

Cover stitch is used in the main in undergarments to conceal elastics or to cover hems and can also serve as a decorative feature.

Blind stitches generally close hems on garments such as trousers or skirts.

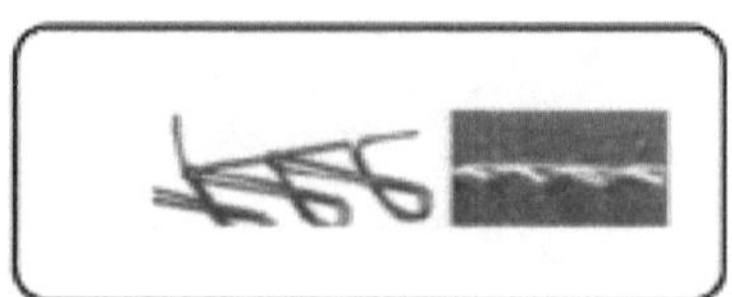

Common defects that must be avoided in the sewing operation is needle and feed damage, skipped or broken stitches and seam grin or pucker.

CASE STUDY

In the manufacture of a formal shirt for the CH Clothing Company a number of stitch types displayed above would probably be utilised in the garment.

CHALLENGE #30

List at least three of the following used in the makeup of the formal shirt.

1. **The type of stitch used.**
2. **Where these would probably be evident.**

The characteristics of a seam that is well constructed is that they are strong, durable, have a good relative elasticity, are secure and neat.

The performance of the seam will be influenced the weight, strength and durability of the fabric together with the seam construction, stitches per centimetre, strength and elasticity of thread used.

Specialised seaming such as darts, pleats, tucks, binding and piping as well as gauging require higher levels of operator skills.

The most common seam types are:

Plain seams are the simplest and used most often in various products from pillows to pants.

French seams have a clean finished look and are used successfully on high slippage fabrics which are susceptible to fraying and are also used with sheer materials to conceal the thread. Such seams are commonly employed on fabrics such as satin, sateen, voile and organza types.

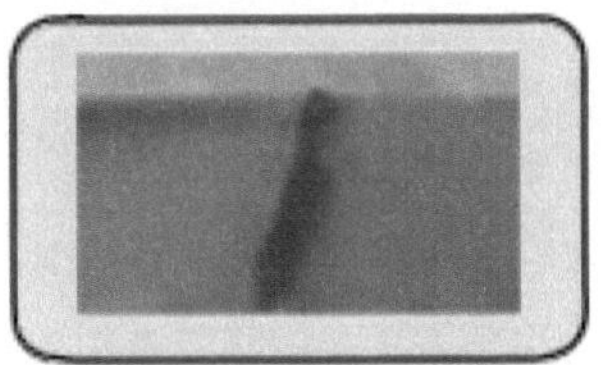

Lap or posted seams are used typically on bulky fabrics that do not ravel like leathers, felt and denim.

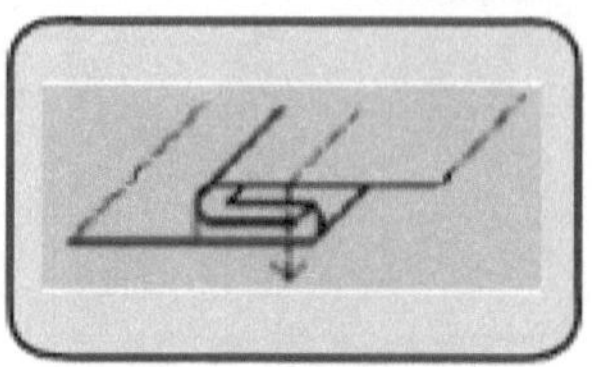

Bound seams provide a cleaner finish and aesthetic appeal on mainly light weight fabrics more often for silk or linings of jackets.

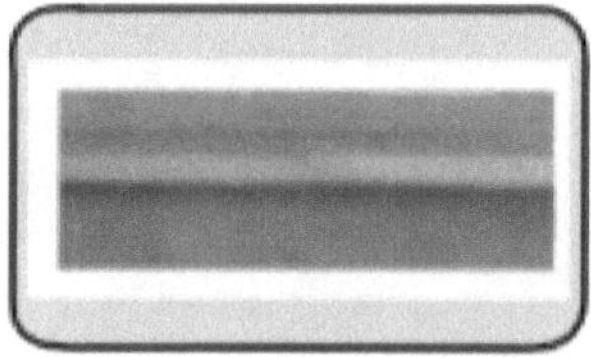

Blind seams deliver a neat appearance and prevent rough edges for products as in lined drapes, curtains, blinds and denim side seams.

Pleats, darts, tucks and gauging are at the best if they lie correctly with no distortion with secure stitching at the end, the marking of which should not be visible from the outside of garment and paired tucks must be equal in length and balanced.

    Hems should be level if straight but if curved must be balanced without any twisting or roping and secure.

Binding and piping should be without roping or twisting, of consistent width and without visible joining. The fabric should not be visible through the binding and allow for adequate extensibility.

Collars require precise cutting of fabric and interlinings and should be accurately centred, balanced in the creation of the mirrored finished appearance.

Pockets need to have adequate width, depth and strength to effectively functional and where the corners are mitred, these should be equally balanced and where they are a styling feature they should be perfectly shaped, positioned with superior sewing detail.

Zips must be stitched clear of the coil of teeth to allow for the free ride of the slider.

Buttonholes need to be compatible with the size of the button with a stitch density that does not allow the buttonhole to fray away from the fabric which is mostly common on knitted garments where they may need to be reinforced with a woven interlining.

Buttons are attached with a secure lock stitch or chain stitch. Two buttonhole buttons should have the holes running horizontally and where there are four buttonholes buttons they should be attached with the holes facing square on.

Processed garments require stricter controls due to their nature to achieve the best end result. Particular attention needs to be given to thread selection which has to be stronger, the selection of fusing and wadding in jackets must be such that it will not delaminate or disintegrate and fabric shrinkage needs to be closely monitored so that the garment does not become distorted during the washing process and the extent of shrinkage is carefully monitored.

CASE STUDY

In the manufacture of a formal shirt for the CH Clothing Company a number of quality characteristics are essential features that need to appear in the garment.

CHALLENGE #31

List three characteristics that need to be evident in the

1. Collars
2. Pockets
3. Button holes

Ironing and finishing

After the sewing process is complete the final stage of finishing can take place where the garment will get its final look which may include some form of decoration like that of the stitching of a cuff, the addition of a pocket or emblems, buttons or Velcro snap fasteners.

The garment needs to be made neat and tidy through the removal of loose threads, fibre and fluff, elimination of stains and final checks are done which include the detection of needles for obvious safety reasons.

Pressing is an essential part of the garment presentation. The methods and equipment will be dependent on product and fabric type in order to achieve the desired garment appeal.

The finished garment is sent to the packing section where it is ticketed, labelled and packaged.

Inspection

Inspection of the product is done during the production process at each critical key point and the type of defects that are watched out for are open seams, incorrect stitching techniques, non-matching threads or improper creasing.

After production is complete the detection of defects is repeated but attention is also given to any possible colour mismatches, incorrect sizing of components, missing buttons and inappropriate trimmings.

Audits of quality standards take place at various stages and places to make sure that the best possible product is delivered. The audit process starts with the pre-production sample where all stakeholders agree on the standards that must be met to set the established benchmarks to which the end of line garments will be compared. Tolerances are set up front such as the percentage defects that will be accepted before a declaration of failure for each category of imperfections. Such declared tolerances will avoid future disputes in the event of whether or not a garment with defects qualifies as a reject.

Roving in line inspections also take place at various points during production for both measurement and construction to ensure the set criteria is being met.

The inspection points that take place during the garment production process can be illustrated as follows

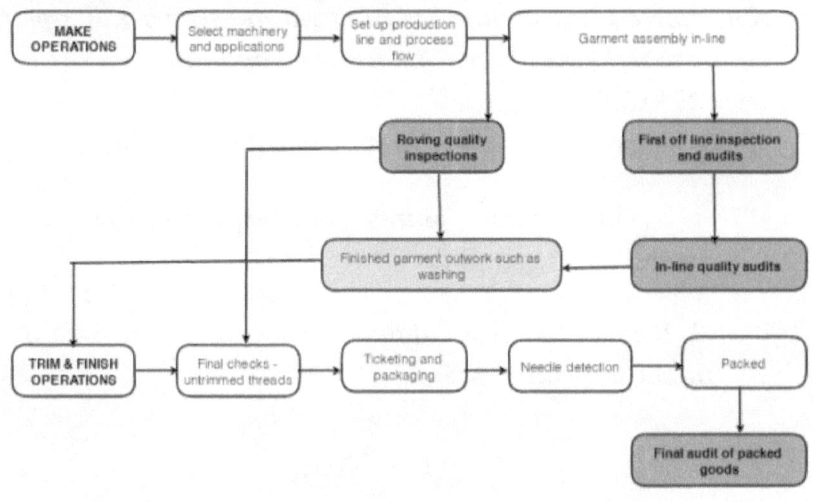

A zero defect would be where the imperfection could be a safety risk to the consumer like insecure studs or protruding metal ribbing in corsetry.

A serious defect is such that the consequence would result in product failure or render the product to be unsaleable as in the case of broken stitches, excessive grinning and holes.

Minor defects are classified where the product would still be useable but does not meet the acceptable standards like loose threads that could result in reduced sales. Other options of random testing may exist at picking and packing stage by either the retailer's representatives or an authorized agent.

It is important that a system is in place whereby it is ensured that reject garments are isolated, labels removed and clearly marked in order that they do not get included again with passed garments. The rate of rejects should be measured and analysed as an endeavour to minimise the failure rate.

CASE STUDY

During the manufacture of the CH Clothing Company formal shirts there is intense inspection at various points and aspects to ensure that the standard of quality is maintained.

CHALLENGE #32

Based on the statement above name the following.

1. **Name three points of inspection in the manufacturing process.**

2. **Identify five types of defects that are looked out for in the inspection process.**

Packing

The packing of the product is done according to specified techniques possibly using templates in such a way to ensure that the quality and integrity of the garment is maintained. Tagging with appropriate ticketing and promotional material is attached in accordance to the retailer's specification.

Cartons

Placing product into cartons is the final packing operation of the garment prior to shipment. The quantity per carton and the configuration within must be consistent. The labelling and markings on the carton has to be as per the regulatory requirements and as part of the quality check there should be a reconciliation of what the contents should be and what they actually are.

Sampling stages

Sampling takes place at different stages during the manufacturing process and serve differing purposes and in essence the main object is achieving absolute clarity in terms of what is expected in terms of styling, required quality standards, confirming the practicality of the patterns and getting the approval of the retailer.

The main types of samples that exist are the following:

Design concept sample is the very first sample which is developed by either the supplier or the retailer with the primary objective to get acceptance and decision to proceed with the garment.

Proto type sample which is prepared as the sample that accompanies the order and is frequently that sample which is utilised in initial range presentations which may or not be in the actual fabric and is really used acquaint those who need to progress further and changes may be made to some styling details, fit or trims and accessories.

Fit samples are made up in order that the buyer is able to confirm the fit on dummies or live models and check the garment for construction acceptability and should be in the fabric that is going to be used for bulk production.

Marketing sample is for use in the promotion of the garment and is used for photo shoots which would include the on line channel.

Size set samples for the buyer to assess that the garment fits properly across all sizes and will serve as a point of reference once production commences.

Technology sample is for technical tests to be conducted on such as wash tests for testing the feel and handling after washing, chemical and physical performance tests to ensure that they meet the required standards.

Pre-production sample is probably the most important sample as it is the signed off sample that is representative in all ways as to what can be expected in production and should there be any dispute during or after production it will serve as the point of reference.

Production sample is the first representative sample that comes off the production line and is sent to the buyer to confirm that it matches the pre-production sample.

Shipment sample is usually the sample received from off shore suppliers by the retailer to authorise the shipment of orders.

CASE STUDY

In order to get approval of the final product for CH Clothing Company a number of different samples need to be submitted to the customer

CHALLENGE#33

Describe the purpose of the following different samples.

1. **Design concept sample.**
2. **Fit samples.**
3. **Marketing samples.**
4. **Pre-production sample.**
5. **Shipment sample.**

During the manufacturing process the pitfalls to be aware of can be depicted at the various stages as follows

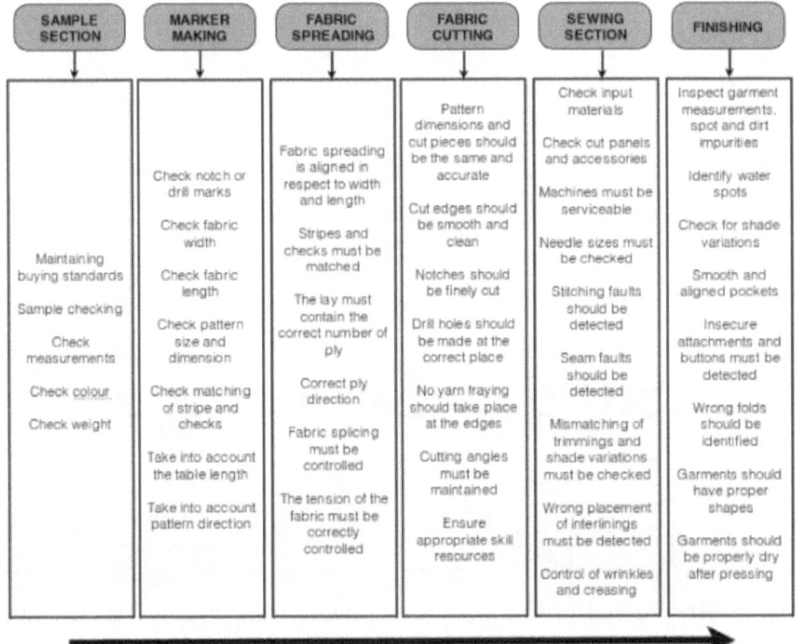

Production systems

The variety of configurations of the layout of sewing machine production lines can be set out in several ways and the selection of the most appropriate arrangement will be determined by the nature and quantity of product being manufactured.

Examples of typical optional configurations for a production line

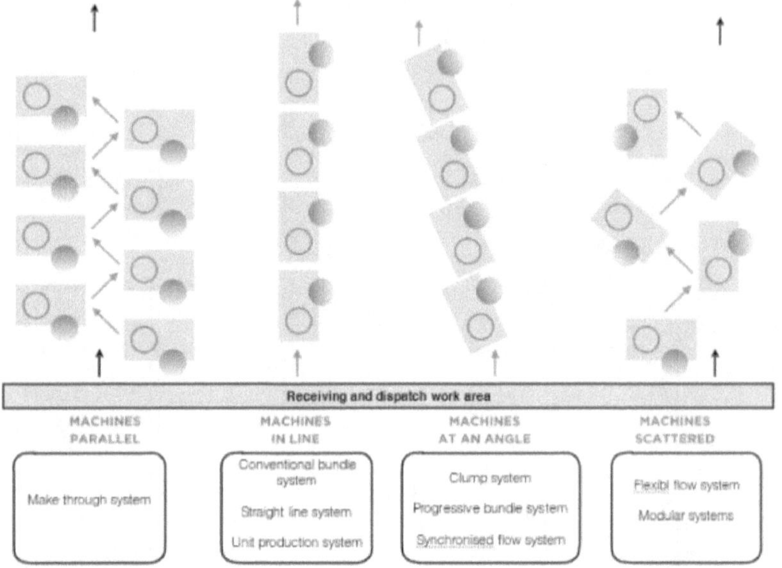

In the main the appropriate production system is set up based on the product style, types of machines and availability of the required operator skill level.

The layout of the equipment will also vary dependent on the nature of the product type in the factory and the system employed may well include the smooth integration of the material handling, production process and the personnel that will direct the workflow to deliver the finished product.

Make through system is one of the typical production systems that is generally used is the where one operator will do all the stages of the sewing operation from beginning to end and after completion will commence with the next garment. Although this is easy to supervise it delivers a comparatively low productivity and is dependent on highly experienced operators and therefore comes with a high labour cost. This type of format is suited to the manufacture of couture garments and sample making.

Conventional bundle system is also employed on a line system of sewing machines in a line configuration where work flows from a central areas to the first machine and then back to the next machine and so forth. The person stationed at the central area is responsible for the control of the work flow of the movement of the bundles.

Clump system is where the worker collects a clump of work from the work central area and completes a specific operation. After this is completed the clump is returned to the central area after which a second operator will collect the clump and complete the second operation and so it will carry on until the garment is finished.

Progressive bundle system is where the sewing operations are laid out in sequence. Each operator receives the bundle and completes their specific task and passes the bundle on via a container or conveyer belt to the next operator who performs the next task. This system is a very common method in many clothing factories these days typically in the case of shirt, jackets, and jeans.

Flexible flow systems is where the operators are positioned in such a way where the correct number of operators arranged in organised groups dependent on the each type of task and the layout is usually in a parallel formation planned in detail to ensure a balanced output until the garment is completed.

Straight line systems is similar in principle to the flexible flow system except each operation takes a similar time to complete and operators only handle one garment at a time. Garments will possibly pass from on work station to the next on a conveyer belt at a rate that is manageable.

Synchronised flow systems apply where the garments of a specific colour and size are passed from station to the next for assembly while components such as collars, cuffs and other features are done simultaneously down another line and at the end the two completed operations are brought together and processed to complete the garment.

Unit production system is a computer controlled production line where an overhead conveyer system move the product from one operation station to the next utilising a hanger carrier for assembly. The automated materials handling replaces the traditional method of bundling, tying, marking and manual movement of product. The advantage of the computerised aspect is that data gathering enables the productivity to be measured, establishing the input of information to the payroll and tracking of styles.

Modular systems of production are where an organised group of individuals work together to accomplish a common purpose where the team works on one or a few garments at a time and the layout is sequential in a parallel formation where each operator is assigned at least one task or a few adjacent to each other.

Example of detailed operation at each station for the manufacture of a t-shirt in order that the plan is such that it ensures maximum operational and time efficiency

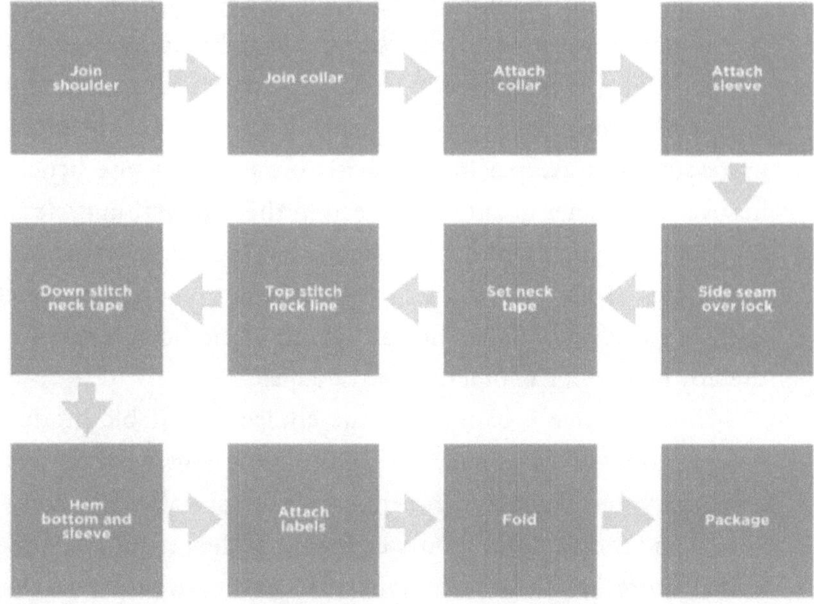

The flow will naturally influence the selection of the production line configuration and in all likelihood the t-shirt will possibly follow the path as illustrated in the first figure above.

CASE STUDY

In the manufacture of the formal shirt for CH Clothing Company the production line configuration may well differ dependent on the type of product, detail and quantity.

CHALLENGE #34

1. **Name five production systems that would be suitable in the production of a formal shirt.**

2. **Why would the modular system not be appropriate?**

Quick response manufacturing

In recent years the substantial shift to high volume cost effective garment off shore manufacturers, the majority of which are based in the East has enforced domestically established suppliers and retailers in traditional manufacturing markets to review their modus operandi in order to keep their plants viable. As a result more and more suppliers are placing emphasis on achieving the benefits of innovation, higher quality and speed in the production cycle where they may be manufacturing in lesser or varying volumes with shorter lead times. This enables them to be nimble enough to react to fashion swings rapidly particularly in an unpredictable market and thereby maintain a competitive advantage.

This objective is assisted by the choice of suitable production process configurations such as cellular groupings with the correct machinery and right attachments such as specialised folders. The needle and thread types should be such that they enable the efficient manufacture of the product type with lower inventory levels and lesser mark downs.

The advantage of quick response manufacturing is that it increases machine up time and therefore delivers an improved quality and subsequently less rework. Where this process is linked to a team incentive programme a consequence is lower staff turnover with fewer social noncompliance issues while also empowering employees and higher productivity.

Typical quick response initiatives is to have product stored at various stages of production so that it is possible to react swiftly to current consumer sales patterns. A prime example is where garments such as knitwear, sweaters, t-shirts, tank tops and the like are made up in uncoloured greige yarn and as the demand happens the garments are then piece dyed to whatever colours the market calls for. Not only in such cases is the benefit of improved sales achieved but it also reduces the build-up of unwanted garments or yarns.

Other tactics include the reservation of production capacity but holding back the ordering of fabric and finalisation of the style for as long as possible in order to react more closely to trends as quickly as possible.

The logistics and supply chain functions need to be as streamlined as possible to allow the goods to reach the point of sale as quickly as possible which will require focus on storage, pick and pack operations, format in which the goods are best stored and transported, for example, whether they should be moved in a boxed or in a hanging state where the benefits of speed to market should be offset against the additional costs that will be incurred in setting up a hanging infra-structure.

With the explosion of sophisticated and faster computer systems sales data is transferred in all sorts of variations and is thoroughly analysed in order to rapidly reveal the wants and preferences of consumers that enables quick collaborative decisions and forecast adjustments across the spectrum of mills, suppliers and retailers and through these actions the retailer is able to better serve their customer in a faster time with less product proliferation which increases their competitiveness and offers the opportunity of potential growth of market share.

PACKAGING TECHNOLOGY

The packaging of a product is largely the responsibility of a packaging technologist and plays a critical role in the presentation, protection and communication of information to the consumer as well as taking into account the ecological demands of the environment.

The common purpose of packaging is that it physically protects the product against mechanical shocks, vibrations, varying temperatures, humidity and excessive handling during transit or warehousing. The usual provision of information whether it is on the packaging itself or through the use of labels, indicate any regulations that may apply, the usage and safety instructions, transport guidelines and lists the components and chemicals that were used in the production process.

Packaging assists in the sale of the product in that it serves as a "silent salesman". There is a communication of information through clever graphic design that encompasses the properties of the product, instructions as how to use the merchandise and the provision of safety warnings. Convenience is added by way of easy storage configurations, display conformity and the accommodation of barcoding information which is easily accessible for scanners to capture sales and stock keeping records and store them on a common data base.

Specialised packaging plays an important part in securing the product through the use of tamper proof mechanisms and can also be engineered to reduce the pilferage.

Over packaging should be avoided and where possible the utilisation of recycled or recyclable materials in the manufacturing process is encouraged without affecting the functional properties.

Outer cartons must adhere to weight and dimension stipulations and should be able to be easily handled on warehouse equipment such as conveyer belts, pallets and storage slots.

Of the two types, primary packaging enjoys the journey of the product right to the end user while secondary packaging is that which is discarded at various points during the journey.

Examples of primary packaging are self- adhesive tickets which carry the barcode detail, price, reference numbers, colour and size as well as date codes. Swing tickets are used where adhesive tickets are not appropriate and may also be independently attached in order to highlight any unique features of the product. Invariably adhesive tickets are applied to presentation packs, wallets and plastic bags.

Sew in labels are typically a satin tape which is sewn into the garment side or neck seam and carry wash care instructions, product reference numbers, size information, fabric composition, country of origin as well as safety instructions. The fibre content must be described by its generic name but may be accompanied by a brand name or a trade mark. An example would be where woollen products will display the wool mark for which the supplier will have qualified to utilise through their manufacturing process.

An example of garment care and reference label

EXAMPLE OF A GARMENT CARE AND REFERENCE LABEL

Care markings are not legally required but are commonly indicated by the universal symbols that are consistent and accurate, for example, where a garment needs to be hand washed only and not machine washed it will be highlighted using the relevant symbol

Universal care instruction symbols are key to the garment label and the most common are outlined below

Symbol	Meaning	Symbol	Meaning
	WASHING WATER TEMPERATURE		DO NOT TUMBLE DRY
	HAND WASH ONLY		DRIP DRY IN SHADE
	WASH ON SENSITIVE PROGRAMMES		DRIP DRY
	DO NOT WASH		DRY FLAT
	DRY CLEANABLE		DRY ON HANGER
	DO NOT DRY CLEAN		DO NOT IRON
	DO NOT USE BLEACH		IRON WITH WARM IRON
	DO NOT TUMBLE DRY		IRON WITH HOT IRON

Country of origin is displayed on labels to indicate geographically where the significant stage of production took place. In most countries this is a legal requirement even if the garment may have some components that originate from other parts of the world. Apart from it being law, the identification gives the consumer the choice of which countries that they may wish to support or not support for political or emotional reasons and participate in buy local promotional campaigns that are designed to stimulate local employment.

Swing tags that describe features or unique properties of products have to be truthful in terms of fit for purpose and of the quality standard that is expected by the customer. Where the product does not meet these claims they can be deemed to be misleading and could have legal implications that can be enforced either by the user or competitors who may feel unfairly disadvantaged. An example of this could be that where a ticket describes the garment as being non-iron but after a few washes it has to be ironed.

Secondary packaging are items such as outer cartons, over bags for hanging product, hanger size indicators, stock room and store address labels, the outer carton product detail and supplier detail stamps.

The procuring and specifying of ecologically friendly packaging should always be done keeping the safety of the environs top of mind. Printing should be done keeping volatile compound emissions to a minimum through, for example, the use of vegetable based ink that are free from heavy metals.

Measures need to be put in place to keep waste of inks, ink tins, and paper to a minimum and the cleaning and recirculation of polluted water should be promoted. Paper packaging and corrugated cartons ought to contain a percentage of recycled papers and must not to have been bleached using chlorine. Plastic packaging should be of recyclable materials such as polypropylene and polyethylene.

CASE STUDY

Care labels are essential to give guidelines to maintain the consistent form and function of the product. CH Clothing Company being a quality conscious entity will certainly focus on this information.

CHALLENGE #35

In the case of CH Clothing Company name five care symbols that are likely to appear on the label of the formal cotton shirt.

SUPPLIERS

Sourcing suppliers

The assessment of a prospective supplier or vendor, mill, dye house, fibre producer, processor, trimming and component contractor, packaging supplier and printer is a process that needs to be done thoroughly in order to ensure that they meet all the required criteria to manufacture the product in mind.

In principle there are four different methodologies of purchasing product.

The majority of garment purchases conducted by the retailer is as per the processes described in this book which is conceived based on inputs from the design, buying, merchandising and technical teams whereby the criteria of fabric, components, style and manufacturing as well as the packaging are dictated to the supplier.

Secondly, as is practiced by the more traditional retailers is where they buy their own fabric and allocate it out to a cut, make and trim supplier. The supplier may or may not offer a style, which could be provided by the retailer to a number of different suppliers to obtain a quote for the manufacture of the product according to a labour minute rating. The price of the fabric is static as it is supplied by the retailer. The downside of this methodology is that the retailer must have a technical understanding of fabrics which means that the buying team needs to be more knowledgeable and have added skills which are not always readily available in the labour market. There is also the need to invest in fabric stocks and have a detailed understanding of minute rates or manufacturing costs of the supplier. On the plus side of cut, make and trim manufacturing is that it enables the ability to cost accurately, be more flexible in selection of styling and achieve a greater speed to market.

A third methodology of sourcing is the direct purchase of a completed ready designed garment from the supplier where the retailer's brand label is inserted and the style is procured exclusively for the retailer.

Lastly there is the option to procure popular brands directly out of the supplier's range. In this case it is likely that there will be no flexibility in terms of modifying the style and often the investment of building a store within a store concept may be required. Pricing tends to be at a premium and commonly minimum order quantities apply.

The researching of new, cheaper, innovative and exciting sources of supply in order to maintain a competitive advantage in the market place is an ongoing process, as is the need to maintain a sustainable relationship with current core suppliers which comes with a continual effort to improve their delivery standards of product. Suppliers are expected to be consistently reliable, effective and efficient to retain the business of their clients as the success of the retailers is the guarantee of continued acceptance of the product that they produce.

A constant balance of those products which are sourced from local suppliers and that which are manufactured off shore is important. As off shore suppliers improve in terms of quality, equipment and workforce living standards there is an increasing pressure on costs and therefore the sources do not remain geographically static.

Fashion buying was originally focused in the Far East in Hong Kong and Taiwan but costs are increasing faster than they have in the past as well as pressure is being placed on authorities to elevate minimum wage bands. It is therefore not surprising that production is moving to more cost efficient areas such as Indonesia, Bangladesh, Pakistan, Cambodia, and Vietnam while production in Madagascar and Mauritius has also become prevalent.

Hong Kong and Taiwan have now become more the management and design centres who procure from alternative production plants. The ease of increased technology, the relaxing of bureaucratic barriers as well as cheaper travel has enabled the transfer of production to be relatively easy and flexible. Migration of production to newer countries brings limitations and therefore it is important to maximise efficiencies in the current countries where goods are produced while at the same time sourcing alternative manufacturing plants that will meet the ethical and quality standards of the retailer.

Added to this is the probability that the larger the offshore supplier is, the more the likelihood is that the retailer will be less important in their lives and if need be, the order can be more easily forfeited. The converse is that if the overseas supplier is small the possibility exists that the production may be outsourced to other vendors who the retailer may not even know about. Overseas factories seldom readily have excess production capacity and that this together with the longer transport lead times make the possibility of repeat orders within the same season improbable.

Sourcing internationally does, at face value, often appear to be very attractive but there are factors that need to be taken into account which can lead to additional unforeseen costs as well as logistical challenges particularly in terms of lead times. The re-organisation of production can therefore be perplexing and the savings that may be apparent up front could indeed be decimated later down the line.

Keeping track of the off shore supply chain at times presents some complex challenges and makes it very difficult to monitor the progress of product at all times. An extreme illustration of such a scenario is where the process commences with the raw material producer who passes the product onto the commodities traders whose purchasing agents sells them onto the garment manufacturers.

In the procedure local distributors could be involved to deliver the raw materials to the garment manufacturing plant. Secondary vendors for outsourced processes are frequently utilised before the product is delivered eventually to the local exporters and freighters administered by agents on behalf of the larger trading houses who are the frontline liaison with the retailer.

Advantages may be enjoyed by having a dedicated foreign office in key cities to control the management of suppliers and product. Obviously this does come at an added cost and should only be considered when a critical mass in that foreign country is achieved. However, the formation of such an organisation must be assessed on merit as to whether it is viable or not. Typically such a team will consist of two or three merchandisers, possibly buying and sourcing specialists together with maybe three or four quality controllers who spend two to three days a week in the factories focusing exclusively on the retailer's orders. The foreign office owns the relationship with the supplier and are able to exert pressure to ensure critical deadlines are met. Communication is easier and faster as such teams are self-managed and can be flexible in evaluating priorities.

The extreme example of the complexity of dealing with offshore suppliers is that of the world's largest trading house being the Hong Kong based sourcing and logistical company, Li Fung. They own no factories or mills but simply play matchmaker between poor countries factories and vendors which have favourable labour rates and costs and the global retailers for whom Li Fung handle the logistics.

Li Fung represent some fifteen thousand suppliers across sixty countries which enable them to procure very high volumes and have them produced in a fraction of a time that a single supplier would take to complete. It is not surprising that consequently they are known as the "Walmart of purchasing" and the sheer size of the organisation makes it difficult to pin point the true sources of the product and they have been alleged from time to time to be linked to several calamities in some dubious factories.

Where the retailer is dominant in their target market and the volumes are substantial enough it is advantageous for them to cut out the middleman agent and procure directly from the source. By doing this an advantage is gained over their competitors and they do not end up subsidising the supply chain for their rivals especially where full containers are bought on a repeat basis. Advantage is also to be gained through using a buying agent or consolidator to combine the products into full container loads where they purchase from multiple off shore suppliers.

Currency exchange rate fluctuations may well change the advantage of buying off shore, as will quota limitations which could change in the exporting country due to the fact that costs will probably increase should the availability of the quotas become scarcer.

The management of offshore deliveries is more complex and if minimum order quantities are imposed they can lead to higher storage costs and inventory investment together with varying transport charges.

The intricate nature of international freight forwarding requires either an in house dedicated team or the need to outsource this function to an agency to take on the responsibility.

Often the additional travelling and increased management costs are not taken into account when considering product quotations. The opening of foreign offices with sourcing, quality control and buying teams in itself can be a considerable additional overhead that needs to be established, staffed and equipped and is excluded from the base garment cost.

Frequently the bulk offshore deliveries have to be unpacked and repacked and labelled after allocation that results in multiple handling which adds considerable cost and time delay.

For the reasons above the viability of sourcing from foreign suppliers has to be carefully considered in terms of the minimum volumes that need to be procured to achieve the benefits while at the same time being able to exceed the sales potential without putting strain on the warehouse storage capabilities.

It is therefore strategically beneficial if the supply chain from overseas is as short as possible with the minimum of cross over proprietorship points, for example, the allocation of product while it is in transit lessens the pressure of receiving and warehousing of the goods before being withdrawn for picking and packing. The possibility exists that the goods can bypass the storage stage and be delivered directly to the pick pack areas of the distribution centre. This type of approach might be appropriate for one off promotions and special events.

The advantages of a local supplier base is quicker potential delivery to market, more flexible production with easily manageable inventory quantities and less complicated administration, quality control and payment methodologies. For local suppliers the trend has also shifted towards smaller production infrastructures with specialisation on exclusivity and individualistic styling.

The relationship between retailers and local suppliers is most often one of mutual interdependence all of which has to be weighed up against the cost and innovation advantages of off shore suppliers. The manufacture of replenishment core type product is better suited to local manufacturers as it calls for the fine-tuning of styles, colour and size ratios which are easier to adjust. There may also be pressure from the authorities to encourage local production through the various "Buy Local" promotions in order to stimulate the local industry and satisfy the employment initiatives in the political arena.

It stands to reason that the less suppliers there are, the less the burden of supplier management will be with regard to different administration models, quality control and varying costs.

A strategy to rationalise suppliers eliminates smaller, incompatible, problematic suppliers who are often more demanding in terms of the time required to manage them compared to the effort spent on more substantial, streamlined producers and enable effective performance management.

The larger the quantities allocated to fewer suppliers will lead to lower cost prices through the economies of scale advantage as well as the benefit of the delivery of improved quality and reliability. Management communication and the mutual interdependence with specialised service provision will undoubtedly lead to a competitive advantage.

There are however risks involved in dealing with too few suppliers in that the exposure to greater innovation is limited and complacent suppliers tend to offer more and more of the same or wait for the retailer to provide ideas and designs. Often the production methods are inflexible which could result in a relationship of mistrust and frustration.

Newer suppliers can be added to the core base of suppliers, however, the number of suppliers in total should remain constant through the consistent measurement of performance including formal review processes being in place for existing suppliers. If they do not meet the performance criteria they run the risk of elimination.

The performance review and assessment of suppliers should not be done in isolation by each department that they supply but preferably conducted across the business as a whole which will deliver more objective and consistent results and thereby will avoid mixed messages being given to suppliers.

Other pitfalls that retailers need to be aware of is the differing perceptions of the suppliers versus that of the buyers. Typically buyers view suppliers as being frequently older and more experienced, full of excuses and promise the world. From the suppliers point of view the buyers are young and inexperienced, abuse their buying power and utilise threats to make unrealistic demands and apart from being busy all the time, the formation of a sustainable relationship is disrupted due to the regular changing of staffing in departments.

It is not uncommon that buyers and designers tend to make last minute changes to designs, trims, quantities and colours which puts immense pressure on suppliers and consequently leads to the need to work excessive overtime hours or over book production capacity. As a result they may end up using unqualified outside vendors in an effort to accommodate the revised unreasonable deadlines and can thereby easily transgress the compliance criteria.

Conscious efforts are essential to influence the relationship to be one of joint co-operation and respect, the conducting of informed cost price negotiations with better transparency with regard to each other's needs and the working together to achieve solutions that will be for their mutual benefit.

CASE STUDY

CH Clothing Company prefers to source local suppliers as opposed to off shore suppliers for a variety of reasons.

CHALLENGE #36

List five reasons as to why they would choose this philosophy to source from local suppliers.

There are some key questions that need to be answered before embarking on a relationship with a potential supplier which are:

What are the supplier's capabilities and specific skills?

Do they have design facilities and what level of innovation is evident?

Do they have the capacity requirements to meet the required volumes?

Is the planning of production stable in that it minimises changeovers and keeps labour fully utilised so that orders are not shifted around dependent on which customer is shouting the loudest.

Are they financially stable? Do they meet the criteria that ensures payment to their raw material suppliers being secure and guaranteed?

Do they have the appropriate equipment to deliver the envisioned product?

Is the production sub contracted to other vendors and do these producers also meet the same required compliance standards?

What are the initial costing indications in comparison to alternative sources?

Which other major retailers do they supply?

What management and liaison structures are in place?

What are their quality standards like and do they have current valid compliance audits from an accredited recognised test house?

Do they have the ability to produce or source in smaller batches to maximise flexibility and speed?

How close are they to their component suppliers?

Where are they located and will that have any bearing on meeting the delivery lead times, delivery demand schedules and costs?

Do they have any long term strategic expansion plans?

Does the physical building structure meet all building specifications, safety requirements and provide the appropriate facilities to accommodate a production environment?

Is there evidence that they are ethically compliant in terms of staff hours of work, remuneration policies and adherence to accepted norms of terms of employment?

Do they meet the environmental requirements in terms of health and safety of the workers?

Do they utilise any banned substances in the production process and what is the policy for the safe disposal of waste effluent?

Are the raw material suppliers reputable and certified?

What are their laboratory facilities or which testing facilities do they use?

The format of these initial audits can be formalized in a matrix form and scorecard values can be weighted according to the level of importance that can be depicted through a relative score compared to other suppliers which ensures a more objective assessment and structured plans of action for suppler selection.

A simple example of such a supplier rating matrix is as follows

	QUALITY	CAPACITY	GROWTH	COSTING	ENVIRON-MENT	SOCIAL	INNO-VATION	LIAISON	TOT	WEIGHTED AVERAGE
WEIGHTED IMPORTANCE	6	6	5	7	5	5	5	6		
SUPPLIER A	20	15	25	30	15	15	10	20	150	108
SUPPLIER B	25	20	30	25	20	20	25	10	175	123
SUPPLIER C	30	30	10	25	20	20	30	20	185	132

Key areas of compliance focus in the drafting of an audit report

Social compliance refers in the main as to how the company treats its employees and their perspective on social responsibility. The point of reference is to a minimal code of conduct that directs how employees are treated with regards to wages, working hours, work conditions, safety signage and preventative measures such as lighting, electrical wiring and use of face masks, recruitment criteria, human resource policies in terms of disputes and promotions. What is absolutely essential is that they adhere to a set code of ethics to meet the compliance requirements.

Environmental compliance speaks to the respect that they have for environmental aspects such as the use of chemicals that may harm employees, disposal of waste products, pollution of water sources and the utilisation of environmental enhancing components such as the use of organic cottons. Compliance audits ensure that they meet the minimum standards of various environmental laws.

Capabilities refers to the standards of vendors and their sources such as mills, trimming manufacturers, distributors and other collaborators in the supply chain who are audited and assessed. They need to provide vital management control for process safety, security and risk management. Audits focus on the policies and procedures to verify compliance with regulatory requirements and industry standards. The programmes must be properly designed and implemented as well as identify deficiencies and recommendations can be made as to where corrective actions may be required.

Audits are done by stages, the first being the gathering of information through visual observation, documented reviews and interviews with staff. This data is then compared to the regulatory requirements and an evaluation is made as to how they conform to the legal stipulations which forms part of the pre audit. The second phase of the audit would be an intense on-site inspection which includes the conducting of interviews and review of records to assess the effectiveness of the implementation of programmes. Lastly the post audit consists of the briefing of management on the findings and the preparation of a final report and the relevant rating with corrective action recommendations.

Such audits should be conducted on an annual basis by a recognized audit company such as SMETA, WRAP or SA 8000. This should be followed up by physical visits to the plants. Audits are not limited to the point of manufacture but ought to also include the raw material sources, processing houses or any other out sourced functions at other vendors.

It is important that such reports are kept on record and up to date as in the event of a disaster such as a fire, building collapse or accident they will serve as critical points of reference.

Supplier introduction

Prior to commencing business with a new supplier it is required that the retailer briefs the supplier on all aspects of conducting business with them. This will apply to all processes that are in place to get them up and running and what is needed to be adhered to in order to maintain healthy relations thereafter.

The type of information that should be provided to the supplier is the background of the retail company and the philosophies as well as the type of operations in place so that they have a high level understanding of the company values that are subscribed to.

The supplier needs to have a crystal clear understanding of the end to end process which must be followed to become a certified supplier. This process will include the complete account registration, bank details and references, contractual agreements, settlement of payment terms and conditions and subscription to any software programmes that may be required to conduct business.

All conditions and guidelines in doing business should be outlined in a manual so that there is a detailed point of reference in the event of any dispute that may arise. Often the manual and other relevant information is available on the retailer's website for easy reference as is any training material together with ongoing updates and communications. The site may be access controlled even to the point that the information available is specific to the supplier. An example of such information is where the supplier is able to monitor the sales performance of their product in real time. It is essential that the channels of communication are structured and very clear as poor exchange of information has a negative impact and causes additional cost through wasted time, effort and resources which could result in late deliveries which will undoubtedly reflect in the end as lost sales.

Processes should be outlined for support and training usually in the form of instruction guides or is done practically in a lecture room environment. Representative topics would be for example, best practices for picking and packing, processing of orders and reporting availability of product. More technical training could be the procedures for the use of specific software packages, analysis and use of management reports or the use of a product critical management tool.

Performance management reports of the supplier should also be available in order that any shortcomings may be addressed promptly and enable the supplier to improve the efficiency of their operation. The type of key performance indicators that are measured, reported on and tolerances set are the analysis of customer returns, the measurement of actual variances to ordered quantities, the accuracy of picking and packing of product as well as the lead times of deliveries between receipt of orders and delivery to the retailer's receiving point.

A vital point to be measured is the rate of attrition during the production process which is the loss of product through rejects, under production through short delivery of raw materials or pilferage in the factory which results in loss of sales and needs to be analysed to keep these pre delivery instances to a minimum.

Customer returns must not only be quantified but the nature of the complaints have to be categorised and thresholds set to determine when a bulk return to supplier is warranted. The real danger lies where it is essential to retain the brand integrity when the nature of the defect can be considered dangerous or maybe life threatening and requires urgent withdrawal of the product from all points in the supply chain as well as the need to communicate a recall of the affected product through the media.

Where tolerances are set and the agreed criteria are not met, a consequence of some form or other may well be applied which usually has a financial implication through penalty discounts being enforced, rejection of delivery and the implementation of sale or return agreements.

Supplier manuals

The topics and information which is usually covered in the manual that may well form part of the memorandum of agreement between the retailer and the supplier are as follows

- The process that has to be followed to set up an account and the registration of the administrative details such as contact details, payment terms and logistical addresses. Retailer contact and help desk information is also published.

- Where the retailer may have unique software programmes for the conducting business such as the processing of orders, reporting of stock availability, the transfer of delivery instructions and product critical path management may require the supplier to invest in the packages and if need be upgrade the hardware to meet specifications to run such packages.

- All details of systems and reports generated should be described in sufficient detail to allow the supplier to be able to refer to in order to resolve any queries they may have.

- Some retailers have an internet based portal system which may be accessed by all accredited suppliers each with their unique login where they will be able to view vital information, notifications, performance reports training documentation and operational manuals be able to order SKU tickets, view and download delivery instructions and any other critical information required to efficiently conduct business with the retailer

A typical greeting page after completing the login process would typically look like the illustration below

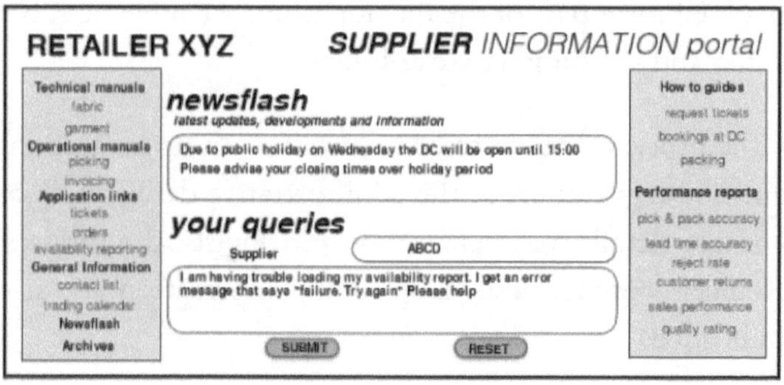

- The manual must outline technical guidelines and testing requirements as well as packaging specifications and approved suppliers should be listed.

- Invoicing methods and the information that needs to be appear on such documents as well as the payment channels and methods have to be described in detail.

- Ticketing details, ticket examples, reference numbers and order process should appear together with a list of approved ticket printing houses as well as the consequences which are in place should goods be delivered without or with incorrect ticketing.

- Packaging specifications should be itemised with regard to outer cartons, pack quantities, sealing guidelines, weight tolerances and markings which have to appear on the cartons.

- The guidelines and processes that need to be followed to complete the delivery of product to the retailer's receiving point in terms of equipment handling, time slot booking, descriptive labelling and the like must be described in detail.

- The shipping documents utilised and the information that is required for off shore need to be noted as well as any specific administration processes that have to be followed.

- A detailed description is included of performance indicators and tolerances that are measured.

- The penalty levels which are applied where performance criteria are not met should be clearly stated in the manual as well as the methodology of the calculation to avoid disputes if and when the occasion arises.

After the decision to consider an agreement with a supplier the retailer's technical team or an approved representative will visit the plant and perform an audit to ensure that the retailer's set down specifications and requirements are adequately met in terms of social, environmental and quality standards in order to be registered as an approved supplier.

If the supplier successfully meets the requirements a process will follow where the account is setup which will include the allocation of a supplier code which makes for easy identification on packaging and garment labels as well as administration of orders, deliveries supplier performance management.

Typical contractual contraventions are where the supplier's quality is found to be substandard and to be eligible for penalisation. Examples are quality failures in production, in cases where the safety of the product is compromised in the form of needle points or staples being found in the product, the use of poor attachments which carry the danger creating sharp edges on the garment that may pose a hazard to the consumer and the subcontracting of production to unauthorised vendors.

Clear guidelines and procedures as to the disposal of product need to be stated in the instances of the total withdrawal of product, production overruns, rejects and after what time period and which labelling or ticketing must be removed. Options that exist will be agreed on by the two parties for settlement of claims, for example, it may not be viable to incur reverse logistical costs to return distressed goods back to offshore suppliers and would be better to dispose of them locally. The recovery value would then be part of the settlement agreement with the supplier.

Protection of the retailer's intellectual property must be made very clear to all suppliers and this will pertain in the main to the safety of patents such as those relating to invention, utility or design. Trademarks are unique names, phrases, logos, symbols and can include colours which appear on the products themselves that are undoubtedly associated with the brand.

In the same way that the focus of the manual is on how to do things, the other side of the coin which is as important is the procedures to follow in order to exit from a supplier for whatever reason. It is not simply a case of no longer issuing orders and ceasing contact as there are certain processes which need to be clearly followed and signed off. These will include the deregistration of the account, the removal from all communication channels such as email distribution lists, elimination from access to any sensitive information on company websites and formal notification to all interested parties such as logistics, technology, marketing and financial departments.

The manual at times forms part of the memorandum of agreement between the retailer and the supplier and it is therefore extremely important that the contents are well understood by both parties.

Style briefing

Successful retailing is largely dependent on clear, accurate communication between the retailer and the supplier and therefore it is crucial that innovation and design takes place as quickly as possible in order that the completed product reaches the market place as quickly as possible. It is no longer just good enough to simply knock off samples from other markets or competitors as the modern consumer through the easy access to the latest trends via the internet are now much more knowledgeable in terms of what is the latest looks and are therefore much more demanding in identifying their wants in order to be as fashion relevant as possible.

Initially the supplier will be briefed conceptually what the product entails. The key information that is communicated is typically a sketch, photo, CAD print or sample with details. The detail will indicate design features, entail fabric and finish qualities, measurement guidelines, size range and ratios, colour ways, pricing and number of deliveries.

It is important that the supplier is provided with as much information as possible that is easily understood by even the most junior staff of the supplier especially in cases where English is not the first language. A principle of over communication and simplification should be followed to ensure complete clarity.

Meetings need to be handled professionally and follow a well prepared agenda and response to any queries have to be concise, well communicated and understanding needs to be tested. Detailed minutes and action plans with time scales attached should be clearly documented. Apart from the formal meetings, ongoing communications can be conducted via Skype and e-mail threads or conference calls.

Other information that can be included on a product specification document apart from the general information above is that pertaining to the inner packing, inserts and labelling. The product packaging minimum requirements and the methodology of the packing must be of a quality to withstand the rigours of transport, varying temperatures, inter warehouse transporting and mechanical handling.

A simple example of a style briefing sheet would look as follows

STYLE BRIEF		DATE	1 March
DEPARTMENT	Ladies T-Shirts	SUPPLIER	ABC
REFERENCE NUMBER	12345678	MNFR NUMBER	44455
DESCRIPTION	Ladies T-Shirt	SILHOUETTE	Top
DELIVERY DATE	20 September	NECKLINE	Round
UNITS	1,000	SLEEVE	Short
SIZES	Small 20% Medium 50% Large 30%	FIT	Regular
COLOURS	White 40% Beige 30% Red 30%	PRICE	129.00
FABRIC / YARN	100% Cotton Single Jersey Quality 12345	PHOTO / SKETCH	
STYLE COMMENTS	Piping must be contrast white.		

Specification pack

The product specification pack is the detailed briefing document managed by the buyer to clearly communicate the product details to the buying, design and technical teams as well as suppliers. The pack serves as a standardised way of clearly capturing all the information associated with a particular product. This is done at the highest level of detail which the supplier will need to achieve in order to meet the requirements

Components of the product specification pack

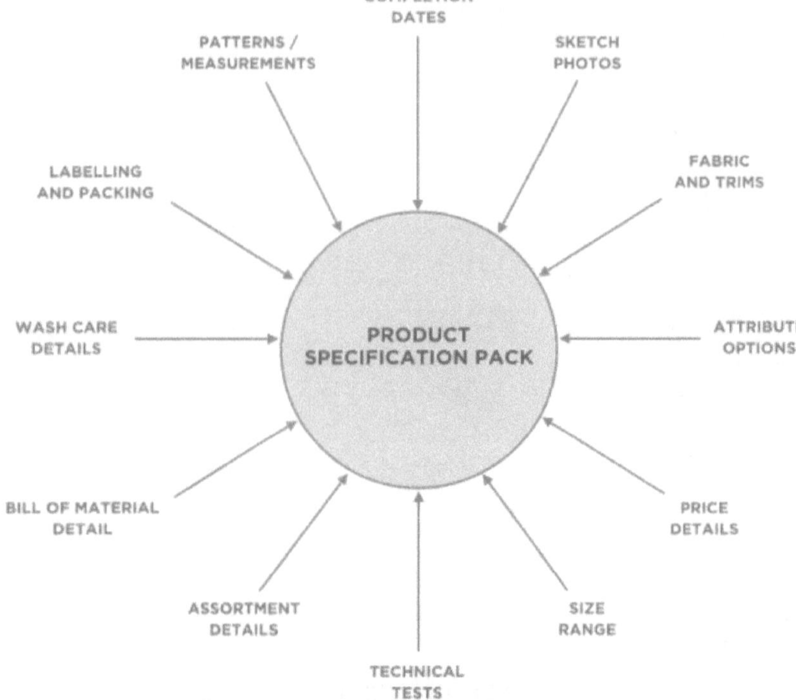

The type of information that should be included is

A sketch or digital picture, the season, the product name and reference number, fabric technical information, fit specifications, size details, quantities, sample sizes, delivery dates, packaging and placement of ticketing, outer packaging requirements, display materials such as hanger reference number, folding guidelines, details of required stitches and seams, trim card and placement details, garment sewing instructions, etc.,

This will enable the supplier to produce a first sample and provide a detailed quote of cost price. The. The technologist will be responsible to provide the bill of materials, the test requirements for the fabric, trim and product, any finishes that are required, safety requirements, fit and block stipulations, wash care instructions as well as provide an assessment together with the sourcing team of the supplier capabilities to produce the product.

The roles and responsibilities of the key buying team members can be depicted as follows

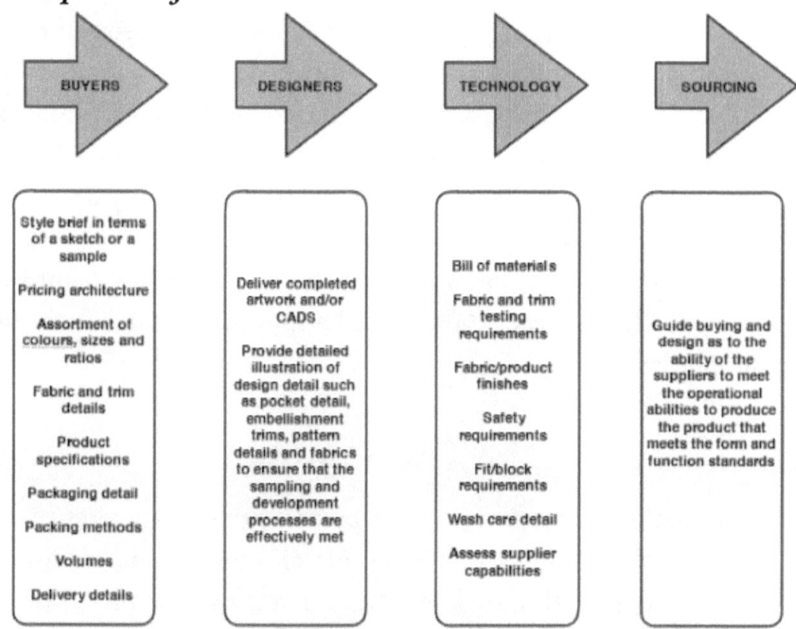

Supplier meetings

Once the product specification pack is formulated for a particular style, the retailer is in a position to initiate detailed meetings in order to prepare the supplier prior to the commencement of the production process.

During the meeting the specification pack will be discussed in detail with specific reference to the style as referenced on the style sheet, any print details or embellishments such as embroidery, accessories and trim details.

Any queries the supplier may have regarding fabric programmes, the logistical aspects, packaging need to be clarified and resolved.

It is extremely important that the meetings are well structured, prepared with an agenda, are clear and professional. Most importantly it is critical that the appropriate people are assigned tasks and completion dates are recorded for follow up.

Live information capture using a laptop and projector is very effective as meetings tend to be shorter, decisions and assignments are clear and results can be managed and tracked. The other advantage is that the publication of the minutes is immediate with the action tasks for those accountable being explicitly defined with completion dates.

It is also important to conduct meetings courteously, respectfully and where applicable be mindful of the culture of the supplier or vendor.

Negotiating

Negotiation is the process whereby through dialogue between two or more parties an agreement is met and the outcome satisfies the needs of both within the boundaries that the situation will allow.

In the retail environment, negotiations typically revolve around topics such as price, garment content, costs, innovation and profitability. The discussions can take place under high pressure where the expectations of both parties are elevated and the rivalry is intense. Often the relationship may be under threat which may or may not add another dimension depending how significant the association is. The opposite of this can be, and the most suitable, where the two parties collaborate to reach the most desired outcome.

To achieve a situation where both parties benefit, requires maturity, a clear understanding of the end objectives with informed discussions by both parties and the development of a plan to achieve a mutual objective.

Notwithstanding the above the supplier and the retailer will still have their own agendas. The supplier will wish to sell as much as he can for the best price while the retailer will want the product for as cheap as possible for the best quality. If the retailer does not have an insightful understanding of the manufacturing process the chances are that they might end up paying too much or sacrificing content.

Negotiating can be a traumatic experience and not all may have the appetite for the heightened discussion. In the case of the supplier there could be a tendency to avoid the confrontation and at times simply give the product to the retailer for the price requested, while the retailer, on the other hand, will similarly pay the supplier's more expensive proposal without exploring all options to get the best deal.

The retailer must always be well prepared with all relevant facts regarding fabric, trim, ratings and costs, prevailing exchange rate trends, wage structures, margin policies including other external and internal factors at hand in order to be able to have an informed sincere discussion. The persuasion process must be done in a way that the argument is convincing and the acceptance by the other party is seen to be mutually beneficial, trustworthy and incorporates the other participant's needs.

The progression of negotiation follows the steps of preparation, conducting the discussion and reviewing the outcomes.

Thorough preparation is critical which requires that the issues and opportunities are identified, prioritised and have a value for both parties. Focus must be on both the hard subjects such as the monetary issues and volumes as well as the softer matters such as perceptions.

Boundaries must be set in the types of outcome broken up into which would ideally like to be achieved, or what is likely to be achieved and thirdly the bare minimum that would be accepted.

Analysis of the environment of both businesses must be well defined in terms of the markets, competitor activities and the supplier capability and technical expertise required. These factors coupled to the trading history and what percentage the supplier is of the retailer's business and what the retailer represents of the supplier's total production or put differently, who needs who the most.

Past performance and consistency as well as the growth potential and the degree of product uniqueness or cost advantages are important leverage factors that are to be taken into consideration.

Key bargaining points for the retailer are cost prices, discounts, volumes, exclusivity, return policies, promotional support, delivery scheduling and any other unique service while the supplier's focus is likely to be the volumes that can be achieved, the highest cost price that will be agreed and the long term sustainability of regular business.

There is not always a satisfactory resolution to negotiation discussions and contingency plans need to be in place as to what alternatives are available should a deadlock situation be reached. These may include the possibility of moving production to different suppliers, reduce volumes and increasing the levels of other substitution ranges, the consideration of sale or return agreements and although not desirable, possibly increasing the selling price above the norm.

Behaviour and strategies during the meeting are extremely important. Asking for more than is expected will give room for negotiation to what is acceptable without simply accepting the first offer. It is also essential to remain flexible and creative in an effort to avoid a deadlock situation. A vital point to bear in mind is that at all costs to avoid haggling as this practice runs the risk of destroying a relationship.

If confrontation does transpire, it should be tactically done and at all costs does not include any personal attack or involve the use of threats and ultimatums. The power of silence should be remembered as it can be effective and if needs be, try and concede to small bits at a time, park potentially unresolvable issues even if it means that the meeting has to be temporarily adjourned.

There are personal factors that can influence the final negotiation. Different partakers follow different processes, they have diverse experience levels as well as possess varying understandings and personality traits which may be unpredictable.

There is an added complexity in dealing with off shore suppliers where there are duties, logistical challenges, and culture and language differences.

Once the negotiations are concluded, a documented summary of the agreements, commitment of resources, capacity to deliver and action plans is absolutely critical to ensure complete understanding. The record will enable an amicable resolution should any misinterpretation which could possibly become a point of dispute at a later stage.

Costings

It goes without saying that cost forms an integral part of the negotiation process. It is therefore imperative that the retailer has a good understanding of the components and the proportions of a costing sheet thus permitting the ability to test the validity and understanding of any costing presented by a supplier.

The cost of a product is broken down into two distinct categories, namely direct product costs and the costs associated in getting the completed product to the retailer.

Factors that will influence the cost of a product will be the size ratio, which if weighted towards the larger sizes will utilise more fabric or affect the wastage of fabric because of a less efficient marking of the lay of fabric on the cutting table.

The level of detail of the styling may not only affect fabric consumption, it will probably also influence the manufacture time or minute rating.

The width of the fabric can also affect the usage of fabric and the general rule is that the narrower the width of fabric the more expensive the product is likely to be. Specialist fabrics tend to be on narrow width such as 110cm while the full width is 148cm. Woven fabrics can be as wide as 160cm.

Plain or printed fabrics will also affect fabric usage particularly where stripes need to be matched on different components such as sleeve and body and is likely to result in more wastage of fabric.

The components of the cost of the products can be divided into those that are considered to be fixed such as raw materials, overheads which include services such as design, technology and logistics and those that are variable which are in the main the constituents that are squeezed down to meet the demands of the retailer like wages, working hours and production methods.

Packaging costs will also vary for different types of product. The size of the cartons required to transport the product is determined by the dimensions of height and width that must protect and accommodate the garment comfortably. The in store presentation requirements will also affect the overall cost from the point of view that allowance may be needed for hangers as well as additional swing tickets.

Where goods are imported, duties need to be taken into consideration. Duties are normally determined against the free on board value or in other words the cost to place it on the deck of the ship. They can also be calculated as ex works which is the cost as at the completion of production.

Exchange rates are a critical factor. The option to purchase currency ahead of time at a fixed rate to finance the cost provides the peace of mind that the costs will be stable even if the day to day rates fluctuate. If currency is not bought ahead but goods are purchased at the prevailing rates the retailer may be forced to revise selling prices to ensure the achievement of the target margin.

Different categories of products attract different tariff duties at the receiving country depending on country of origin and manufacture as well as protection policies of local production.

The cost to transport the goods from the place of manufacture will vary for local goods or from the port by the clearing agent, depending on the location of the retailer in relation to the supplier or port, the size of the cartons or container and the mode of transport. Included in this section would be freight and warehousing charges.

The typical elements of a product costing and examples of approximate proportions will be

ELEMENT	DEPENDENCY	CATEGORY
TRANSPORT 5%	Different methods of transport used.	Transport / landing 20%
DUTY 30 - 40%	Taxes levied against the import of goods as specified by the local government.	
SUPPLIER MARGIN 10%	Supplier margin can vary between 5% and 15%.	Production costs 80%
WASH AND TRIMS 5%	Costs allocated to special processes or trims.	
PACKAGING 7%	Total cost of all packaging, including presentation.	
LABOUR 28%	The standard minute rates will differ from country to country, depending on operational complexity.	
FABRIC AND MATERIAL 50%	Will be influenced by the garment rating, which will dictate how much fabric is used to manufacture the garment.	

In addition to the product costs as outlined above there are other costs that need to be taken into account in order to get product to market. These can be categorised basically into two categories, firstly being additional costs to the supplier such as the base overhead costs being the total for rent, electricity, administration costs and the like that will always be there and which must be apportioned per product unit.

The second category can be described as being unrelated to the product directly that have to be paid. The main type of such costs are settlement discount agreements, marketing contributions, finance costs and royalties. These together with the product costs will deliver the final cost of the garment.

Points to note in the review of costs are in cases where the supplier throws in vague and unsubstantiated reasons to justify increases. It is essential that the retailer tests such requests to ensure they carry merit.

A typical instance is where the statement is made that wages have gone up and a new costing is proposed. A cross check is required to determine the proportion of what labour represents of the total costing. In the above example this would be the 28% for labour and apply the increase to this part and reconcile to the proposal.

Where increases are attributed to material increases an effort should be made to investigate the trend in the industry and do some comparisons even if they may be a bit crude. If your research shows that the increase is not in line with the trend, the supplier should be encouraged to find a better source and not to pass on the cost of their inefficiencies.

The use of exchange rate fluctuations to motivate cost price changes is more easily resolved as the average movement can be tracked over a period of time and applied. It is a possibility that in fact there might have been an improvement. Foreign currency could also have an influence depending at what price the supplier or retailer may have covered forward.

If the retailer's volumes are increasing significantly the opportunity exists to negotiate a discount in cost price to share the benefits of the improved scale of efficiencies. A point to note is that while this practice is not discouraged, the smaller retailer may not be able to finance the larger volumes of product or growth based incentives. Even with the benefit of a greater margin, the viability remains to be dependent on the organic growth of the chain, for example, the addition of new stores in order to accommodate the higher buying volumes.

A costing approach which is often employed by retailers is that of requesting appropriate suppliers to tender for a product. In order that this is done fairly and equitably the exact same specifications need to be provided to the potential suppliers. Cross costing comparison between suppliers is a popular option where there are large programmes up for grabs and is unlikely to be used for once off high fashion inputs.

For a retailer to commit to high volume programmes, it is a key requisite that the potential suppliers fulfil some basic requirements in that they must be financially stable, have a reliable track record in terms of delivery performance, provide consistent quality with up to date compliancy audits and will be able to cope with the required volumes which could include the agreement to hold a minimum stock holding. The supplier should also be flexible enough to be able to make styling changes to the product where necessary.

The key stipulations for use with cross costing or tenders which will be provided is a detailed style sheet, comprehensive specifications of fabric and trims, the garment measurements with the range of sizes, volumes, a target cost price, packaging requirements and packing methods, delivery dates or production flow.

CASE STUDY

CH Clothing Company have been presented with a costing of 110.00 for the formal core long sleeve shirt in their range which is manufactured locally How this is derived based on the costing components needs to be investigated in order to ensure that the cost is realistic.

CHALLENGE #37

The fabric and components contribute 45%, labour is 25%, and packaging is 10% while distribution and warehousing is 5%.

1. What % margin does the supplier make?
2. What monetary value does this represent?
3. What % does the production costs contribute to the total cost?

ORDERING

After the negotiations are completed and the decision to award the production of a style to the supplier is taken, an order has to be drafted to reflect the commitment to the supplier.

The signed order for the supplier is created and placed by the retailer for the entire season in the case of a continuity product or possibly monthly for input styles. It is imperative that it must be done timeously to ensure the required completion date is realistically achievable and the production lead time required will be determined by careful critical path production management.

While the order is in essence a contractual document it will be subject to the overall terms and conditions that are entered into in a memorandum of agreement that is drawn up separately when a manufacturer is appointed as a certified supplier. Production can only commence once the final approved order is in the possession of the supplier.

The contract or the order is the document that details the terms by which the retailer takes ownership of the goods in exchange or payment of an agreed price.

The timing of orders is done according to the range plan guidelines and each supplier will be provided with an extract specific to them for the season. This production programme will indicate the style details, quantities, size ratios and colour specifications which will enable them to plan the production capacity and will be used as the point of reference during follow up production progress meetings. Each style will also have a corresponding style specification sheet which confirm the costs, pack quantities, labels and tickets, wash and care details, testing requirements and the fabric as well as component information.

Orders may be amended where required. These adjustments are normally for quantities, dates, prices and size ratios. The changes need to be recorded on the contract and refer to the date of the alteration as well as the nature of the change.

It is advisable that any style changes require the order to be cancelled and be replaced by a new order as in essence it is a different product.

The order can have two status phases where a pre-production contract enables the supplier to procure fabrics, components, labelling and packaging and make a pre-production or pre shipment sample which will be submitted to the retailer for approval. The sample will serve as the set standard of quality that will be referred to should any disputes evolve in production or in stores.

Production may only commence once a final approved order is received by the supplier.

Documented programmes of continuity lines for the full season may serve as an authorised arrangement from which the supplier will be able to order the raw materials and components but they will only be able to commence production of agreed quantities, for example, for six weekly time periods upon the receipt of an approved contract. This gives the retailer the flexibility to make adjustments based on current performance. Such amendments may take the form of changes to quantities, size ratios and colour quantities.

Dependent on whether the supplier is local or offshore the delivery requirements need to be clearly outlined with all relevant contact details, delivery stipulations, carton markings and delivery addresses.

In the case of a local supplier, delivery is normally to a designated warehouse at an approved time. Off shore suppliers may have to deliver to an offshore centralised consolidation centre where the goods will be amalgamated by shipping agents into containers prior to shipping. Payment will be made in the foreign currency and will be dictated by the international commercial (INCO) terms applied.

Common INCO terms for the payment of imported goods will be FOB (Sea Freight) which is where payment is prior to shipment by sea either by bank wire or a letter of credit. The purchaser's bank releases payment upon receipt of certain documentation such as the bill of lading, packing lists or commercial invoice and is due when the goods are loaded on the ship and ownership is then transferred to the retailer. If the INCO term is FCA it carries the same conditions as FOB except that the transportation is by air.

CFR (Sea and Air Freight) describes the situation where the supplier is responsible for the costs of transport to the destination port. While ownership only transfers when the goods reach the destination, the retailer is responsible for the goods while they are in transit and therefore they would have to take out insurance for this period. If the supplier does this then the INCO term applied is CIF (cost, insurance, freight).

Added to the costs are government duties which can be applied in the form of a percentage dependent on the various customs categories that the product falls into.

In terms of air freight it should be noted that the cost is often prohibitive as it is dictated by volume and weight and therefore is usually only applied to small and high value items or where an urgent stock need is required in order to meet a launch date.

When placing orders for imports it is critical to take into account the lead times that need to be added on to ensure the required delivery and launch dates are met. Lead time can be described loosely as the time that it takes for product to be delivered from the factory to the back door of the retailer's warehouse or distribution centre. This becomes increasingly complex when the factory is off shore as there are a whole host of additional activities that have to take place before the retailer eventually receives the goods.

Pre shipment activities may involve the delivery to an off shore consolidation centre where different orders may be combined to make the full use of a container cost effective. Part deliveries in different containers can also make the consolidation and sequence of packing more complicated where there are different orders possibly also for different retailers.

In terms of the pre shipment critical path that needs to be adhered to prior to shipment is triggered by the supplier's confirmation that this will be met about three weeks before the ship date and approximately a week later the forwarder will advise the vessel and booking details at which time the supplier will send the pre shipment sample to the retailer with quality audit reports to request approval to ship.

A typical order for imported and local products will probably be as follows

ORDER

RETAILER XYZ

ORDER NO.
SUPPLIER
SUPPLIER REFERENCE
PAYMENT TERMS
DELIVERY METHOD
DELIVER TO

DATE
ORDER STATUS — Pre production / Production
COMPLETE/SHIP DATE
LAUNCH DATE
PACK QUANTITY
TOTAL QUANTITY
COST VALUE
SELLING VALUE

SKU NUMBER	STYLE NUMBER	STYLE DESCRIPTION	COLOUR	TOTAL COLOUR UNITS	SIZE	TOTAL SIZE UNITS	COST PRICE	SELLING PRICE
100023564	12345	Basic t-shirt	White	1000	S	200	45.00	99.99
100023565					M	400	45.00	99.99
100023566					L	300	50.00	110.00
100023567					XL	100	50.00	110.00
100023568	12345	Basic t-shirt	Black	2000	S	400	45.00	99.99
100023569					M	800	45.00	99.99
100023570					L	600	50.00	110.00
100023571					XL	200	50.00	110.00

BUYER SIGN   MANAGEMENT SIGN

MERCHANDISER SIGN   SUPPLIER SIGN   DATE

The information typically included on the order is as follows and will be stored on a data base system for any interested party that needs to access the detail.

Supplier reference number and name

Order number

Date that order was raised
Port of loading
Shipment date and launch dates
Shipping method
Method of payment
Payment terms
Point of delivery
Style number
Style description
Colour break down and quantity
Labelling instructions
Special terms or conditions of trade
SKU number
Size breakdown
Quantities
Cost Price less any negotiated discounts
Selling Price
Number of cartons
Carton dimensions
Number of units per inner pack
Number of inner packs per outer carton

Signatures of authorization to buy are most commonly those of the buyer, merchandiser and a member of senior management. The omission of any of the signatures could result in the order being rendered invalid in the case of a disagreement. A supplier signature is often the rule but the acceptance of the order is in essence the recognition of all the terms and conditions of the order.

It is not uncommon for planning production schedules or provisional orders to be handed over to the supplier prior to the issuing of an official order, particularly in the case of replenishment product where the supplier needs to plan capacity requirements, order raw materials and components but this is by no means the go ahead to commence production. Without the completed signed order no knife may be put to the fabric.

The higher level order may be supplemented by a detailed specification pack and a critical path management document that serves as an appendage to the order and reflect the details and quality references of the fabric and components, sample submission requirements, technical tests, labelling instructions, packaging reference numbers and specifications.

The buying and merchandising team will use the basic information to interrogate orders at any time to check, monitor and if required will amend the orders which may be, for example, quantity or date related. Other areas of operation or parties will also need to have access to orders in order that their activities are completed timeously to safeguard that the final completion date is met.

Technology has to utilise the detail to ensure in the process of managing the critical path that all tests, quality control during the manufacturing process, garment fittings and rail samples are completed timeously.

The finance department need to know all the costing details and terms of payment as well as the proposed selling price to ensure that there is sufficient cash flow available to enable payment and be able to monitor the achievement of the gross profit margins.

The IT departments need to be aware of all orders for the provision of the SKU numbers as well as cater for the generation of the swing tickets or labels that are attached to the garments indicating the style number, colour, size and price detail which are either sent to the suppliers in bulk or the data files are transmitted to those suppliers that have the facilities to generate their own SKU tickets.

The distribution centre must have sight of the orders in the pipeline to assess the size of proposed deliveries going forward to ensure that they are in a position to plan sufficient resources in terms of staffing, equipment, space capacity and that sufficient transport is booked to deliver the goods speedily to stores.

The space capacity requirements both in the warehouse and stores will depend largely on the packing configurations in terms of the storage outer carton which is how the goods will be stored, allocated and transported to stores and the inner packs which are otherwise known as the saleable unit that will be presented to the potential consumer.

Examples of packing configuration below where selling units of t-shirts is singles and are packed ten in an outer carton and where socks selling units is in a three pack and there are ten three packs in the outer carton

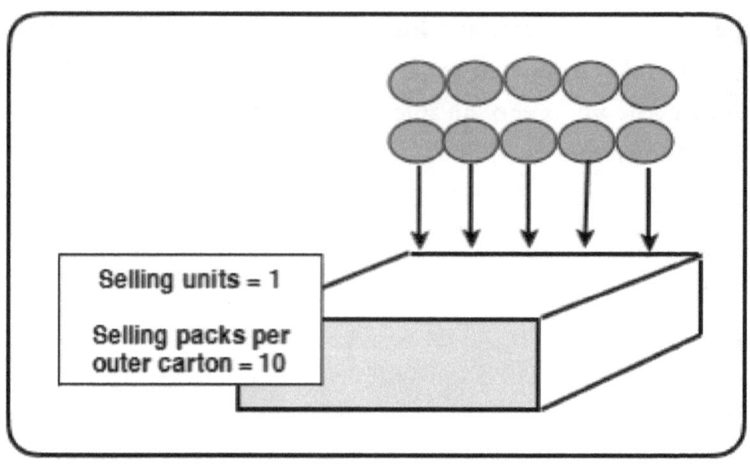

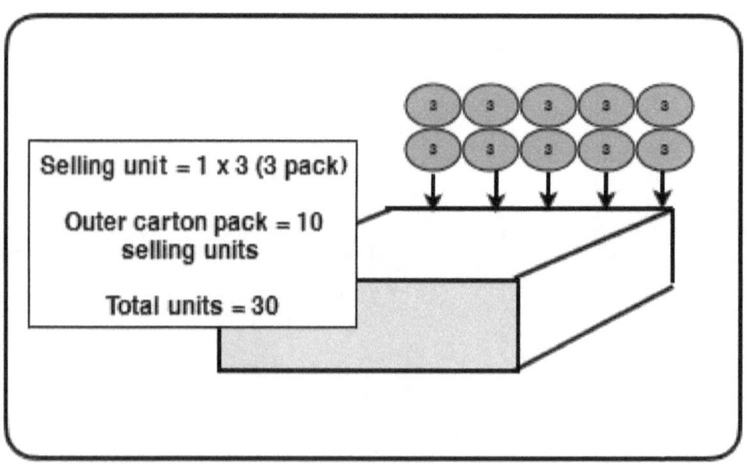

CASE STUDY

CH Clothing Company uses varying approaches of storing and transporting its product so that they arrive at their destination in a pristine state and maintaining the quality specified quality standards. The selection of the mode will be determined by the type of product and the cost effectiveness of the model.

CHALLENGE #38

In the example of the formal shirt the product is displayed on the counter in a branded presentation poly propylene bag with all the relevant ticketing detail. Describe the most appropriate methodology with the reason why it would be so.

CRITICAL PATH MANAGEMENT

Critical path management is undoubtedly one of the key philosophies that needs to be applied in production management in order to have control and knowledge of the work flow in the production of garments. This achieved by the setting up of a timeline that reflects the anticipated critical deadlines that have to be achieved in order to meet the required delivery date of the order and being completely aware of the impact of late deliveries of fabric and components on the realisation of this objective. Without the knowledge of all statuses the consequence could well be the late deliveries with the application of penalties or even worse the cancellation of orders.

Through the management the entire flow of product workflow through the view of progress from concept to completion allows the effective planning of tasks and reallocation of resources to minimises bottlenecks, identify due dates and milestones as well as highlight areas where attention is required. And thereby keep suppliers on schedule as well as encourages collaboration between the different teams. A major benefit is that critical path management allows management to move away from day to day reactive management into a more strategic management role aligned with strategic business objectives.

Ideally a critical path management tool should possess characteristics such as flexibility that enables the tool to be configured to meet the customised requirements of the user. Alerts should be built in to notify stakeholders directly through SMS, emails or pings and Information should be able to be automatically rolled up with an analytical ability to be able to drill down to prescribed levels or issues.

The interface ought to be user friendly and easy to learn, easy to update and where web based tools exist they should be compatible and easily accessible within a range of internet speeds, browsers and levels of internet sophistication that allows global interaction with suppliers in order to track the progress of the product from the sampling stage through to delivery. As supply chains grow in complexity with increased production volumes and links in the supply chain information visibility is imperative in order to facilitate complete transparency while also highlighting the ramifications of poor decision making and poor capacity management.

Some of the software tools that are available in the market place which assist in the monitoring of production progress and are accessible to all stakeholders do come at a cost and albeit expensive the benefits of the investment may well be justified.

Alternatively if the product is too expensive it is well worth developing one's own instrument even though the tool may well be cumbersome and more complex to apply but at least it will provide rough idea of the lead times required for the procurement of fabrics and components for the completion of orders and therefore In order to guarantee the on time launch of the product and the management of the path of product development. Without this the retailer ends up flying blind and often only finds out about delays from the supplier close to the expected delivery date when it is invariably too late to take corrective action. It is not uncommon to hear of the cancellation of large volume contracts worth great values as a result of the relatively low cost care labels not being available on time and thus the completion of the delivery date is compromised. It is not only the physical components that can cause issues the added value outsourced services such as embroideries, pattern making or packaging can in the same manner impact the delivery status if they are not completed on time.

Unfortunately with multiple versions of documents such as cost sheets, design samples and supplier scorecards in differing formats which provide an inadequate platform to share information can result in a lack of awareness into potential supply chain problems and an inability to provide early warnings and synchronise real time responsiveness.

All stakeholders involved in the process, which includes the buyers, suppliers, product technologists, fabric technologists and commercial management need to focus on the critical path management of the product.

The key stages or milestones which are in the main controlled by the buyers and technologists that need to be scrutinised are the style briefing and finalisation, colour approval, fit approval, bulk test of fabrics and components, approval of the pre-production sample, pre-production meetings with the supplier and final approval of the pre-shipment or rail sample prior to production at which point the product development can be considered complete and the launch date is able to be confirmed.

The monitoring of the process needs to documented and highlighted in some form in order that key players are able to measure the actual accomplishment of tasks compared to the required completion dates. If collaboration and communication is ineffective, bottlenecks are likely to occur, production and delivery deadlines may be missed, and penalties will be applied with the resultant squeezing of margins. The purpose of such reports is not only to ensure that the critical milestones are met on time but also serve as a reference for meetings to identify possible delays and decide what actions need to be taken to improve or correct the situation.

In principle the lead times are measured in weeks and the relevant dates are attached starting from launch date which represents zero days and progressively working backwards taking the time for the completion of each stage into account and ending up where the no later than date for the starting style brief stage is determined.

The format of the critical path action plan may well vary from retailer to retailer dependant on the level of detail the measurement takes place in terms of each operation.

The hierarchy of the reporting and performance measurement is usually done at style level and all the styles for a department can be rolled up to departmental level and then up to group level. These together with supplier extracts and other filters make for effective performance management of both the retail teams and the supplier.

An example of a basic critical path management tool which highlights the key milestones, time line and progress monitoring with analytical properties is illustrated below.

PRODUCT DEVELOPMENT MANAGEMENT							Style Brief		Style Finalised		Colour Approved		Fit Approved	
Supplier	Grp	Dept.	Style	Colour		Total	Complete	In-complete	Complete	In-complete	Complete	In-complete	Complete	In-complete
abcd	1	123	44445	Black	Units	1000	900	100	800	200	900	100	750	250
					%	100	90%	10%	80%	20%	90%	10%	75%	25%
					Weeks	39			28		24		11	
					Date	10-Oct			17-Dec		15-Jan		15-Apr	
Supplier	Grp	Dept.	Style	Colour		Total	Complete	In-complete	Complete	In-complete	Complete	In-complete	Complete	In-complete
abcd	1	123	55555	White	Units	1500	1300	200	1400	100	1450	50	1500	0
					%	100	87%	13%	93%	7%	97%	3%	100%	0%
					Weeks	39			28		24		11	
					Date	10-Oct			17-Dec		15-Jan		15-Apr	
Supplier	Grp	Dept.	Style	Colour		Total	Complete	In-complete	Complete	In-complete	Complete	In-complete	Complete	In-complete
bcde	2	124	55556	Yellow	Units	2000	1500	500	1400	600	1600	400	1800	200
					%	100	75%	25%	70%	30%	80%	20%	90%	10%
					Weeks	39			28		24		11	
					Date	10-Nov			17-Jan		15-Feb		15-May	
Supplier	Grp	Dept.	Style	Colour		Total	Complete	In-complete	Complete	In-complete	Complete	In-complete	Complete	In-complete
cdef	3	128	44445	Green	Units	1000	700	300	900	100	800	200	750	250
					%	100	70%	30%	90%	10%	80%	20%	75%	25%
					Weeks	39			28		24		11	
					Date	10-Dec			17-Feb		15-Mar		15-Jun	

PRODUCT DEVELOPMENT MANAGEMENT							Pre-production sample & supplier meeting		Pre-shipment sample		Launch Date	
Supplier	Grp	Dept.	Style	Colour		Total	Complete	In-complete	Complete	In-complete	Complete	In-complete
abcd	1	123	44445	Black	Units	1000	750	250	750	250	750	250
					%	100	75%	25%	75%	25%	75%	25%
					Weeks	39	8		2		0	
					Date	10-Oct	06-May		17-Jun		01-Jul	
Supplier	Grp	Dept.	Style	Colour		Total	Complete	In-complete	Complete	In-complete	Complete	In-complete
abcd	1	123	55555	White	Units	1500	1500	0	1450	50	1500	0
					%	100	100%	0%	97%	3%	100%	0%
					Weeks	39	8		2		0	
					Date	10-Oct	06-May		17-Jun		01-Jul	
Supplier	Grp	Dept.	Style	Colour		Total	Complete	In-complete	Complete	In-complete	Complete	In-complete
bcda	2	124	55556	Yellow	Units	2000	1800	200	1700	300	1900	100
					%	100	90%	10%	85%	15%	95%	5%
					Weeks	39	8		2		0	
					Date	10-Nov	06-Jun		17-Jul		01-Aug	
Supplier	Grp	Dept.	Style	Colour		Total	Complete	In-complete	Complete	In-complete	Complete	In-complete
cdef	3	128	44445	Green	Units	1000	850	150	950	50	950	50
					%	100	85%	15%	95%	5%	95%	5%
					Weeks	39	8		2		0	
					Date	10-Dec	06-Jul		17-Aug		01-Sep	

QUALITY MANAGEMENT

Quality is defined as the combination of design and properties that are required at an acceptable level to perform the ideal form and function requisite to serve the market for which it is intended. In the textile and apparel industry the quality is calculated in terms of quality and standard of fibres, yarns, fabric construction, colour fastness and the final finished product.

Quality control starts with ensuring that the fabric being utilised meets the required specifications to be transformed into a perfect garment and therefore needs to be managed and inspected for faults which are marked. The length and width of fabric have to be checked to ensure that they meet the specified measurements and thereby do not affect the cutting table lay. It is important that the fabric is inspected upon receipt and meets the finished width and stability while the garment must be sound with regards to seam construction and the stitch forming action.

The supplier will need to have the fabric and trims tested by a recognised laboratory to record that they meet the weight, width and yarn specifications. Tests also need to focus on the performance of fabrics such as rub tests or how the fabric reacts in a washing machine in terms of colour fastness and shrinkage.

In the manufacture of garments the objective is to achieve the right final product on time. The final product specifications are dependent on the level of the quality control present in sampling and development departments that from samples to completed production, including layout and process stipulations, the construction parameters and measurement of performance. In order that this done effectively robust recording systems should be in place as well as checklists for the supervisors to logically ensure that all critical points are covered and are within the set down tolerance levels are measured as per performance analysis and reporting.

Reporting will outline results of quality control during garment assembly, number of marks and stains on garments, analysis of the cost of faults and directives as how to improve garment cleanliness.

It is vital that proper quality control is applied in order that the product presents well on the shop floor, fits well, wears well, washes well, is functional and represents value for money to avoid the loss of sales through customer returns or the depletion of units during production which results in under deliveries and ultimately lost sales. The points of quality control are conducted throughout the supply chain process which includes those prior to production, during in line production, at dispatch stage and on the shop sales floor.

A quality controller needs to possess certain abilities that will equip them to ensure that a thorough and complete monitor is done. The key attribute required is that of the need to pay attention to detail along with assertiveness and transparency. Tasks have to be conducted professionally and ethically. The incumbent must be prepared to be open minded and consider alternative points of view. The nature of the job requires tact and diplomacy and in certain situations the quality controller is required to be culturally sensitive. Decisiveness together with collaboration is paramount to ensure that quality standards are maximised.

The various steps of quality control and types of checks in the manufacturing process is illustrated below

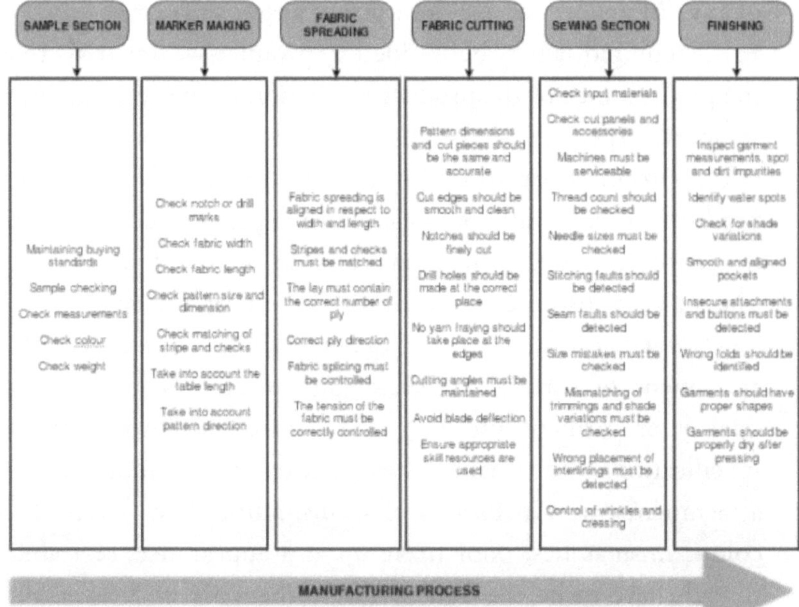

The purpose of the pre-production meeting conducted for every style is to set the standards to which the quality will be measured during production.

The pre-production sample serves as the basis of discussion and all key stakeholders will be present from both the retailer and the supplier. Technology representatives and the buying team must attend together with supplier teams to determine the criteria for sewing, finishing, fabric, trim, quality assurance, cutting, production and packaging management. At these meetings the technical requirements are stipulated and agreed for the make-up, sewing and thread combinations, the special methods that are needed to handle trims in bulk production, the wash and product finishing standards as well as the packaging and shipment methods. Any special processes out of the ordinary must be well documented and the minutes of the meeting must be recorded and signed off by all participants to ensure there are clear reference standards in the event of any difference that may transpire at a later stage.

If required it may be decided to produce wearer trials to assess the performance of the product in relation to the technological test standards especially where physical or chemical laboratory tests are not appropriate or it is not able to be spot checked in bulk production. All in all the purpose of the pre-production meeting is to identify risk areas which may result in product failure or possible injury to the customer and establish preventative measures.

During production the quality audits must include the assessment of care labels, packaging, price tags, colour and the quality of garment finishing and conformance to measurement specifications. The main visual checks will include the button attachments, non-inclusions of seams, fabric flaws, elastic failures, colour mismatches, poor make up and appearance, sew ability of threads have to be checked to ensure there are no broken threads, evidence of skipped stitches and that the stitch spacing is balanced. Safety issues such as needle points or staples in the product are also watched out for.

Final inspection will include will focus on ensuring the consistent colour shading of all parts of the garment, that the garment is balanced in terms of collar, pockets and cuff attachments as well as the critical measurements and weight are within the acceptable tolerances and that all accessories are securely applied and are functional.

It is important that the audit report is completed speedily in order that preventative measures can be documented and action plans are implemented. The number of garments that must be measured and assessed is determined by agreeing the sample survey percentage that will represent the total quantity and what tolerances are allowed before rejection takes place.

The amount to be inspected may vary from no inspection to 100% inspection and may or may not include random inspections. Statistical sampling may be determined that would represent the amount that could be extrapolated to be the character of the total quantity.

It is assumed that 5000 pieces are purchased with the breakdown and sample survey quantities as follows

	WHITE	BLACK
SIZE M	1 500	1 200
SIZE L	1 500	800

Of the 5 000 units, it is agreed to check 30% visually and measure 10%

VISUALLY INSPECTED	WHITE	BLACK
SIZE M	450	360
SIZE L	450	240

MEASURED	WHITE	BLACK
SIZE M	150	120
SIZE L	150	80

Graphically the inspection sample can be depicted as follows

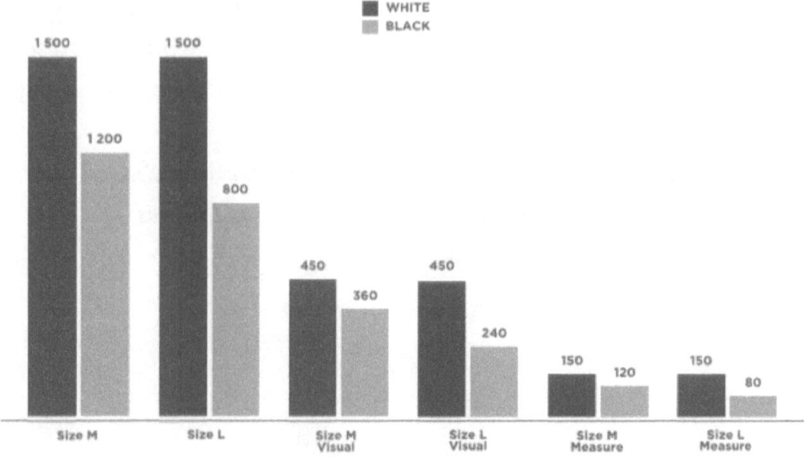

A typical measurement sheet will look like the example below

QUALITY MEASUREMENT AUDIT REPORT														
DEPARTMENT	XYZ	STYLE	STYLE DESCRIPTION											
COLOUR	WHITE	SIZE	SMALL				MEDIUM				LARGE			
OP NO	DESCRIPTION		SPEC (cm)	1	2	3	SPEC (cm)	1	2	3	SPEC (cm)	1	2	3
1	Across front		35				37.5				40			
2	1/2 chest		48				53				56			
3	1/2 hem		46				51				53			
4	Shoulder		13.5				14				16			
5	Overarm sleeve		18				21				23			
6	Underarm sleeve		7.5				9				11			
7	Across back		38				40				43			
8	Neck drop front		8.2				9.5				11			
9	Neck width		18.2				19				21			
10	Neck drop back		1.5				2				2.5			
INSPECTED BY			TOTAL MEASURED					COMMENTS						
			RESULTS											
SUPPLIER			Out of tolerance											
			In tolerance											

In addition to the production line audits it is also necessary to conduct quality inspection in stores which apart from identifying and resolving quality issues there is the added advantage of interacting with sales teams and share knowledge and learnings from those at the coal face who interact with the customer.

Apart from the skill levels and components which may affect the quality of a garment there are other factors which need to be taken into account. For Chinese suppliers it is important to consider production which takes place close to the Chinese New Year holidays. Not only is it the completion of orders prior to the commencement of holidays which could put pressure on the rate of production the other real risk is the start-up time taken by factories after the holidays. This is often a slow process due to the fact that many of the workers who travel inland to their villages are tardy in returning back to work or take extended leave which results in broken production and the use of lower skill levels to complete more complex operations. This phenomenon is part and parcel of doing business with Chinese suppliers and contingencies need to be put in place as invariably suppliers who do not have the capacity to complete orders on time which were optimistically accepted as well as the fact that raw material suppliers experience the same phenomenon also puts excessive strain on the production lines to meet deadlines timeously. In summary careful planning with built in safety stocks to ensure continuity of supply to the stores is paramount.

Environmental circumstances such as storms which prevent ships docking or deviate from their routes, power failures, strikes, goods being held up at customs or other unforeseen events can delay the arrival of raw materials and finished product and may impact eventually on the timing, quality and quantity being delivered.

SUPPLIER PERFORMANCE MANAGEMENT

In order that supplier performance will be at consistently high standards there must be a solid foundation of core requirements in order to achieve the objective at hand. While it is important that performance is influenced external environmental factors and the customers that are served the most influential factor that impacts the operational efficiencies is undoubtedly the management of the organisation.

While the day to day measures are important, some of which may be minor such as containing canteen costs, time keeping, rental and logistical costs and the like it is critical that management focus on the longer term issues such as staff training and development, process control, maintenance, production planning and the consistent achievement of set down performance indicators.

Such a set of performance indicators are cascaded down through the organisation and as a result each employee is constantly aware of how they are being evaluated and whether they are adequately meeting the standards for which they are held accountable. The pay structure, including bonus incentives should be in place based on the achievement of the recognised KPI's.

It is equally important that management maintain their visibility on the production floor and interact at all levels in order to keep motivation at high levels with good communication and also when they relate to retail customers they are able to do so with knowledge of the hands on challenges.

Safety has to be promoted to the fullest with respected and assertive safety teams in place that have the support of senior management, and all staff should be equipped with appropriate effective personal equipment.

Research and development departments should continually be innovating, testing and improving products while apart from a robust preventative maintenance programme the reinvestment in the company by the owners is key to maintaining regular customers and attracting new ones.

The objective of achieving zero defects and delivering optimum quality is done through the building and sustaining of relationships by continually assessing, anticipating and fulfilling stated and implied needs.

It is important that service level agreements are set up front and are understood and committed to by all. SLA's clearly define the clients can expect from service providers and outline what their responsibilities are. This ensures protection for both parties and promotes beneficial long term relationships.

The risks that can be encountered are aggravated in certain situations such as with the movement of strategic product to new plants, or existing suppliers being utilised for different types of products which they may not adapt well to. The allocation of high volumes with a minimal quality assurance infrastructure in place as well the ability to meet critical launch dates require that performance measurement is critical for early identification of any potential failure.

A tough line has to be taken on dealing with substandard delivery and quality. Data collected from various sources needs to be accurate and reliable especially where a penalty system is applied for non-performance.

Customer returns have to be analysed and criteria put in place which may result in a penalty being applied for the number of returns in the form of a sliding scale. The analysis of the most common faults also highlights the areas of quality which need to be addressed.

The late or under completion of orders or non-conformance to size and colour ratios translate directly to lost sales and can be assessed and penalized either through a direct fine or a trade discount and possibly a sale or return arrangement. A word of caution with regard to a sale or return arrangement is although the goods that are not sold after a period of time can be returned, the sales of these goods may impact the performance of other similar products that are on offer at the same time which is not always taken into account.

Late deliveries measurement ensures that completion is on time according to the critical path. A typical example of a penalty is one which is on a sliding percentage scale of discount for every week that the delivery date is missed up to a pre-determined stage after which the order faces cancellation.

Lead times can be measured based on the time taken for the supplier to deliver to the retailer's back door. A realistic number of days can be set as a tolerance for the delivery of product based on mode of transport and distance from the retailer thereafter penalties may be activated. It does happen that the supplier may report the full availability of product but in reality part of the order may still be in production and the delivery may take place in the form of a number of split drops which would be unacceptable and is almost equivalent to fraud.

Order fill percentage represents what was actually delivered in comparison to what was ordered. Any deviation to this translates into lost sales from the lowest size level as the retailer is not receiving what was ordered.

Ticketing must be accurate as an incorrect ticket which is scanned in will be captured erroneously on the stock data base and sales at the till point will be incorrect thus distorting the product's data integrity which will only be rectified once a physical product count is completed. Sample checks upon receipt of product will help identify such errors and enforce the implementation of a penalty system. Often the attachment of incorrect SKU tickets could be as a result of poor communication and disciplines between the retailer and supplier, poor control at suppliers or non-destruction of old SKU tickets at times of a price changeover.

The advantage of a controlled performance management system is the quick identification of poor performing suppliers. The more efficient suppliers welcome the performance measurements as it assists supplier management to more effectively manage their business, assign accountability and also be able to assess their contribution to sales performance and strive to benefit from the advantage of incentive schemes applied by the retailer where they exist.

It is not surprising that the garment manufacturers are in turn also applying penalty systems and clauses in the contracts with their raw material suppliers such as the fabric mills and trimmings suppliers.

It is preferable that a reporting system is entrenched and is published on a monthly basis to the supplier and the internal buying groups. Such reports form a good basis of discussion in meetings with the supplier and alerts the buying team to potential problems that may be evolving. It should therefore be no surprise to the supplier if the need to apply penalties is necessary as sometimes the monetary value of the penalties could pose a major financial risk to a supplier.

Supplier meetings where qualitative feedback and their performance measures are discussed encourages commitment between the two parties and promotes collaboration. At such meetings the sales performance of the products specific to the supplier is analysed and understood. This may lead to the formulation of action plans where required and may include cooperation and coordination of marketing activities which could comprise of cooperative advertising and media campaigns. Part of the discussion would include the sharing of information regarding consumer, product, market trends and new innovations.

CASE STUDY

CH Clothing Company apply supplier performance measurement in order to gain the maximum benefit from the advantages that accompany them.

CHALLENGE #39

The overall advantages that are delivered with the application of supplier performance systems are numerous. List five benefits that will be gained.

It is as important that the retailer probes their suppliers in terms of their expectations in the relationship with the various operational and management structures of the retailer. This can be conveniently done through a scheduled survey, possibly annually or seasonally, an example of which is outlined below.

Buying

Is it easy to communicate with the buying team?

Are you clear in terms of what they expect from you with regard to costs and deadlines?

Are the general terms and conditions understood?

Do you have any suggestions to improve the relationship?

Quality and compliance

Do you receive clear guidelines and know what standards need to be followed?

Do you receive sufficient feedback?

Are approvals of samples received timeously?

Do you have any suggestions to improve the relationship?

Product development

Do you receive clear briefing and information about new products

Do we take into account the configuration and specifications of your production processes?

Do you have any suggestions for improvement?

Relationships

Is there sufficient interaction with higher levels of management

Do teams visit frequently enough?

When teams visit you, do they behave in a professional manner?

Our service providers

Are the courier services meeting expected standards?

How efficient are our freight forwarders?

Is our QC audit firms applying similar standards as ourselves?

PRODUCT ALLOCATION

Once production is complete the supplier will advise via a report what volumes by size and colour are complete and packaged ready for dispatch to the addresses as stipulated by the retailer.

In a perfect world the intake will match the volumes as indicated on the intake line in the original plan as highlighted earlier. However, sales will never be exactly as expected as the customers do not have prior knowledge of the plans and will always buy differently. Coupled to this the amount of over or under production due to a reject factor could result in availabilities being higher or lower than what the supplier was meant to make and therefore the actual closing stock at the end of each period will definitely vary to the expectation. Markdown values are also continually different to that planned.

Stocks and sales are the anchor targets that are consistently aimed for with the intake being the balancing variable to bring the plan back in line. In the hypothetical exercise below done for Month 1 of the plan it is illustrated as to how the intake is manipulated over the four weeks of the month in order to meet the original stock targets.

It must be noted that the monetary intake requirement needs to be converted to units at the style/colour level to enable the stock availability to be allocated and distributed.

The allocation of product from the availability reports provided by suppliers or stocks stored in the warehouse takes on two methodologies. The input type products, usually for seasonal launches or fashion styles are described as "push" products while the continuity product which is replenished in empathy to sales performance are known as "pull" products where allocations are triggered by minimum stock level points and stopped by the maximum stock level thresholds.

The key differentiators of these types of products are that "push" styles cater for peak sales before being replaced. These styles attract a higher markdown volume as they are removed off display once the range becomes broken as they need to make way for the new themes that the replacement input styles bring.

"Pull" styles determine the requirements based on replacement of actual sales to a pre-determined build to level of stock. The calculation of the quantity of stock required will be the be determined by the amount of intake needed to meet the stock target that is either dynamically determined by the set weeks sales forward cover or is maintained at a static level over time.

"Pull" styles should typically be continuity items that have a predictable rate of sale and have a balanced availability of sufficient volumes of stock from the lowest level to meet the fluctuating demand. The supplier's production planning therefore has to be consistently reliable and flexible to sustain this condition.

The "pull" principle can be illustrated as follows

The automatic replenishment or distribution of products is often performed through the use of sophisticated technical allocation systems and are most suitable for the basic continuity product that have consistent predictable sales patterns and for store displays which are laid out according to a centralised space planning system.

The application needs to be merged with the historical sales data and the planned overall sales going forward. In order to achieve a constant replenishment over time a technique of smoothing is utilised where a weighting factor is applied to sales which deviate from the norm due to an unusual event and in such cases the system will use the adjusted realistic level of sale in the algorithm to derive the most appropriate forward allocations.

In the case where there is a launch of new lines, the new line can be linked to the pattern of a similar current style. The performance of the new styles must therefore be very carefully monitored early on and adjusted if need be to ensure the best size provision as possible.

The manual overriding of calculated allocations at store level should only take place in exceptional circumstances for specific reasons such as unforeseen special events, competitor activity or natural disasters. Often the temptation exists to manually override allocations based on an inherent gut feel and this should be avoided at all costs.

The delivery instruction which is sent to the supplier specifies the quantities that must be picked and packed per item per store by colour and size.

The primary size refers to the commonly designated size of all products such as waist measurements, neck and chest sizes while the secondary size refers to products which have other options of the main primary size such as different leg lengths for trousers or varying cup size options in case of bras.

If automated replenishment systems do not exist or are not very sophisticated it may occur that the actual sales by size do not mirror those as planned. In such cases it is necessary to review the size patterns using a manual technique and alter contract ratios going forward. A special balancing contract must be raised for production of those specific sizes that are short in order to realign the size sales pattern to that of the amended regular contracts going forward. A very clear indication where the size ratio is out of line is where at the end of range launches the left over stocks or reduced stocks are dominated by one or two sizes. If one applies one's mind to the consequence of this, it is a fact that potential sales have gone drastically astray of better selling sizes and profit is consequently not maximised.

In summary, the sad part about poor performers or the lack of stock control, is that especially in the case of high volume continuity styles, the resultant negative impact can be likened to a lingering illness that lives with the buying team until the situation of overstocks of unwanted product is eventually rectified or doomed to the reduced counter. It is therefore critical that where there is a hint of such an evolving scenario that very swift action is taken.

Where there has been above average performance of categories, a situation may arise where the amount stock available is unable to satisfy the requirements of the entire store catalogue. In such instances the predicament that exists is one of how to keep everybody happy. The choice usually boils down to reducing the quantities proportionately across the entire catalogue dependent on the priority of need whereby at least each store sees a piece of the pie before sell outs are experienced. The other option is to take the view to shrink the number of stores that are serviced and best satisfy the stores that are more likely to deliver the greatest volume of sales. In many cases it is not uncommon for twenty percent of the catalogue to deliver sixty to seventy percent of the sales. The selection of the second option will retain the credibility of the customers in the bigger units but will disappoint the many customers across the balance of the stores. A tactic to alleviate severe situations is by choosing a geographical cross section of stores and if an on-line facility exists, to ensure that stock is available at all times that can be ordered via the internet.

The use of digital imaging has helped develop realistic three dimensional representations which enable the product to be placed efficiently on the various types of equipment in the store. Such systems operate at detail size level so in theory a store will never be out of a size as the principle applied is that as the store sells one it gets one. The key to the success of such a system is that the data integrity has to be as accurate as possible. If this is not the case, for example, where the data base is distorted through incorrect barcode ticketing or pilferage will result in allocations being calculated inaccurately. The only means to rectify the data base is to do a disciplined full manual stock count from time to time and update the data base accordingly.

CASE STUDY

The core white formal shirt of the CH Clothing Company which would be probably be allocated on a regular basis to ensure continuity of availability.

CHALLENGE #40

Which allocation system would be best suited to ensure the objective of continuous availability of all sizes is achieved and provide a reason why.

The automatic replenishment or distribution of products is often performed through the use of sophisticated technical allocation systems and are most suitable for the basic continuity product that have consistent predictable sales patterns and for store displays which are laid out according to a centralised space planning system.

Delivery Instruction note example

ORDER NO	12345	DEPARTMENT	Men's Trousers
SUPPLIER	ABC Manufacturer	STYLE NO	5554
DATE	14 March, 2015	DESCRIPTION	Casual cotton trouser

STORES		COLOUR	GREY					
		PRIMARY SIZE	32	34	36	38	40	42
		SECONDARY SIZE	32	34	36	38	40	42
NO	STORE	TOTAL	120	170	160	140	110	100
141	City Centre	250	38	53	50	44	34	66
145	Main Street	200	30	43	40	35	28	53
148	Back Street	250	38	53	50	44	34	66
151	Country Lane	100	15	21	20	18	14	26

PRODUCT STORAGE AND DISTRIBUTION

Logistical planning and supply chain

Supply chain logistics is described as the product movement comprising of the transport and shipment of goods from the point of origination and clearance through customs where applicable to the distribution centre or warehouse and on to stores where the goods are placed on offer for purchase to the customer. Many stores traditionally have stockroom facilities or at least a backroom to accommodate overflow stocks.

The reality is that the same rates of rental are charged as that for saleable metreage and therefore it is preferable that off-site storage facilities be maintained. The downside of holding stocks in high rental cost stock rooms is that invariably the remnant stocks of promotions or themes are removed from the sales floor and left in the stock room to gather dust waiting for the seasonal write down.

Out of season stocks such as thermal underwear are returned to the stockroom to await the reappearance of the next season to be returned to the sales floor. In such situations, particularly where there are undisciplined controls in the store, stocks get lost in the black hole of the stock room and bad or dead stock will accumulate and affect the data integrity of the stock records. It is therefore essential that redundant stocks are written off and cleared out almost immediately.

The trend is to keep store holding areas as small as possible and enable the regular drawing off from larger economical offsite storage facilities which can be done more effectively through a centralised point whether it be at the warehouse or in the commercial office. The success as to how well this is done is dependent on the responsiveness of the warehouse and reduces the accumulation of isolated pockets of stocks while minimising the corruption of stock data integrity as well as the reduction of double handling of merchandise.

Examples of stock held in the holding room is the accommodation of an overflow of stock where space planning is applied using planograms. End of ranges stock that have to be returned to the centralised storage facility or supplier may need to be held temporarily in the back room awaiting collection. Stock is also temporarily held for consolidation in back room areas until all components of a promotional launch is received and moved to the sales floor on the launch date for maximum impact.

The selection of the various options of supply chain will depend on a number of criteria such as the source of supply, characteristics of the product, the costs of the storage and distribution, selling locations, shelf life and customer demand.

The main channels of supply are a flow through model without storage or warehoused product. Outside of these channels the other formats are direct delivery to stores or displays being fully merchandised by the vendor.

The type of distribution model that is selected will depend on factors such as the size and growth phase of the retailer. For example, smaller or new retailers will probably prefer to operate a cross dock model which does not require investment in large warehouse facilities or the need to carry excessive inventory enabling their efforts to be focused possibly on opening more stores.

For a larger mature retail chain on the other hand, it may be essential to operate through a network of sophisticated warehousing amenities. These enjoy elaborate systems whereby they have better control of the management of the inventory and are able to efficiently allocate, pick and pack and schedule deliveries to stores country wide or even internationally.

Retailers also have the choice to manage their own facilities or outsource them. The main factor that is considered in selecting the most suitable option is the cost saving element. Initially it may have been cheaper to outsource without having to invest in the high setup cost of such an infra-structure, however, as the retailer grows, coupled to the fact that the third party is a profit based operation that delivers expertise in the warehousing field, the time will come when it is more beneficial to move the operation in house.

A workable compromise solution that is often employed is for the retailer to control their own warehouse facilities with the accompanying IT infrastructure and avoid the major upheaval should they change third parties but to still outsource the transport network part to specialised haulage service providers.

Cross dock or flow through model is the arrangement where the goods are pre picked and packed at the supplier and are delivered to the distribution centre with store labels already gummed on the boxes or hanging sets. The alternative model of cross dock is where the order across the stores is delivered in bulk by the supplier to the cross dock facility and the goods are picked by distribution centre staff and deposited directly in the respective store dispatch bays. Eventually the product from all suppliers for the day is consolidated in each store's designated bay awaiting transport.

Stores that are geographically far from the receiving distribution centre have the goods transhipped in bulk to their own respective closest geographical distribution centre where the picking operation will take place. The number of regional distribution centres will be largely dependent on the density of the store network and the operating costs of such facilities.

The added benefit of the goods being picked and packed at the supplier is that the cartons are able to contain a combination of size and colour requirements by store and will therefore eliminate the need to unpack and repack from warehouse stock thus eliminating double handling and is subsequently more cost efficient. It is also possible where the supplier is picking multiple styles for the same store that these can be nested in the same container which reduces the need for additional packaging as well as reduces handling making for a considerable time saving.

In the event that there are over or short deliveries these cause delays as the changed quantity requires that the computer is updated and the store quantities are scaled or recalculated based on varying algorithms that satisfy those stores with the greatest need first rather than simply apportioning equally across all the stores before the picking process can take place.

In the case where the receipt of product from suppliers is pre labelled for stores the testing of the accuracy is done by randomly inspecting a sample of cartons per supplier delivery and should the errors of packing fall outside of a certain tolerance it may result in the entire delivery being rejected. Where inaccuracies are within the tolerance but there is still a measure of incorrectness the error factor will still be extrapolated for the entire delivery and the invoicing is amended accordingly. Dependent on the size of the error it could attract a penalty. While many find this concept difficult to accept, it should be remembered that the time and cost to do a full unpack and reconciliation in all likelihood would render the operation to be considered impracticable. Tests have been statistically done which reveal that the deviation from the sample survey results is also not that large.

The advantage of a flow through supply chain type is that the allocation can be made as late as possible allowing the shortening of the lead time and thereby meeting the customer demand more efficiently. The other benefit is also that the storage space requirement is minimal and dependent on the payment obligation it may be beneficial to the retailer in terms of cash flow in that ownership is only transferred upon receipt at the distribution centre.

There is an argument that utilising cross dock without warehousing is possibly a disadvantage in terms of the speed of delivery to stores as having stock drawn from the warehouse is quicker and smoother than waiting for the supplier delivery. The challenge is therefore to streamline the supplier delivery efficiencies to avoid the cost impact of holding warehoused stock and the handling costs that accompany this option.

Other difficult situations arise where there is a poor performing unreliable supplier for which a contingency is required when they fail to deliver and similarly at key periods such as holidays where the factories shut down for a period and in spite of confirming that there will be a skeleton staff to cope with the execution of orders over this period the level of service is invariably diminished.

Example of a cross dock flow through model

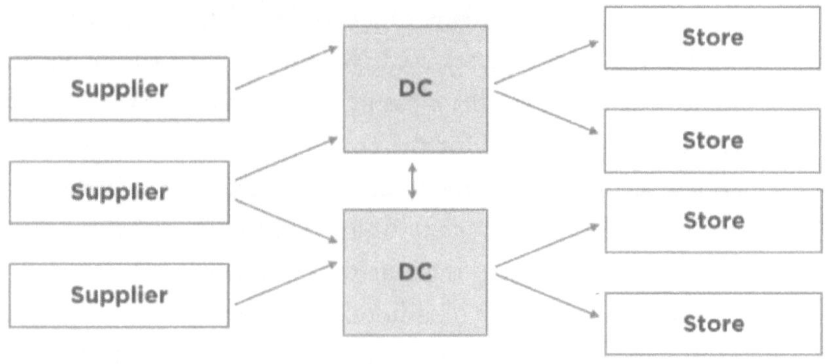

Warehoused product is where the goods are received in bulk and are held in storage awaiting a call off and distribution to stores or to other storage sheds using the cross dock facilities.

The warehouse can be seen to operate in a similar way as the supplier and performance management of indicators such as pick and pack accuracy, lead time measurement and the like can be implemented in the same way.

Warehoused stock tends to be predominantly for imported product but can also include local suppliers particularly where minimum order quantities or negotiated special volume deals apply. In the main the products are continuity items with long supply lead times which are replenished on a regular basis as "pull" allocations.

The challenge with warehouse stock is to manage the stock levels as the investment in high volumes does not only have adverse financial consequences but also a real physical problem can arise in the form of space constraints and the possible requirement of additional operational resources. There are also instances of seasonal goods such as knitwear being produced in the off season to maintain a consistent production throughout the year and therefore creates an accumulation of stocks in the warehouse either at the supplier or the retailer at a cost which needs to be accounted for.

A point to note is that the storage shelving location is restricted to a fixed size which is usually the size of a pallet and may be at multi levels. As goods are withdrawn to the pick and pack locations it does happen that within one storage location a lesser quantity of goods remain behind which results in the space utilisation not being optimal as two different SKU's are not able to share the same location. Technically the warehouse becomes restricted in the capacity availability while physically this may not be the case. Thought needs to be applied to the minimum percentage or quantity that is able to be efficiently maintained and what tactics must be utilised regarding the consolidation of and removal of such stocks to free up the storage slots. This may take the form of allocating the odds to stores or transferring it to a different storage area with smaller slots and take on a high priority for distribution thereafter.

Other space inhibiting practices are where there are poor rates of sales, or volume deals are negotiated or through minimum order quantities that are imposed which cause the warehouses to fill up eventually and consequently result in the total utilisation of palette slots. The alternative then remains to either source outside storage, put the brakes on in terms of accepting intake or to simply stop buying to relieve the space and financial strain. The consequences of this is that availabilities suffer with the disruption of the composition of product and theme launches as well as the service levels of suppliers decline when they put production on hold while they wait for the retailer's stock levels to diminish and inevitably will sell on to other competitors in order to keep their production capacity full and operational.

The siting and the number of warehouses will be reliant on the geographic network of stores, the proximity to suppliers and ports and will be dependent on the achievement of the most economical costs which need to be continually reviewed to ensure the delicate balance of viability is maintained. This balance is particularly important in the case of retail chains which continually open and close stores.

The introduction of higher levels of automation and the possibility of outsourcing operations to contractors or independent logistical organisations for storage and the management of the fleet of transport to tranship between storage points and schedule deliveries to stores also has an impact on the sustainability.

After the unloading of a container or truck at the back door, the cartons are consolidated and received, and then palletized for packing away in the storage facilities with unique identification location barcodes for ease of retrieval upon withdrawal in bulk.

After drawing product in bulk from the shelves the goods are moved to a pick and pack location to satisfy each stores order and are deposited in the unique store bays to await dispatch.

An alternative option is to pick and pack goods directly from storage shelves by store and when the order of the various products for each specific store is complete it is delivered to the store's relevant bay.

The appropriateness of which picking method to apply will depend largely on the size of the withdrawals. The larger volumes are usually removed to a picking area in bulk where the pick and pack operations take place. The smaller the quantities that are required by store, the picking by individual store across the product range into picking bins or shipping units for each store would probably be more suitable. It is possible that some retailer's employ both methods from different areas of the warehouse dependent on the product characteristics and volumes.

The task of picking is activated by the generation of a computer picking sheet which informs the picker as to which location must be accessed and indicates the quantity that must be withdrawn. Together with this the computer will create the store labels which is applied to the shipping container.

There are generally two methods of generating picking lists and labels. The more manual method is where the picking lists are generated up front prior to the picking operation but the downside is that it is susceptible to inaccuracies and at the end of the operation the computer needs to be updated manually and report any exceptions. The implication is that this step must be fulfilled before any goods can be shipped which could cause delays.

The other option is real time picking which is the technique of using hand held terminals that employ radio frequency to give the pickers their instructions on a computer terminal or pad. With the handheld terminal or voice instructions via hands free headsets the picker will scan the barcodes of the product and locations to confirm that the correct product has been identified and the picking can commence which will then update the stock data base in real time. For this reason the accuracy is almost guaranteed and the movement of stock is free flowing.

As all retailers are concerned about shrinkage this method is a big plus and also lessens the possibility of disputes between the warehouse and stores with respect to over or short deliveries. The facility to automatically generate store delivery notes is provided enabling the deliveries to be tracked. Real time control does however come at a much added cost and therefore the viability must be assessed in terms of the benefits it brings with it.

There are sophisticated automated picking systems which lessen the manual handling of product but these require a higher level of investment. The most common system employed is a conveyer belt system whereby the pickers are relatively stationery and are responsible for a section of products in an area where the items are packed onto the conveyer belt from which picking takes place and can be done for either the store or product picking options.

Challenges that the picking operation faces is that different approaches are required to segment activities in cases where fast selling items need to be picked more frequently and others such as for some stores that require less service than others. Consequently there is a prerequisite to carefully schedule actions in order to streamline deliveries.

In a similar way the peaks and valleys of volumes through the week apply undue strain on the operation at certain times while at other spells the warehouse may stand idle. In the case of clothing where there are not many expiry dates involved the approach should possibly be to pick the high volume product outside the peak delivery periods and reserve the ability to prioritise the promotion items during the peak delivery period thereby smoothing the operation and maintain a constant labour utilisation.

The ideal size of the warehouse is difficult to assess but the general rule is obviously the smaller the warehouse the better as the overheads are kept to a minimum and experience often shows whatever the size of the shed is it will inevitably be filled. The size should be tailored to the space required during normal trading and not to accommodate peak periods such as Christmas or the accumulation of stock build up prior to Chinese New Year when at such times additional temporary space can possibly be procured or alternatively implement night shifts to keep stocks moving.

The flow of product within a warehouse environment is illustrated below

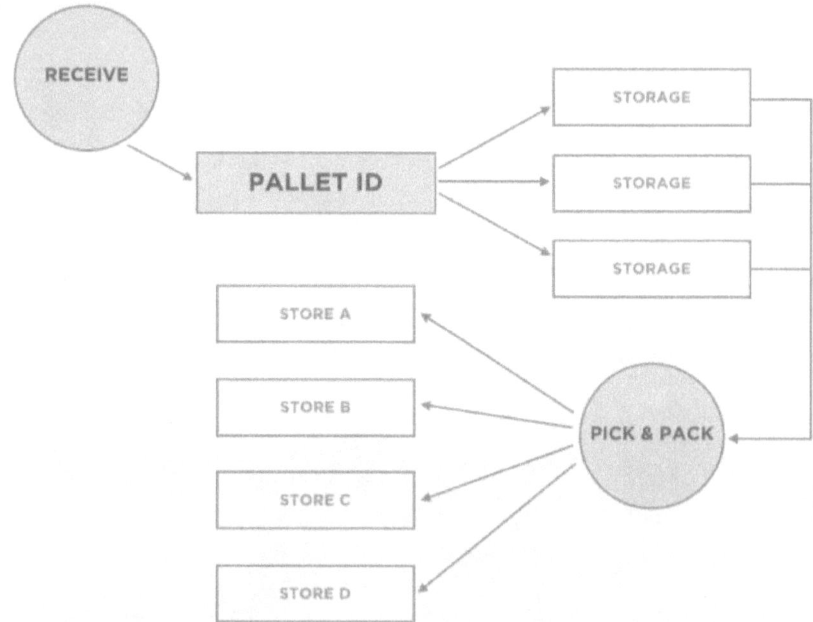

Direct delivery of product to the store location by the supplier is used where the retailer does not have the infrastructure to accommodate certain types of product such as high priced goods like cosmetics and expensive accessories.

This mode of delivery is also required where the vendor completes the end to end merchandising management of the displays whereby slow selling stock is withdrawn and replaced by the supplier. A typical example would be a product such as greeting cards, accessories and magazines.

In summary, a well-managed supply chain enables the retailer to acquire goods from the manufacturer more profitably, facilitate well controlled stock levels, and provide more timeous response to the consumer demand as well as the building of sustainable working relationships between the retailer and the supplier.

VALUE ADDED PROCESSING

The need for additional work on product is frequent and the facilities to do this has to be provided for to make goods store ready. The nature of value added work can take on a variety of forms but typical examples are as follows.

Goods that are received from off shore suppliers may be bulk packed or not be received in their final form in order to achieve optimum space utilisation during transit. Prime examples of this is in the case of cushions or duvets which are space hungry but are relatively light. In order to accomplish the most efficient space usage these goods may be transported without the fibre filling or alternatively are vacuum packed. However, this operation then creates the need for additional work upon receipt to fill the cushions and unpacking of the vacuum packs as well as treating the product through pressing or steaming.

The transport of goods in cartons that eventually will be displayed on hangers, such as men's formal suits or ladies tailored garments, is done to maximise the space efficiency in containers. Upon arrival they will need to be unpacked and placed on hangers and will have to be steamed either with a hand steamer or pass through a steam tunnel. In most cases this will also require the attachment of price tickets and garment information labels.

Repackaging may be required where bulk transit quantities need to be debagged and repackaged into smaller stock room packs ready for allocation to stores.

It does happen that there may be garments received from the supplier with defects or returned from stores which are repairable in order to make them available in a saleable state which has to be done by the value-adder.

The location of the added value service provider can be either at an independent site or be incorporated in the retailer's warehouse facility. The challenge with an offsite location, particularly with the receipt of offshore product is the fact that the goods are received by another facility and reflect on a separate stock record which renders the administration of stock to be more complex.

It is preferable to have the value added processing done in the retailer's warehouse facility as there is control of the receipt of the goods and performance is more easily managed. The operation can possibly be done on a contractual basis whereby the processor rents space within the warehouse or the space is alternatively staffed with warehouse resources as a separate entity and not included in the distribution centre operational costs. It should be noted that the cost of this processing work forms part of the cost of the product and must be included in the determination of the product margin.

The costing structures for work done is a complex one as the type of work is not always consistent and therefore needs to be broken down into some detail.

Value added costing would typically consist of a basic cost for the overheads and handling of the product which is usually relatively stable but may vary depending on the type of product being processed. Charges per operation such as a rate per garment for steaming, labelling, placing on hangers and the like will be added to the base costs. Out of the ordinary operations such as ad hoc repairs will be dependent on the results of negotiation between the processor and the buying departments.

TRANSPORT METHODOLOGIES

The method of transport will be determined by a number of criteria. The option for clothing is either in cartons or in the form of hanging sets. The choice is dependent mainly on the characteristic of the product, the cost comparison between the two models and the equipment infra-structure of the supplier and distribution centres. Many of the more sophisticated production plants have the overhead rail systems that can accommodate hanging goods and which can facilitate the transport of the goods hanging from rails affixed to the ceiling of the vehicle to the retailer.

The cost of the hanging storage and transport of product will come at added expense for the rail systems in comparison to the charge for distribution in cartons. The time saving as a cost offset in the case of moving hanging goods needs to be considered and in many cases it is also dependent on the nature of fabrics such as voiles as well as the structure of garments as is the case for formal wear. If crease sensitive goods are moved in cartons there is a need for an added value processing requirement to steam and bag the goods which can either take place at the distribution centre or at the stores upon receipt which comes at an additional cost. The transport of formal wear in cartons could also lead to persistent creases in the garment such as the fold in pants that may be difficult to eradicate even with intense steaming.

Where retailers insist on receiving goods in boxes, a reverse cost may have to be applied where sophisticated manufacturing plants that only cater for hanging goods to maximise the scales of efficiency will need to purchase cartons and employ additional labour to pack the garments into boxes as well as encounter an additional time delay.

The downsides of the hanging format is that the equipment is expensive, space requirement is greater, and where multiple hangers are hung vertically to save space in the outer bag there could be the danger of bunching of longer garments at the bottom of the bag. Space wastage below the hanging bags in the vehicles also needs to be taken into account.

The advantage of time saving that hanging formats deliver in comparison to goods transported in cartons is that goods in cartons have the benefit of easier handling, better space utilization and less capital investment. However the necessity of capacity planning for processing to steam and place products on hangers together with the additional cost, extended lead time and a risk that the quality may be compromised needs to be weighed up.

Another determining factor will be the aesthetics of the garment that may lend it to be displayed on hangers such as casual shirts made from natural fibres or styled tailored goods which will better highlight the features and promote the unique feel of the special fabrics.

Goods are stored and dispatched as hanging sets that will comprise of a fixed number of garments in the same colour and sizes and are allocated as such. This makes for easier handling and loading into vehicles especially where the equipment is able to access the vehicle or container directly from the despatch area.

The optimisation of the supply chain calls for an end to end cost analysis and monitoring to ensure that the goods reach the sales floors efficiently to best service the customer through consistent availability without the congestion of stock in warehouses and back rooms.

A flow diagram which indicates the garment and fibre types which best suit the method of storage, transport and display can be illustrated as follows

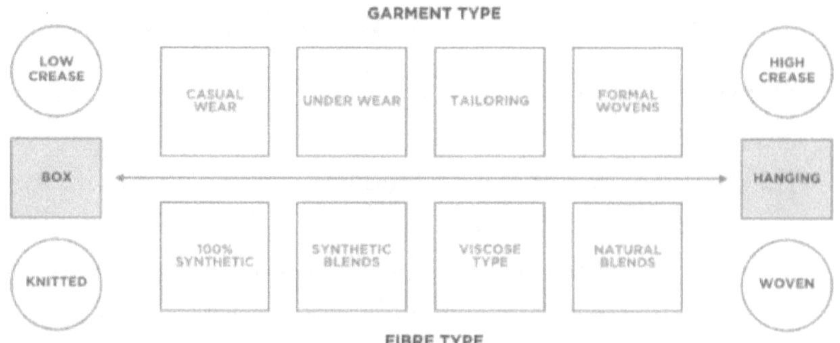

CASE STUDY

The casual linen shirt is manufactured in volume and therefore requires the most appropriate mode to store be transported.

CHALLENGE #41

Based on the scale of box versus hanging above describe where the linen shirt would be best suited and what characteristics qualify it to be so.

Product security

Wastage through pilferage is an important factor that needs attention during the movement of the product. Control is done by various methods but mostly through the use of sealed containers, marked sealing tapes on cartons, sample tests of contents in cartons, locked and sealed back doors on trucks and sophisticated handover procedures. There is a breakeven point where the cost to maintain the security must be weighed up against the shrinkage allowance as it may be overkill to secure cheaper products with refined protection. The additional labour and checkpoints will slow down the movement of product through the pipeline as well as lower the service levels and therefore may not make it meaningful. On the other hand it could well be very worthwhile for the movement of high value product.

Carton specifications and requirements

Transit and outer case cartons need to conform to certain specifications in terms of size, strength, weight, markings and sealing. The characteristics of certain products will dictate modifications to some cartons such as goods that are packed on hangers may require a tape at the ends inside the box to hook the hangers to prevent the shifting of product such as blouses within the cartons. Other products may require separators between the garments such as tissue paper or card board to minimise creasing.

Careful consideration must be given to the number of units per stockroom pack which will usually be by solid colour and solid size and should be equivalent to the unit of allocation. Savings can be achieved through less handling and storage configurations by setting the quantity per pack equivalent to the minimum allocation quantity that a store can accommodate without being overstocked.

Barcode markings enable the scanning in of boxes at the receipt points and alleviate the risk of congestion with less labour. Packing away on palettes into the storage slots is also done more quickly.

Markings on the cartons must be uniform and conform to international regulations and display a recognized certification stamp.

Side 1 marking required on the carton – product description

MARKING	DESCRIPTION
Retailer ABC	Name of the customer who is to take ownership of the product
Fragile	Indicates if the box should be handled with care
Supplier	Source of product where goods were supplied
Order no	Order that the box belongs to
Batch number	Production batch that carton belongs to
Product reference no	Style number of garments inside the box
SKU number	Stock keeping unit or barcode number that will be reflected on the stock records
Contents description	Style / colour / size and style description
Units per carton	Number of units inside the carton
Carton number	Number of carton out of the total (e.g. 'carton no 3 of 10')
Country of origin	Sending country (where carton was packaged)

Side 2 marking required on the carton – weight and measurement information

MARKING	DESCRIPTION
Fragile	Indicates if the box should be handled with care
Stack max	Maximum number of cartons that can be packed on top of each other
Net weight (kg)	Net weight in kg of goods inside the carton
Gross weight (kg)	Total weight of the outer carton and the goods inside the carton
Dimensions (cm or mm)	Dimensions of height, length and width of carton in cm or mm

Apart from conforming to international rules, the size parameters and volume dimensions will also be dictated by the pallette sizes and storage slots of the warehouse to safeguard the most efficient usage of space. The dimensions also need to be considered in terms of what the other equipment such as conveyer belts, vehicle capacities and store storage facilities can accommodate.

Carton critical measurements

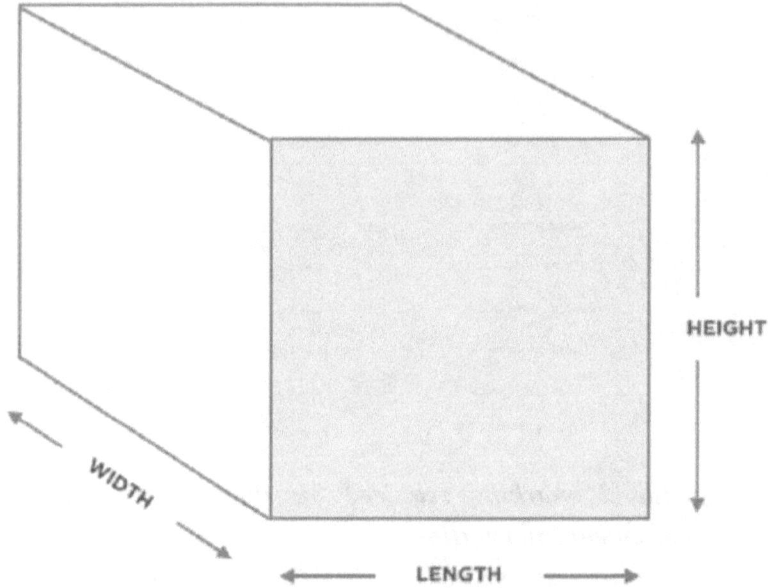

Local logistics should investigate the possible use of returnable cartons or crates by suppliers much in the same way food retailers utilise lugs. Such an operation would be environmentally friendly and would incur a once off investment but the administration of such an operation does come at a cost which may influence the viability.

REVIEW AND ACTION OPTIONS OF IN SEASON TRADING

Process of comparing the actual performance in relation to the plan

No matter how much time and thought is spent in drafting the strategy and planning forecast it is inevitable that the reality will deviate from what is expected as a result of the volatile internal and external factors that exist at the time. Therefore it is critical to continually review actual performance, analyse the trends and take appropriate action to minimise the risks. Where adjustments are not able to be made to remedy a situation the lessons learnt must be taken on board and banked to be avoided in future trading seasons.

The path to follow in the process of comparing the actual performance in relation to the plan can be outlined as follows

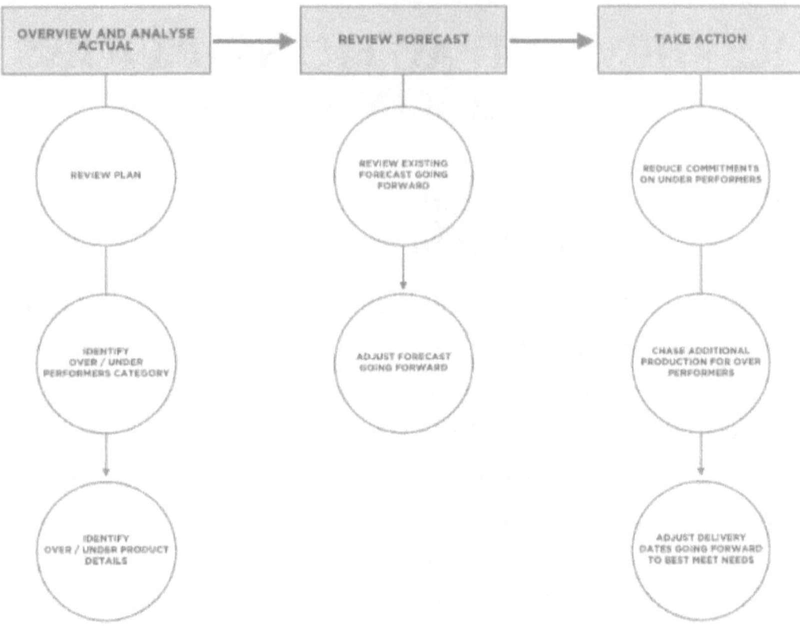

The start point of analysing and comparing the actual performance to the intended plan at a point in time, is to firstly to compare actual sales to date at total departmental level and drill down to product level and based on the result, review the planned sales for the balance of the season.

The potential new sales forecast is then compared to the actual commitment of product in the form of stock on hand at stores, product in transit and that at the supplier as well as the orders in the pipeline to determine the resultant shortage or surplus of stock.

In the scenarios below the assumption is that the department consists of a product which is over performing, another that is under performing and one that is selling to expectation.

The procedure which needs to be followed can be broken down into three distinct activities.

- The recording of the total plan for the season in terms of sales and the planned breaking stocks at the end of the season as well as the current week's performance which has just been completed.

- Based on the comparison of the actual sales to date in relation to that which was budgeted for may require a review of the balance of sales to be achieved and thereby create a revised forecast for the total season. The change in the sales forecast may also then require an adaptation of the planned breaking stocks to reflect the reality of the sales plan.

- Once the realistic revised sales performance has been established, the result then needs to be compared to the total stock commitment and assessed whether there is sufficient stock in the pipeline to achieve the revised targets. If this is not the case, a plan has to be devised in order to determine what action is required to achieve this or conversely there may be a consequent surplus of stock which will have to be reduced.

CASE STUDY

Below is the hypothetical example of CH Clothing Company review of trade during the season and the typical action that is required to modify and fine tune the key components.

Analysis and adjustment of sales and commitment status tabulated in three focus areas

TOTAL SEASON STATUS AND CURRENT SALES

STYLE NO	DESCRIPTION	SELLING PRICE	TOTAL SEASON 26 WEEKS					END SEASON STOCKS		WEEK NO 6			
			LY SALES	SEASON BUDGET	% INC / DEC ON LY	REVISED SEASON F/CAST	% INC / DEC ON LY	BUDGET CLOSING STOCK	REVISED CLOSING STOCK	WEEKS LY ACTUAL SALES	WEEKS SALES BUDGET	WEEKS ACTUAL SALES	% INC / DEC ON LY
1234	Round neck t-shirt	99.99	950 000	1 100 500	15.8%	1 016 500	7.0%	180 000	150 000	35 000	42 800	39 000	11.4%
1235	V-neck t-shirt	120.99	990 000	1 150 100	16.2%	1 260 000	27.8%	250 000	200 000	38 000	43 700	45 000	18.4%
1236	Button down t-shirt	150	1 100 000	1 200 000	9.1%	1 210 000	10.0%	220 000	220 000	38 000	41 100	41 000	7.9%
TOTAL DEPARTMENT			3 040 000	3 450 600	13.5%	3 486 500	14.7%	650 000	570 000	111 000	127 100	125 000	12.6%

PROGRESSIVE SALES STATUS

STYLE NO	DESCRIPTION	SELLING PRICE	6 WEEKS TO DATE							20 WEEKS BALANCE TO ACHIEVE				
			PROGRESS LY SALES TO DATE	PROGRESS BUDGET SALES TO DATE	% INC / DEC ON LY	ACTUAL PROGRESS SALES TO DATE	% INC / DEC ON LY	PROGRESS REVISED SALES TO DATE	% INC / DEC ON LY	BALANCE OF LY SALES	BALANCE OF BUDGET SALES TO ACHIEVE	% INC / DEC ON LY	REVISED BALANCE OF SALES TO ACHIEVE	% INC / DEC ON LY
1234	Round neck t-shirt	99.99	190 000	220 000	15.8%	205 000	7.9%	210 000	10.5%	760 000	880 500	15.9%	811 500	6.8%
1235	V-neck t-shirt	120.99	250 000	290 500	16.2%	318 000	27.2%	300 000	20.0%	740 000	859 600	16.2%	942 000	27.3%
1236	Button down t-shirt	150	235 000	250 505	6.6%	252 000	7.2%	252 000	7.2%	865 000	949 495	9.8%	958 000	10.8%
TOTAL DEPARTMENT			675 000	761 005	12.7%	775 000	14.8%	762 000	12.9%	2 365 000	2 689 595	127 100	2 711 500	14.7%

COMMITMENT STATUS

STYLE NO	DESCRIPTION	SELLING PRICE	COMMITMENT SELLING VALUE					OVER / UNDER STATUS				
			STORE STOCK	TRANSIT STOCK	SUPPLIER STOCK	SUPPLIER OUTSTAND. ORDERS	TOTAL STOCK COMMIT	REVISED SALES BALANCE	REVISED CLOSING STOCK	TOTAL BALANCE OF SALES & STOCK	TOTAL OVER / UNDER SELL VALUE	TOTAL OVER / UNDER UNITS
1234	Round neck t-shirt	99.99	250 000	100 000	280 000	500 000	1 130 000	811 500	150 000	961 500	168 500	1685
1235	V-neck t-shirt	120.99	280 000	70 000	200 000	400 000	950 000	942 000	200 000	1 142 000	-192000	-1587
1236	Button down t-shirt	150	250 000	100 000	120 000	700 000	1 170 000	958 000	220 000	1 178 000	-8000	-53
TOTAL DEPARTMENT			780 000	270 000	600 000	1 600 000	3 250 000	2 711 500	570 000	3 281 500	-31500	45

Logically speaking based on the tabular representation above of the scenarios, the thought process may well progress as follows.

Scenario 1: Style 1234 round neck t-shirt selling for 99.99 currently has an original season's budget of 1,100,500 which represents a 15.8% increase on last year. Based on the actual performance during the past six weeks the budget is set at a value of 220,000 that still represents a 15.8% where in fact the actual 6 weeks have performed to a value of 205,000 which is only 7.9%. Based on this fact the reviewer then thinks that going forward for the balance of the season a potential increase of 6.8% is more probable than the 15.9% originally planned. Adjustment to the revised level will result the total season being 1,016,500 rather than the 1,100,500 originally anticipated. At the same time the view on the breaking stock is that it will be 150,000 based on the reduced sales for the balance of the season rather than the original plan of 180,000. Thus the stock requirement to complete the sales to the end of the season as well as meet the revised closing stock need means the amount of stock necessary is 961,500. However, when the actual stock in stores, stock in transit, and stock at the supplier as well as outstanding orders still planned to be produced totals 1,130,000 it is clear to see that there is a surplus of 168,500 which at a selling price of 99.99 translates into 1685 units. Action is required to deal with this over commitment. Options are described later on in this section.

Scenario 2: Style 1235 v neck t-shirt selling for 120.99 currently has an original season's budget of 1,150,100 which represents a 16.2% increase on last year. Based on the actual performance during the past six weeks there have been revisions to a value of 300,000 that represents a good 20.0%, however the actual 6 weeks have over performed to a value of 318,000 which is 27.2%. The reviewer then thinks that going forward for the balance of the season an increase of 27.3% is therefore more probable than the 16.2% originally planned which will result in the total season being 1,260,000 rather than the 1,150,100 originally anticipated. At the same time the view on the breaking stock is that it will be 200,000 based on the higher sales going forward will erode stocks and will be less than the original plan of 250,000. The stock requirement to complete the sales to the end of the season and to meet the revised closing stock need means the amount of stock required is 1,142,000. However when the actual stock in stores, stock in transit, and stock at the supplier as well as outstanding orders still planned to be produced it is clear to see that there is a shortfall of 192,000 which at a selling price of 120.99 translates into a deficit of 1587 units. Action is required to deal with this under commitment.

Scenario 3: Style 1236 Button down t-shirt. In this scenario the same process as followed in scenarios 1 and 2 delivers the result that the style performed closely to what was planned and was only 53 units short of target which therefore resulted in no need for any action.

Analysis options

Before deciding on what action is required there are consistent questions that need to be answered. In terms of why the sales differ to the plan one needs to determine whether the sales were early or late possibly due to seasonal factors or extraordinary events. However if they are low the question must be asked whether it is because the appeal to the customer is below expectation.

Measurement against key targets should also be considered as well as the guidelines that are outlined in the strategy. The proportions of the customer segmentation may be incorrectly projected. The pricing policy such as price tiering could be incorrectly balanced, new initiatives may be over optimistic or colour trends are not be as expected and therefore the deviation should be examined down to the lowest level of the hierarchy.

Key performance measures to focus on are forward cover targets to confirm that they are in line or if they are too low the reason may be that there is not enough stock in the system to enable achievement of targeted sales. The measures at store level need to be evaluated as the bigger selling stores may be significantly impacting sales if their individual targets are not being achieved.

Sell off percentage which is defined as the total stock received divided by sales expressed as a percentage, is often used as a key measure but a word of caution is that this needs to carefully assessed as sales with low stocks may deliver a flattering result that leaves a lot better impression than deserved or conversely a disappointing sell off percentage of a product may be due to a full delivery having been received in the latter part of the period and therefore the opportunity to sell was restricted. The value that this measurement has is only truly valid when all products being measured are for the same period of time when full stocks were in place and then can be used as a fair relativity measure between products or to the comparable acceptable levels of sell off.

It is key that all planned promotions and deliveries are still in line to be launched as scheduled and that there are no risks of late or non-delivery from the supplier as this will impact on performance for the balance of the season.

Historical comparison must be considered carefully especially in the case where events fall differently in that this year they may fall on the weekend instead of a week day as may have been the case in the previous year. Special events unique to the season could also have a significant effect. Much of this type of insight is gained through regular store and supplier visits, as well as strict adherence to meeting schedules that include all of the stakeholders comprising of buyers, merchandisers, allocators, designers and technologists. Working as a team keeps everyone involved and committed to an action plan complete with assignments and timelines and a system of updates that monitor the progress of action items.

Differing trends or patterns to that expected may have evolved such as prints which may emerge to be in higher demand than plains.

The review of better selling products as well as the worst sellers needs to be analytically done in an attempt to understand as to why they are performing as they are. Factors that may be common are styling features, colourations, functionality or fabrications. Styles programmed going forward should be reviewed for the identification of opportunities to adapt or change, move out or pull forward and if possible turn on or cancel production.

Regular probes on the sales floor and interaction with sales staff and customers often reveal obvious reasons which are commonly overlooked particularly when one is, as is typical, too close to the detail. Customer focus groups can also provide valuable comprehensions into the practical needs of the consumers and highlight opportunities where sales can be improved and poor quality issues may be exposed.

Action options

In scenario 1 the various possibilities should be considered where action is needed to reduce the commitment in order to minimise potential markdowns.

The stage of completion of the outstanding orders must be determined and if the fabric has yet to be cut, an immediate hold should be put on the order. It is preferable to be left with uncut fabric than with made up garments. The fabric can possibly be converted into other areas of need and be made up in faster selling styles if it is appropriate. Fabric can be held over to be incorporated into a future season's programme if suitable but if it is not right, the last resort would be to sell the fabric off and take the loss on the fabric alone.

Outstanding orders or made up goods at suppliers may need, where possible, to move out the delivery dates or alternatively cancel unmade orders. A point to note is that this decision may require sensitive negotiations with the supplier's in order that they fully understand reasoning and it is encouraged that the resolution of the situation becomes a collaboration of problem solving.

The sales performance at individual store level should be carefully analysed and where there are stores that are selling the product at acceptable levels, that stock is moved from underperforming stores to those where there is a likelihood of improved sell offs. When this is considered as an option it is important to weigh up the cost of the relocation of the product against the possibility of clearing the goods at an acceptable rate. If it is deemed not to be workable it should not be done. Where the product is not in all stores, the temptation is often to extend the catalogue in the hope that the goods may be cleared through greater exposure. This may, however simply spread the problem so should be contemplated with great caution.

A successful strategy could possibly be to launch a promotion and sell the goods at a discounted price in whatever form. The practice may be a simple price reduction, a "two for one" campaign or special discount offers to loyalty programme members.

If all else fails, the last resort is to remove the product from display as it is possibly clogging saleable space and hold back from allocating any stock at the supplier and wait for the major seasonal sale launch to clear the goods. What is essential is that it needs to be clearly understood as to why the product was not wanted and bank the lessons for future seasons to ensure the errors are not repeated.

In the scenario 2 the net result showed that there was a shortfall of required stock due to over performance and the action required would enable the maximisation of the opportunities to achieve additional sales.

The first investigation that should take place is to see whether additional product can be turned on which is dependent on the availability of fabric, components and production capacity. The possibility of converting slower selling styles planned for the balance of the season is frequently a feasible option. Any existing outstanding orders should be pulled forward and the gap that evolves be replaced with the turn on orders. A word of warning is that while the temptation exists to turn on product it is critical that the delivery timeline will allow the full achievement of potential additional sales. If the delivery is too close to the end of the trading period particularly in the case of seasonal product it may result in the product landing up on the reduced counter and thereby eradicating the benefit of extra profits.

The analysis of sales at store level may reveal that certain stores are underperforming in relation to other stores and therefore the catalogue could be reduced to ensure continuity of stock in those stores that are delivering above average sales.

In the same light as the identification of the unique feature of the underperforming product, it is equally important to understand the features that can be attributed to the good performance of other products and put on file for future referral.

CHALLENGE #42

CH Clothing Company finds itself in a situation where a product is underperforming and the commitment to product is increasing. List five action options that can be adopted to rectify the situation.

POST SEASON TRADE ANALYSIS

A key focus in the assessment of the past performance for the season is to compare the actual key numbers to that what was expected and understand the deviations whether they were positive or negative. The learnings are imperative in the compilation of a new season's strategy and setting of targets.

The key topics that need to be questioned and evaluated are:

Product

- Were the trends which were anticipated in line with what actually materialised? What needs to be taken into account when predicting the future season's trends?

- Did the strategy that was set for the brand and customer together with that of the group and department as well as the supplier selection deliver the envisaged objectives? What needs to be done differently for the new season?

Customers and competitors

- Did the information on customer segmentation and the action plans cater effectively in the satisfaction of the needs? What adaptations and additional resources are needed for the future season?

- Did the competitor initiatives which were anticipated actually happen and was it possible to effectively counteract them? What other methodologies are available to keep up to date with the market place activities?

Key performance Indicators

- Were the targets of sales, margins, stock levels and turns, gross and net profits achieved as per plan or were they unrealistic? What measures require review and which activities are needed to be put in place to achieve them in the new season?

- Was the product assortment in the right proportions and did they perform to acceptable levels to cater for all customer segments effectively? Were the product innovations and promotions that were implemented successful and at the right levels?

- What were the actual colours and sizes sold in comparison to the volumes purchased and what should have been bought instead?

- Identify product sales which need to be adjusted to a realistic level as a result of product failure, poor availabilities and any other factors such as competitive activity and what special events were there that may have influenced sales either positively or negatively.

Suppliers

- Did the suppliers perform to the levels that maximised availability in the right quantities and on time?

- Did the selected suppliers possess the right capabilities to deliver the programmes that were allotted in terms of innovation, complexity, capacity, quality and on time delivery? Are there other suppliers who should be considered?

- Was the feedback received from suppliers of a nature that can help improve the working relationships going forward?

Stores

- Were stores able to understand the structure of the ranges and easily display them to emphasize the thinking of the buying team? What improvements to guidelines can be made to assist them?

- Was the feedback received from stores valuable and what mechanisms can be implemented to improve the quality of feedback?

Marketing

- Were the marketing channels that were utilised effective and was the uplift in sales able to be measured accurately against control products? Which other communication mediums would be considered?

- Were the promotions successful and what was the extent of substitution purchases?

- What was the feedback from store staff and customers?

- Were the social initiative objectives achieved?

CONCLUSION

Up to now the book has tried to adequately describe in the main the principles and theory to follow in order to logically embark on the journey, perform the key activities and utilise the mechanisms involved in the complex retail network required from conceptualisation stage right through to presenting it to the customer as an offer to purchase.

There are however crucial elements of stewardship required to guarantee that the future is both successful and sustainable. The demonstration of those elements which are characteristic to a true merchant are outlined below.

Integrity is an absolute unconditional prerequisite that should be evident in all the interactions with all stake holders. In short it is important to uphold the promise of doing what you say you are going to do and maintain a policy of under promising and over delivering.

Passion is clearly illustrated through attributes such as the visible demonstration of the love for the organisation, the product and relationships in such a way that it is contagious and serves as a great motivator to all those who come in contact with a sincere energised trader. An underlying sense of urgency to cope with the continual changes that the marketplace pitches at the retail participants. The response to such events whether they originate from the customers or other competitors needs to be such that it remains composed and the analysis of the situation prepares a clear path of creative action to withstand such onslaughts.

Humility is demonstrated through the focussed retailer from all levels of seniority who listens to customer and sales staff feedback and opinions with an enquiring mind and courteously probes and takes heed of their comments. Often there is a temptation to arrogantly brush disagreeable criticisms aside as being irrelevant but this should be avoided at all costs and every effort should be made to seek to understand and apply different thought processes. This is especially evident in this day and age where the social media has become an indispensable part of day to day living where something that was thought to be initially insignificant can in a matter of hours demand full attention and therefore the need to be sensitive to outside inputs is intensified.

Vigilance and alertness is a precondition to keep the finger on the pulse. An example of this is in the same way that the customer is the reason for the existence of the retailer so are the competitors in a way. The retailer needs to know their rivals intimately and keep watch on them like a hawk. It is so often easy to treat the smaller minnow contestants with contempt and scoff at any hint of threat. However it should be remembered that there are many success stories of such upstart retailers that have rattled the foundations of well-established traders, some of whom are today no more than romantic memories of the past. It is therefore important to admire the boldness of new and emerging entrants and possibly learn from the courageous innovations that many bring with them as they make their way up the ladder in the industry. In the same way there are other competitors who are on the way down the ladder and from them there are many lessons to be learnt as to why they are in decline. In essence therefore the competitors have a valuable input into the sustainability of their counterparts.

Partnerships between the retailer and the supplier is an essential pre-requisite to ensure the success of the retailer. There has to be a circle of trust to promote collaboration and mutual respect. As has been highlighted the only guarantee about change is that there will be change and it is without doubt that the retailers' greatest ally when change happens, whether it be positive or negative, is their source of supply. The support of the supplier through their flexibility and ability to appreciate the need for revolution is vital for the shared destiny and the celebration of success for both businesses through maintaining healthy relationships with the customer.

Complacency is probably the greatest enemy of the retailer, particularly those who are enjoying great trading performance or who have been a major player for many years and with it often comes an air of arrogance as well as a belief of invincibility. It is therefore critical to be obsessed with trying to keep one step ahead of the market through the deliverance of continual innovations, being open to new opportunities and supporting the reinvention of operations. If this is not maintained but rather the belief is taken steadfastly that the position is rock steady and stores are consequently allowed to deteriorate to a stage where they look old and tired. Similarly if the merchandise is allowed to become much of the same old same old it is inevitable that dwindling sales figures will reflect the result of such complacency. The sad thing is that by the time that the alarm bells are rung, the damage may already be done and the sales rate suddenly does not support the investment required to fix the situation. The more likely solutions which are applied in an attempt to salvage the situation are to dramatically cut costs of anything and everything which in turn inhibits any rejuvenation initiatives and the implementation of staff retrenchment drives not only adds to the burden to those who are left behind but also does irreparable damage to morale. The tactic to increase profit margins in order to generate additional income is often seen as the saving grace but this is in turn is frequently rejected by the consumer who is now being asked to pay more probably for less appealing product in very ordinary facilities which results in her crossing the road to explore alternative options.

In summary, having a farsighted view of the overall big picture of the retail environment, with an all-inclusive attention to detail and being aware of early warning signs to effectively avoid challenges through the optimised use of the tools, mechanisms and talents at hand is without doubt a key factor in delivering a successful and sustainable retail business.

Healthy partnerships between the retailer and the supplier is an essential pre-requisite to ensure the success of both parties. From get go there has to be a circle of trust to promote collaboration and mutual respect. As has been highlighted frequently the only guarantee about change is that there will be change and it is without doubt that the retailers' greatest ally when change happens, whether it be positive or negative, is their source of supply. The support of the supplier through their flexibility and ability to appreciate the need for revolution is vital for the shared destiny and the celebration of success for both businesses.

The sourcing setting has evolved into a highly complex process environment, where the multiple processes, functions and suppliers in many different factories need to collaborate and work together in such a way in order to produce products in as short as time as possible.

In the past it was possible for retailers to have a limited assortment of offer for a season which demanded a much lower level of rotation of stock whereas today the market is demanding a quicker reaction to trends and a greater variety of style changes that calls for far more frequent rotation of stock. It is those global retailers who understand this phenomena and are able to respond quickly that are successful.

The seamless integration of roles and activities of all stakeholders is essential to ensure that the end objective of servicing the customer with the highest quality product that is fully functional which effectively meets the consumer's aspirations and expectations in terms of style, price and consistent availability.

In today's difficult economic retail environment failures are not uncommon and retailers and brands face a myriad of challenges simply to maintain margins and a competitive advantage simply to just survive through the reliance of carefully crafted innovative strategies involved from concept stage through to the delivery in the customer's shopping basket. For the viable strategies to be successful, retailers need to ensure that the plans are optimised with built in visibility, efficiency and integration with other strategies.

Hopefully the book has achieved the objective of entrenching the realisation of the critical need to mesh the activities of the multiple stakeholders in such a way that they are aligned with a common purpose and the successful end result is perceived by the customer to be the work of one united unit.

SUGGESTED CHALLENGE SOLUTIONS

Below are suggested solutions to each of the challenges that followed the mini case studies

CHALLENGE #1

Based on the different store formats for CH Clothing Company and their relevant contributions to the total company sales consider the following

1. What will the main influences be that will influence the range selection in Mall stores?

2. Regional stores customer profiles may differ from one store to another as a result of different factors that need to be taken into consideration. List four of these factors.

3. City centre stores will not necessarily be evident in all cities. What are at least two drivers that will determine the need to establish a store in a city?

4. The on line facility can have various options of the distribution channels available to deliver the order to the customer. List three possible methodologies of fulfilling the customer orders.

Suggested solutions

1. *Age demographics, lifestyle and income profile*
2. *Age demographics, lifestyles, income profiles, cultural ifluences*
3. *Level of apartment living and the number of offices*
4. *There may be a centralised warehouse that fulfils and delivers*

all orders, nearest store to the customer that fulfils and delivers the order, "click and collect" concept whereby the customers collects from the nearest facility

CHALLENGE #2

In the hierarchy of product selection for Menswear shirts illustrated above with the intention to create a balanced selection option for the customer comment on the following:

1. Consider an alternative method of creating the sub category and product group splits for shirts.

2. In the more conservative older customer profile type of stores versus the high fashion stores serving the younger markets list the comparative percentage proportions of fabric types for each customer personality.

3. In the size category where provision is made for secondary sizes such as in addition to the collar size there may be a choice of different sleeve lengths. Name other types of products which may also offer similar different choices of secondary sizes.

Suggested solutions

1. *Sub category could be split into formal and casual with product groups divided into long sleeve and short sleeve*
2. *The apportionment of fabrics across the two profiles could possibly be:*

Conservative Fashion

Poly Cotton 70% 30%

Cotton 20% 40%
Linen 5% 20%
Voiles 5% 10%

3 Other types of product that also carry secondary sizes are cup sizes of bra's and trous and different trouser lengths

CHALLENGE #3

Based on the basic layout plan for a CH Clothing Company store answer the following questions

1. In each of the product group sections what will determine which product groupings will flank the aisle?

2. What product will be featured in the cameo displays and windows?

3. What factor will determine which group will be situated at the door?

Suggested solutions

1. Product which sell in the highest volume will flank the high traffic areas

2. Co-ordinated looks and promotion items to suggest to potential customers the advantages of the featured product

3. The group that is best suited to the dominant customer profile applicable to the store will be that which welcomes the customer into the store

CHALLENGE #4

Comment on the advantages or disadvantages of the use of following the options highlighted in the scenario above

1. The benefit of the CD option for the participant pack

2. The dangers of "death by power point " in presentations

3. The advantage of break out group excersize

4. The advantage of groups in the feedback for the improvement of the session

Suggested solutions

1. The benefit of having the presentation in a digital format either on a CD or on file enables easy reference.

2. Very often if there are too many slides or the slides are too busy results in the audience getting overwhelmed and the succinct points are lost. It is beneficial if the presentation is supplemented with video material.

3. Break out groups are very appropriate as there is a sharing of knowledge and views which involve participation and group resolutions.

4. Course feedback in whatever format provides the opportunity for the presenters to modify course content and methodologies to enhance the presentation session.

CHALLENGE #5
Based on the CH Clothing Company individual landscape diagramme above – complete the following

1. Utilizing the three types of knowledge and the examples of the situations, select for each one those that will be either PROBABLE, POSSIBLE PREFERABLE or PLAUSIBLE

2. Once the selections have been made list what possible actions could possibly be taken for each item "JS knows what JS does not know" knowledge grouping.

Suggested solutions

1. *Will there be any political disruptions? – PROBABLE: Will there be any new competitors?-POSSIBLE: Will raw materials always be available?- PREFERABLE: Know of technical advancements – PLAUSIBLE*

2. *Will there be any new competitors? – Review marketing strategy: What new innovations will there be? – Consider global trends and research: Will raw materials always be available? Research and if need be review stock levels accordingly*

CHALLENGE #6

From the illustration above you are required to perform the following

1. Identify and categorise the factors under the internal headings to those depicted in the respective circles.

2. Identify and categorise the factors under the external headings to those depicted in the respective circles.

Suggested solutions

1. Lack of skilled staff in close locations: THREAT: Unreliable technological infra-structure-THREAT: Key suppliers close to CCC storage and distribution facilities – OPPORTUNITIES: Competitors have low profit margins – BARRIER TO ENTER INDUSTRY: 2. Customers are becoming older and more conservative- CUSTOMER BASE

Laws passed to increase taxes on sin products – ECONOMIC: - Elections are imminent and outcome uncertain – POLITICAL: Import tariffs are to be relaxed – ECONOMIC: Incentives introduced to encourage buy local – ECONOMIC: Higher subsidies for education – ECONOMIC/SOCIAL

CHALLENGE #7

Taking into account the above example of the distribution of sales turnover across the total number of stores respond to the following

1. Provide two other examples where the eighty twenty principle may apply

2. What commercial decision may be taken should the tail-enders with low results be considered unviable?

Suggested solutions

1. *The offer of sizes is likely to be dominated by the most popular sizes such as medium and large as will the sales of the core basic colours such as white and beige.*
2. *The most probable commercial decision would to possibly discontinue the slowest sellers which will minimise markdowns and enable additional investment in the more*

lucrative areas.

CHALLENGE #8

After assessing the possible impacts that the possible events may have describe what action or preventative could be taken in the following situations

1. Under the political grouping what action can be taken to make shopping more secure?

2. In terms of the changing work behaviour what are examples of the different technical options available to enable these changes?

3. With the changing weather patterns what methodologies can be applied to confirm the validity of these theories?

Suggested solutions

1. Employ additional security measures in the form of personnel or modifications to physical formats in order to keep customers and staff safe.

2. There will be a need for new tech equipment such as scanners, pads with the corresponding technical training and coaching to maximise efficiency.

3. The weather patterns need to be monitored and compared to historical data in order to determine any changes in trends and thereby attempt to forecast the expected patterns going forward and adjust launch dates and products accordingly.

CHALLENGE #9

1. In order to try and achieve the goal of the measurement of supplier performance list three factors that could be monitored to evaluate performance of the supplier

2. A strength that is highlighted is that of a reliable supplier base. What attributes are essential to the making of a dependable supplier

3. One of the weaknesses is noted as a substandard on line facility. Name three factors that are essential to rate the facility to be above standard

Suggested solutions

1. In order to rate suppliers three measures that can be applied is factors such as the actual delivery quantities to that which was ordered, the ability to meet the set down delivery dates and the reject factor or number of customer returns.

2. Some of the attributes that need to be met is the consistent acceptable levels of delivery performance, quality levels, innovation and good values.

On line facilities need to be user friendly, reliable with superb speed of response and delivery.

CHALLENGE #10

1. Three examples of different types of loyalty programmes are listed. Note an additional two types of loyalty programmes that could be beneficial.

2. Implementing a store expansion programme, in the identification of new locations, list three components that would make for suitable locations

3. In the measurement of supplier performance provide an example of an incentive reward and three models of penalties systems

Suggested solutions

1. A system whereby points are allocated to account holders which are accumulated and cashed in at a later stage or a competition programme such as the presentation of novelty characters for purchases above a certain amount and when the collection goal is completed some form of reward is received.

2. New locations should be easy to access with plentiful parking facilities, housing a complementary mix of tenants that meet the consumer profile of the surrounding area.

3. Supplier incentive programmes may take the form of a monetary reward or award while penalties could be extra discounts or fines being applied, a sale or return system whereby the unsold goods are sent back after an agreed period of time or even a cancellation of an order.

CHALLENGE #11

In the above setting of performance indicators for the middle of the road retailer how will the following be affected how if they were a high fahion retailer?

1. Markdowns?
2. Buying margin?
3. Stock forward cover?
4. Stock annual turn?

Suggested solutions

1. Because high fashion product carries more risk of non-acceptance to customers and the time on offer will normally much shorter than the more basic higher volume product it is probable that the percentage of write down in relation to the sales will tend to be much higher. A typical relationship is that it may be double or more, a typical example could be that high fashion could be 15% of sales whereas more stable product may only be in the region of 8 Markdowns will also tend to be more frequent to flush out the broken ranges.

2. In terms of buying margin it would be likely that the target would be a lot greater in order to accommodate the greater write off risk of fashion goods.

3. As fashion goods are normally contained in theme launches and need to be an ongoing generation of newness the time on offer is much less than more basic or continuity merchandise which is replenished on a regular basis.

4. As the time on offer is shorter with lower quantities and more frequent markdowns it will therefore result in the number of the stock is replaced is more than continuity items and consequently the profit benefit will occur more often.

CHALLENGE #12

1. Add under the qualitative factors of customer service and brand awareness an additional key factor for each

2. What additional action can be taken in the case of the shortcoming of organisation capacity?

3. What means of communication would be effective in promoting environmental awareness?

Suggested solutions

1. Another indicator of level of customer satisfaction will be the number of repeat purchases while a measure of market penetration would provide a distinct indication of brand awareness.

2. A measure as to whether the capacity of trading space is adequate is to compare individual unit's takings per metre to the company's total target takings per square metre measure.

3. The use of social media vehicles and blogs specific to environmental initiatives would be a suitable means of promoting environmental awareness.

CHALLENGE #13

1. Should a regional store consist of a predominantly more mature age group name at least three

modifications that will be applied to enhance their shopping experience?

2. List three optional loyalty programme methodologies that can be employed to improve the marketing strategy.

3. Apart from assisting the efficiency of a marketing strategy name two other benefits that loyalty programmes bring.

Suggested solutions

1. Where the majority of customers fall into a mature age group of a store there may be a review of the facilities such as shelf heights, pack sizes, font sizes on signage and shelf ticketing which will accommodate such profiles more adequately.

2. Generally loyalty programmes may take the form of a system of point accumulation as purchases made which can be utilised at a later stage, cash discounts at point of purchase for account holders and specific campaigns such as a monetary benefit upon registering as an account holder.

3. The great benefit of loyalty programmes is the harvesting of customer data which will enable better profile analysis and the improved product cataloguing at specific locations.

CHALLENGE #14

After considering the definition of the CH Clothing Company profile determine in which quadrant and roughly where in the selected quadrant the following attributes will live

1. Mass retailer
2. Price
3. Quality
4. Location
5. Customer
6. The total chain

Suggested solutions

1. Mass retailer – Top left quadrant (high volume)

2. Price – Top left quadrant (mid-price)

3. Quality – Top left quadrant (mid quality)

4. Location – Top left quadrant (broad representation of high volume)

5. Customer – Top left (on trend)

6. The total chain Top left quadrant (as all key factors fall squarely in the top left quadrant it is logical that the overall chain will

CHALLENGE #15

Using the earlier example of the Menswear group product division provide examples that could be applied to the following blocks as depicted in the illustration.

1. Company
2. Group A
3. Sub Group 2
4. Dept 1
5. Dept 2

Suggested solutions

1. CH Clothing Company
2. Menswear
3. Shirts
4. Long sleeve shirts
5. Short sleeve shirts

CHALLENGE #16

After focusing on the roles of Merchandisers and Location planners research the role descriptions earlier in the introductory section of the procurement team and comment the following

1. The fundamental difference of the two roles
2. The disadvantages of combining the roles
3. The additional advantages of a separate team of location planners

Suggested solutions

1. *Merchandisers focus on the procurement of product whereas location planners perform the task of allocating the goods to the most appropriate catalogue of stores.*
2. *The combination of the two roles leads to a complex integration of procurement and allocation systems and processes which can be an excessive workload for one resource across what is really two functions.*
3. *The advantage of a pool of location planners is that there is a consolidation of intense knowledge of stores and cross department initiatives can be effectively coordinated.*

CHALLENGE #17

While there are the technological tools available to analyse the customer profile specific to a particular store a view should be able to be formulated through the simple observation of various elements in and around the store.

Using a hypothetical visit a store based on the observations listed below compile a description of the likely general profile of the store's customers.

1. In the cark park it is noted that out of every ten cars three are Mercedes or BMW, two are SUV types while the rest are Toyotas or Volkswagens.

2. While sitting in a general eatery it is noted that out of ten tables six are eating snack meals such as burgers or toasted sandwiches, two tables are eating steaks or sushi while the other two tables are simply drinking cold drinks.

3. It is noticed that at four out of ten couples are pushing prams.

4. Judging by what clothing is being worn it appears that out of ten people five are conservatively clothed while three others are reasonably trendy while two are wearing high fashion branded attire.

Suggested solutions

1. *The observations reveal that the majority of the populace are younger families of a middle income group who are in the main middle of the road fashion relevant.*

CHALLENGE #18

Using the data displayed in the table derive the following measures for the basic white shirt

1. The percentage growth for the 26 weeks
2. The markdown percentage
3. The number of forward weeks cover as at the end of February
4. Dependant on the forward cover derived determine the stock turn value for the year
5. The buying margin percentage

Suggested solutions

1. *Last year sales was 497000 and this year sales are 579000. The sales growth would therefore be [(579000-497000)/579000] x 100=14.2%*
2. *The value of markdown for the period was 46000 and the corresponding sales were 579000. The markdown percentage would therefore be (46000/579000) x 100=8%*
3. *The number of weeks that the 103000 worth of stock will last before running out will be +22000+20000+18000+19000+24000 therefore this will represent 5 weeks forward cover of stock required to achieve targeted sales.*
4. *If the forward stock cover remains at five weeks the stock turn for the year will be 52 / 5 = 10.4 times.*
5. *The cost price is 110 and the selling price is 199.99 therefore the buying margin will be (199.00 – 110.00)/199.00 *100 = 44.7%*

CHALLENGE #19

Taking the sales margin of 260,521.00 and given the following extra expenditures and revenues listed below the actual NET PROFIT and GROSS PROFIT needs to determined according to the methodology described above

1. 20,000.00 worth of product is stolen

2. 5,000.00 worth of product are used for advertising shoots

3. 10,000.00 worth is used for design origination costs and packaging.

4. 15,000.00 is recouped from the supplier in the form of settlement discounts

Suggested solution
Sales Margin 260,521.00

=============

Less stolen product 20,000.00
Less advertising expenditure 5,000.00

=============

NET PROFIT 235,521.00

=============

Less design origination and packaging costs 10,000.00
Add revenue from settlement discounts 15,000.00

=============

GROSS PROFIT 240,521.00

=============

CHALLENGE #20
From the diagramme above identify examples of the following

1. Two organisational hierarchy data specimens
2. Two merchandise hierarchy data specimens
3. Two examples of attributes
4. Three examples of differentiators

Suggested solutions

1. *Menswear, Shirts*
2. *Category, product group*
3. *Long sleeve, short sleeve*
4. *Designs, colours, sizes*

CHALLENGE #21

Referring to the matrix above determine the intake value for the 26 week period

Suggested solution

1. *Intake = Closing stock plus sales and markdown less opening stock*
2. *Therefore (140,000+579,000+46,000)-70,000 = 679,000*

CHALLENGE #22

With reference to the table above determine the values that should be reflected in the row for the total season

1. **Open Stock**
2. **Sales**
3. **Markdown**
4. **Intake**
5. **Close Stock**

Suggested solution

1. *Open Stock =580*
2. *Sales =5030*
3. *Markdown =430*
4. *Intake =5880*
5. *Close Stock =1000*

CHALLENGE #23

Knowing the above it is possible to determine the various values of the Product plan combined to the Location plan. Based on this provide the following monetary values.

1. The value of Menswear Group.
2. The value of Menswear in Region 1.
3. The value of the Men's Shirts department.
4. The value of Store A in Region 1.
5. The value of Men's Shirts department in Store A.

Suggested solution

1. *The Menswear group is 20% of the total Company, therefore the group is 5,030,000x (20/100) = 1,006,000.*
2. *Region 1 represents 15% of the total Location plan therefore the value is 5,030,000x (15/100) = 754,500*
3. *The Men's shirt department is 8% of the Menswear group which is 1,006,000x (8/100) = 80,480.*
4. *Store A is 5% of Region 1 which equals 754,500x (5/100) = 37,725..*
5. *Men's shirt is 8% of the total therefore in Store A the shirt product plan will be equal to 37,725x (8/100) = 3,018.*

CHALLENGE #24
The following needs to be explained

1. The selling price in the total row are not rounded and do not resemble those at line level. Why is this?

2. While the LY sales match those in the previous shirts department matrix the TY sales do not match. Why is this?

Suggested solution

1. *The total row selling prices are the weighted average selling price taking the total sales and units into account.*
2. *The sales in the previous matrix represent actuals which is influenced by different sales and mark downs while the departmental sales summary is a budget document prior to the season and reflects the anticipated performance*

CHALLENGE #25
Make comment about the yarn best utilised in terms of

1. **The type and advantage of the yarn.**
2. **The treatment and advantage of the yarn.**
3. **The count and the advantage of the yarn.**

Suggested solution

1. The best type of yarns utilised would be a blend of cotton and polyester fibres that are of defined length and have the comfort of cotton and the strength and easy care properties of polyester.

2. The cotton yarn component will be combed rather than carded to ensure a clean hair free finish that is durable.

3. The count of the cotton yarn will be as fine as possible which will provide a lighter luxurious feel compared to alternative cheaper options.

CHALLENGE #26
Name three reasons as to why preference is given to woven fabrics instead of knitted products in the formal shirt area.
Suggested solutions

1. Knitted garments lack the crispness of formal woven products.

2. Knitted garments are more prone to shrinkage than the stable woven fabrics.

3. Knitted garments tend to stretch more easily and lose shape than formal shirts.

CHALLENGE #27

1. In the main what type of weaves will be used for plain, yarn dyed or printed garments?

2. What typical weave will be used in the surface interest garments?

Suggested solutions

1. Plain weaves is best suited to plain shirting as the simple criss cross weave forms a stable pattern.

2. Jacquard and dobby weaves enable the creation of jacquard or self-interest designs on the garment.

CHALLENGE #28
Describe three chemical finishes and three mechanical finishes that will be used on the following

1. Three chemical finishing on woven products such as shirts or trousers
2. Three manual finishing on knitted products such as jerseys or tracksuits

Suggested solutions

1. Chemical finishes on woven products could be chemicals to improve sewing, more crease resistant or more water resistant.

2. Mechanical finishing on knitted products would typically be cropping to reduce pilling, compacting to reduce shrinkage while milling or felting gives a feeling of felt on woollen products.

CHALLENGE #29

Describe what the following tests are applied to achieve

1. **Abrasion test**
2. **Tensile test**
3. **Stability test**
4. **Weight of fabric test**
5. **Wash test**
6. **Spirality test**
7. **Fabric slippage test**
8. **Perspiration test**
9. **Light test**
10. **Pilling test**

Suggested solutions

1. Abrasion testing to test for resistance to wear such as the knees of children's bottom garments.

2. Tensile strength tests measure the amount of force required to rip or tear the fabric.

3. Stability tests check the level of shrinkage of the fabric which does not impair the fit, the shape and the comfort of the garment.

4. Weight of fabric tests are performed to make sure the fabric is within the grams per square metre parameters of the specifications.

5. Wash tests determine if there is an unacceptable loss or bleeding of colour that will stain other garments in a wash load.

6. Spirality tests measures the extent of side seam skewing after the garment has been washed.

7. Fabric slippage tests measure to what degree the seams can absorb pressure.

8. Perspiration tests determine the potential of cross staining or discolouration of garments when exposed to perspiration.

9. Light tests measure the effect of exposure to sun.

10. Pilling tests assess the susceptibility to little balls of fibres being formed on knitted and woven garments.

CHALLENGE #30

List at least three of the following used in the makeup of the formal shirt.

1. **The type of stitch used.**
2. **Where these would probably be evident.**

Suggested solutions

1. Lock stitch - which is used mainly in visible areas such as top stitching and on collars.

2. Over locking stitches - are utilised to cover raw edges of exposed seams.

3. Safety stitches - which are predominantly used for the joining seams.

CHALLENGE #31
List three characteristics that need to be evident in the

1. **Collars**
2. **Pockets**
3. **Button holes**

Suggested solutions

1. Require precise cutting of fabric, Should be accurately centred, collar points must be balanced.

2. Pockets must be functional, mitred pockets must be balanced, should have superior sewing.

3. Buttonholes need to be compatible with the size of the button, the stitch density must not allow the buttonhole to fray away from the fabric, and buttons are attached with a secure lock stitch or chain stitch.

CHALLENGE #32
Based on the statement above name the following.

1. **Name three points of inspection in the manufacturing process.**

2. **Identify five types of defects that are looked out for in the inspection process.**

Suggested solutions

1. First off line. In line inspection audits and final audit of packed products.

2. The types of defects that are identified are loose threads, improper stitching, creasing, holes and oil spots.

CHALLENGE #33

Describe the purpose of the following different samples.
1. Design concept sample.
2. Fit samples.
3. Marketing samples.
4. Pre-production sample.
5. Shipment sample.

Suggested solutions

1. Design concept sample is the very first sample which is developed by either the supplier or the retailer with the primary objective to get acceptance and decision to proceed with the garment.

2. Fit samples are made up in order that the buyer is able to confirm the fit on dummies or live models and check the garment for construction acceptability.

3. Marketing sample is for use in the promotion of the garment and is used for photo shoots.

*4. Pre-production sample is probably the most important sample as it is the signed off sample that is representative in *all ways as to what can be expected in production and should there be any dispute during or after production it will serve as the point of reference.*

5. Shipment sample is usually the sample received from off shore suppliers by the retailer to authorise the shipment of orders.

CHALLENGE #34

1. Name five production systems that would be suitable in the production of a formal shirt.

2. Why would the modular system not be appropriate?

Suggested solutions

1. Make through system, Conventional bundle system, Straight line systems, Synchronised flow system, Unit production system.

2. The modular system consists of a group of people work on one or a few tasks at a time.

CHALLENGE #35

In the case of CH Clothing Company name five care symbols that are likely to appear on the label of the formal cotton shirt.
Suggested solutions

1. Washing machine temperature.
2. Do not use bleach.
3. Iron with a warm iron.
4. Do not dry clean.
5. Do not tumble dry.

CHALLENGE #36

List five reasons as to why they would choose this philosophy to source from local suppliers.

Suggested solutions

1. There is a potentially quicker delivery to the market.

2. More flexibility in switching styles during production.

3. More manageable inventory control with less complicated administration.

4. Opportunity to focus on exclusivity and individualistic styling.

5. Less likely to be restricted to minimum order quantities.

CHALLENGE #37

The fabric and components contribute 45%, labour is 25%, and packaging is 10% while distribution and warehousing is 5%.

1. What % margin does the supplier make?

2. What monetary value does this represent?

3. What % does the production costs contribute to the total cost?

Suggested solutions

1. The supplier makes a margin of 15%

2. The monetary value that the supplier puts in the bank is 16.50

3. The production costs are 95% of the total cost.

CHALLENGE #38

In the example of the formal shirt the product is displayed on the counter in a branded presentation poly propylene bag with all the relevant ticketing detail. Describe the most appropriate methodology with the reason why it would be so.

Suggested solutions

1. Because the product is pre-packed it would be most appropriate to store and transport the product in a carton.

2. Because the product is counter displayed it can be stockroom packed in multiples (for example three) in an outer bag which is discarded for time saving during withdrawal and cost effectiveness.

The overall advantages that are delivered with the application of supplier performance systems are numerous. List five benefits that will be gained.

Suggested solutions

1. Accurate deliveries that match the order quantity.

2. The consistent maintenance of accurate data integrity.

3. The reduction of lead times from supplier to retailer due less need for rechecking.

4. The quick identification of poor performing suppliers.

5. Supplier management is able to more effectively manage their business.

CHALLENGE #40

Which allocation system would be best suited to ensure the objective of continuous availability of all sizes is achieved and provide a reason why.

Suggested solutions

1. A "pull" system or automatic replenishment and distribution of products.

2. Such a system is most suitable for the basic continuity product that have consistent predictable sales patterns and for store displays which are laid out according to a centralised space planning system.

CHALLENGE #41
Based on the scale of box versus hanging above describe where the linen shirt would be best suited and what characteristics qualify it to be so.
Suggested solutions

1. The product would be best suited to be transported hanging.
It has a tendency to crease easily.
2. It is woven.
3. It is a natural fibre product.

CHALLENGE #42
CH Clothing Company finds itself in a situation where a product is underperforming and the commitment to product is increasing. List five action options that can be adopted to rectify the situation.
Suggested solutions

1. An immediate hold should be put on outstanding orders, rescheduled or cancelled.

2. The transfer of stock from poor performing locations to better performing stores should be considered.

About the Author

CHARLES NESBITT graduated with a degree in Economics specialising in Business Economics from Stellenbosch University, South Africa. He spent thirty five years at a leading retailer in Southern Africa where he was exposed to all the key disciplines of retailing during this period.